A2 MEDIA STUDIES
FOR OCR
SECOND EDITION

A2 MEDIA STUDIES

FOR OCR
SECOND EDITION

Jacqueline Bennett, Tanya Jones and Julian MacDougall
Consultant Editor: Peter Fraser

Hodder Arnold

A MEMBER OF THE HODDER HEADLINE GROUP

Orders: please contact Bookpoint Ltd, 130 Milton Park, Abingdon, Oxon OX14 4SB. Telephone: (44) 01235 827720. Fax: (44) 01235 400454. Lines are open from 9.00 – 6.00, Monday to Saturday, with a 24 hour message answering service. You can also order through our website www.hoddereducation.co.uk

If you have any comments to make about this, or any of our other titles, please send them to educationenquiries@hodder.co.uk

British Library Cataloguing in Publication Data
A catalogue record for this title is available from the British Library

ISBN-10: 0 340 89990 5
ISBN-13: 978 0 340 89990 8

First Edition Published 2002
This Edition Published 2006
Impression number   1   2   3   4   5
Year   2006   2007   2008   2009

Copyright © 2006 Jacqueline Bennett, Tanya Jones, Julian McDougall and Peter Fraser
Copyright © 2002 Jacqueline Bennett, Tanya Jones, Julian McDougall and Richard Harvey

Typeset by Fakenham Photosetting Limited, Fakenham, Norfolk.
Printed in Dubai for Hodder Arnold, an imprint of Hodder Education, a member of the Hodder Headline Group, 338 Euston Road, London NW1 3BH

CONTENTS

Preface

In completing the work for your AS Level in Media Studies, you will have studied a range of media texts and topics, developing skills of analysis and production and learning about the four key concept areas of Media Forms and Conventions, Media Institutions, Media Audiences and Media Representations. These key concepts carry through to A2 and will form a more explicit framework for your studies. This book builds on the work you have done at AS Level and, although it is freestanding, you will benefit from using it in conjunction with its complementary publication, *AS Media Studies for OCR*. Although the content and structure of this book is targeted specifically at the OCR Specification, it also relates well to the A2 Specifications currently available from other awarding bodies.

Media Studies offers an unusual space within the education system, bringing opportunities to discuss things most students would choose to consume anyway: magazines, websites, music, films, games, radio and TV programmes. The OCR Specification offers the chance to study examples from each of these media, to analyse them in depth and to find out more about how they are produced. With practical work, it also brings the chance to develop skills of teamwork, organisation and planning, alongside the particular skills developed in using the equipment. At A2 an additional consideration is the opportunity to undertake in-depth independent research, a skill that will prove essential in higher education.

This book offers a clear and comprehensive framework for students taking the A2 course. You will find clear explanations and applications of key terms and sections on each of the course units, where the authors describe the range of possible options for the two exams and the coursework and provide helpful case studies as possible models for student work. The tips on production should enable you to produce better structured work, which will be good enough to show to audiences, and allow you to reflect on how media texts function. The range of ideas for the Critical Research unit will give you the basis for your own independent study and give you the confidence to approach the exam. The variety of approaches for the Issues and Debates unit will introduce you to many of the arguments involved and prepare you for the exam.

This textbook will act as the foundation for your studies as you will be pointed towards resources such as other books, newspapers, video and particularly the web. Media Studies is a living and ever-changing subject and keeping up-to-date is crucial for success.

Of the many good textbooks on Media Studies now available, this is the only one specifically aimed at the OCR Specification, the most popular of the A2 Level options. This latest version of the book has been updated to reflect the changes for the third version of the Specification for first examination in 2007, and now includes 'Music on TV' for Unit 2735 and many new topics for Unit 2734. The media texts referred to have been updated to include more contemporary examples. The Production section has now been streamlined to reflect some of the more popular choices made at A2.

Using this book

Although ideal as a whole-class textbook, *A2 Media Studies for OCR* is designed for you to use for independent study as you work through your course.

- Section 1 offers clear guidance on the processes of production for the Advanced Production coursework.
- Section 2 covers the Critical Research Study, with advice on choosing your topic and undertaking different types of research.
- Section 3 deals with all nine topics in the Media Issues and Debates unit.
- Section 4 looks in detail at how best to handle written assignments for all three units.

At the end of the book there is a glossary of key terms and a selection of resources, websites and books that you may find useful.

Throughout the book, you will find a variety of clearly defined suggested activities, most of which can be undertaken on your own at any time. However, there are some areas of discussion where you will find it helpful to work with others.

This course follows on from Media Studies at AS Level; it is pitched at a more sophisticated level and does test more advanced skills. However, with systematic application and sensible use of content, it is possible for any diligent and well-organised student to succeed. I hope this book will help you in that process.

Pete Fraser (Chief Examiner, 2005)

Acknowledgements

The authors and publishers should like to thank the following for permission to reproduce illustrative copyright material:

MGM/EON/The Kobal Collection and Keith Hamshere for the film poster of *Die Another Day* on page 9; *The Guardian* for the front page on p22; Mirrorpix for the *Daily Mirror* front page on page 23; NI Syndication for the front page of *The Sun* on page 24; NI Syndication for the front page of *The Times* on page 25; Aardman Animation Ltd for the set for Morph on page 52 © 1998 Aardman Animation Ltd; Matt Baron/Rex Features for the photo of Jodie Foster on page 62; SNAP/Rex Features for the film still from *Little Man Tate*; Rex Features for the photo of Gurinder Chadhra on p65; UMBI Films/Channel Four/The Kobal Collection for the film *Bhaji on the Beach*; Sipa Press/Rex Features for the image of health warnings on cigarette packs on page 68; Nicholas Bailey/Rex Features for the image of an anti drugs poster on page 69; Francis Dean/Rex Features for the image of Britney Spears' Curious perfume advert on page 69; The *Daily Mail*/John Frost Newspapers for the front page on page 76; *The Guardian* for the front page on page 78; The BBC for the photo of *Blue Peter* presenters © The BBC on page 81; The BBC for the photo of *The Tweenies* © The BBC on page 81; *Girl Talk*/BBC Magazines for the front cover on page 82; The BBC for the film still from *Silent Witness* © The BBC on page 87; CBS-TV/The Kobal Collection for the film still from *CSI: Crime Scene Investigation* on page 88; *True Crime*/Forum Press for the front cover on page 89; BSkyB for the screen grab from *Sky Sports* on page 93; AP Photo/Fernando Bustamante/Empics for the photo of Wayne Rooney on page 93; Andy Clark/Reuters/Corbis for the photo of Nicolas Huet © Andy Clark/Reuters/Corbis on page 94; HBO/Everett/Rex Features for the film still from The Sopranos © HBO/Everett/Rex Features on page 104; the BBC for the film still from *Eastenders* © The BBC on page 104; Miramax/Everett/Rex Features for the poster of *City of God* © Miramax/Everett/Rex Features on page 107; Miramax/Everett/Rex Features for the poster of *Amelie* © Miramax/Everett/Rex Features on page 108; The Ronald Grant Archive for the poster of *Goodbye Lenin!* On page 109; The Ronald Grant Archive for the poster of *House of Flying Daggers* on page 110; Rex Features for the photo of the panel of *X Factor* on page 120; Rex Features for the image of Tony Blair speaking from Gleneagles on page 127; Assassin Films/The Kobal Collection/ Buitendijk, Jaap for the film still from *East is East* on page 144; the Ronald Grant Archive for the poster of *Lagaan* on page 149; Richard Young/Rex Features for the photo of JK Rowling, Rupert Grint, Daniel Radcliffe and Emma Watson on page 152; *Mojo Magazine* and Emap for the front cover on page 165.

The authors and publishers should like to thank the following for permission to reproduce copyright material:

Philip French for his review of *Bride and Prejudice* on pages 66–67; the ASA for text from the ASA website on pages 70–71; the *Daily Mail* for the article 'Blair backs Bush over Iraq threat' on pages 75–77; *The Guardian* for the article 'Blair's Black Day' © Guardian Newspapers Ltd 2003 on pages 77–80; *The Guardian* for the article 'Is television destroying our children's minds?' © Guardian Newspapers Ltd 2004 on pages 83–86; *The Guardian* for the article 'New bill offers pets protection' © Guardian Newspapers Ltd 2005 on pages 90–91; The *Daily Mirror* for the article 'Government plans new rights for pets' on pages 90–91; BBC News website for the article 'Pets may get "Bill of Rights"' on pages 91–2; Ken Livingstone for the article 'We must go for gold with London's Olympic bid' on pages 95–97; *The Guardian* for the article 'The real-life Ali G' © Guardian Newspapers Ltd 2000 on pages 99–102; BBC Radio 1 website for the article on Tim Westwood on pages 102–103; BBC Drama website for the article on 'Deronda v Zhivago' on page 106; the BFI for the review of *Spirited Away* on pages 111–113.

Every effort has been made to obtain necessary permission with reference to copyright material. The publishers apologise if inadvertently any sources remain unacknowledged and will be glad to make the necessary arrangements to correct any omissions at the earliest opportunity.

SECTION 1
ADVANCED PRACTICAL PRODUCTION

Introduction

At AS Level, practical **production** required the creation of a media text from a set brief. At A2, the choice of which text to create is open. There are no set briefs. However, the requirements for the project are rather different and more demanding.

The most important point to remember when beginning to prepare for A2 production is that you are *not* allowed to work in the same medium as you did at AS Level. As part of your evaluation for A2, you are asked to identify which of the designated AS briefs you completed and to state that you are not working in the same medium. This is done to ensure that you get practical experience with at least *two* media during your course and to give you a chance to demonstrate and translate your skills across media. Remember that you are allowed to use the same medium for delivery if the textual intention is different. For example, you may choose to be assessed on film for A2, having done television at AS Level (both submitted on video), or choose a magazine at A2, having done print advertising at AS Level (both submitted on paper).

You should be aware that the work is expected to be of a far higher standard at A2, with highly competent use of the necessary technology. Several times throughout this section we reiterate that you should be competent with the equipment before you start this project. You will be marked down if your work suffers because of your technical skills. However, you will not be penalised in any way for technical limitations that are outside your control, such as minor loss of tape quality due to being recorded from VHS to computer and then back again. Nevertheless, you could lose marks if this process has been repeated several times unnecessarily, resulting in significant distortion.

The A2 Specification stipulates that the purpose of this unit '*is to assess the origination and construction of a media text, demonstrating technical skills and conceptual understanding (Assessment Objective 8). Candidates should also demonstrate critical evaluation of the process and outcome of their own media production (Assessment Objective 9)*'.

Here, the key differences from AS are that the work is expected to be realised to a high standard, both technically (an extension of AS standards) and conceptually. At A2 the choice of brief is intentionally open so that candidates can demonstrate significant research and ownership of their chosen text. This text must not be created in isolation, but in direct relation to the chosen **genre** and medium, with explicit address to **audience** and institution. In other words, all the factors that are part of professional practice are required at this level.

Thus, the Critical Evaluation is significantly different from AS and this is reflected in the higher proportion of marks allocated and the requirement to produce 3000 words. For each of the topic areas discussed below, some comments have been made about the content of the four different sections of the evaluation, directly related to the medium and task discussed. However, in Section 4 of this book, there is far more information about how to structure your writing tasks for A2 and how to approach an evaluation. You should make sure you read Section 4 in conjunction with this section.

You are free to choose your own topic area for A2, using *one* of the specified media: Film, Television, Video, Print, Radio and ICT/New Media. You may also construct a project that uses more than one medium (such as a marketing campaign for a film using video to make a trailer and print to create posters).You must remember that it is central to this unit to show synoptic knowledge and understanding of key conceptual areas. Therefore, it may be sensible for your whole class to work within one topic area or related area. This will allow for shared knowledge and understanding and the opportunity for detailed analysis of relevant texts and exploration of key concepts in relation to this area. Your teacher will tell you whether he or she has chosen the task or whether you are being offered complete freedom.

As at AS Level, the permitted maximum group number is four, to ensure equal and comparable work distribution among group members. There is no minimum group size so you could work on your own, but A2 projects are fairly substantial conceptually and individual work may be excessively demanding. Each group member must produce an individual evaluation (although the research and preparation can be shared) and it should be obvious that the evaluations have been completed individually. Your group can duplicate **storyboards** and other planning sheets or deconstruction examples for the appendices of your evaluations, as long as you have all been involved in them.

It is important that you write about your particular role and responsibilities within the group as part of your evaluation. You must highlight your individual contribution and reflect upon your individual learning and group practice in the evaluation. Again, you will find more comments about this in Section 4 of the book.

Your project will be marked out of 120 and the breakdown is as follows:

- Planning – 30 marks
- Construction – 60 marks
- Critical Evaluation – 30 marks.

As you can see, at A2 half of the marks are awarded for planning and evaluation to reflect the importance placed on conceptual learning and organisation, not just technical competence.

Planning

Marks will be awarded for time and equipment being organised properly and the production schedule being sustained. It is a requirement that you submit a storyboard or equivalent documentation for all time-based work and evidence of several stages of drafting for print-based work. If this evidence is excluded from your evaluation, you cannot be credited with the marks for planning, no matter how much thought has gone into your project. Your teacher will write about how you have planned and organised your time and what planning documentation you have used, so make sure that you provide the evidence to support the work you undertake. It is not permitted at A2 to submit a storyboard as a realised project in its own right, only as supporting documentation for planning evidence.

Notice as well that you are required to define a specific target audience and to test your project on that audience for assessment in the evaluation. You should identify this audience and plan how you will test your artefact during the planning process. Remember to allow time between completion of the artefact and your final submission date to test-market your artefact properly and to analyse the feedback you receive.

Construction

You are expected to be technically competent at this level and this is fundamental for your construction marks. Work that is not technically secure will not be very successful at A2 Level, despite its potential. You are expected to use and/or subvert established forms and conventions to make meaning and to make this meaning clear to your target audience as required. You must ensure that your artefact is a credible media product, realised to a high standard and evidencing awareness and understanding of the relevant conceptual areas for your chosen medium and task.

Do not send in your master copy of your work for assessment. You should always retain the master copy and submit a copy instead. If the work is mislaid or lost during transit, for example, and you do not retain a copy, you may find you cannot submit. Allowances cannot usually be made for work lost in this way. As at AS Level, you may find that your work is not returned by the Board for some reason, and so, unless you have your master copy, your work could be lost to you.

Critical Evaluation

As already indicated, the approach to the Critical Evaluation is discussed in detail in Section 4 of this book. Suggestions about possible content are made in Section 4 for the various examples offered during this section. You should provide your planning evidence as appendices to your evaluation and it is important that you word-process this evaluation and present it clearly. It is usually worth numbering the pages as 3000 words is a substantial essay. Make sure you have your name on each page in case your work becomes separated.

Before you begin

It is worth reading this section of the book in conjunction with *AS Media Studies for OCR*. Because you worked in a different medium at AS Level, you should look at the relevant section for the medium you are working in now to identify and reflect upon the relevant technical competencies and to refresh your memory about the technical standards expected. It is recommended that you read all the material in this chapter and not just that related to your chosen medium, since there may be useful information in other sections that will help you with your work.

Part One

Film Production

Film remains the cornerstone of media production and analysis and it is a global industry. As a medium, film is the oldest form of moving-image media and thus, arguably, far more mature and sophisticated in nature than television. Television also tends to be a more realist form, whereas film runs the gamut from archetypal Hollywood realist traditions, through **art-house** and more complex texts to **avant-garde** and experimental texts that may be considered too obscure for the majority of television audiences. As a medium for production work, therefore, film offers a vast range of possibilities. In this section we will consider two possible productions, but you should bear in mind the range of opportunities available and reflect carefully upon **form**, **style** and **genre** before you begin.

Audience and institution

You may have studied some aspects of film institution in detail elsewhere in your course. Remember to consider the type of institution that would produce your film and how this will affect and influence the production. If a film is to be produced by a Hollywood studio, the studio is unlikely to invest substantial amounts of money unless a clear audience is identified. The genre, stars and format of the film will be directly related to the audience expectations. Hollywood studios do not always take risks with new films or with divergent approaches. Investors do not usually wish to invest in speculative ventures, but prefer tried and tested formats. You may wish to read some of the work of Rick Altman or Richard Dyer about the importance of genre for institutions and audience expectations.

However, many art-house and avant-garde films are produced as aesthetic projects with substantially less focus on audience and institution. This is one of the reasons that such films are frequently perceived as 'non-commercial'. The director, cast and crew are able to focus on the film itself, without having to compromise for commercial purposes. At times, this can lead to accusations of self-indulgence and to films that become too obscure to communicate to an audience on any level. If you decide to create an experimental or avant-garde piece, be careful not to allow this to happen to your film. For the purposes of A2 Media Studies, you must produce a mass media text that is credible in a commercial market. This does not mean that you cannot work experimentally, but you should be aware of the inherent dangers.

Production facilities

It is important not to attempt a production in this medium unless you are competent with the equipment. If you want a particular effect, it can often be added during **editing** or **post-production**. If you are working with non-linear editing equipment you can add 'film noise' effects, for example, in most editing or post-production software, as well as the range of filters, effects, distortions and so forth which might be used in less conventional film formats. The use of a **fish-eye lens** to distort a picture and intensify the focus on the middle of the picture, for instance, can be added fairly easily in post-production if you do not have access to a fish-eye lens for your camera.

You are likely to have access to conventional video equipment, which is more than sufficient for this production module. A digital editing program such as iMovie is perfectly adequate, as is domestic camcorder equipment used well.

Remember that although the rules for AS and A2 production stipulate that you may not work in the same medium twice, the exception is that you may choose to use video to present television work and film work, since they are substantially different products but are presented using the same technology. Nevertheless, if you have access to non-linear film and editing equipment, you may decide to work with a 16:9 screen size to reflect film rather than television. Make sure you do not distort your work by rendering out to a different screen size.

Technical quality of final production

Remember that you are assessed on your skills with filming, editing and post-production work. Your work is marked for technical competence in relation to these skills. If poor framing, wobbly shots and awkward **jumpcuts** mar your work, this will be deemed unsuccessful against the specified technical criteria for A2 Level work. If, however, the final quality of your video is not as strong as you would like due to the equipment available to you (for example, if your rushes are uploaded to a computer over an ordinary VHS cable, edited and then exported back to VHS using domestic video equipment), this will not impact on your assessment.

The technical quality of final production is an important point with sound as well. Good quality live sound for your film work is difficult to achieve without professional equipment, but there are some things you can do to improve the sound quality. Whenever possible, avoid using the built-in microphones on the video camera, using the 'mic in' socket for a better microphone. Set up a simple boom mike (tie the microphone onto a broom handle if you need to) and point it at the action while keeping it out of shot, or use radio mikes attached to your actors if you can. You may find it helpful to look back at the information on sound quality when recording in *AS Media Studies for OCR*.

It is also worth remembering at this point that you do not lose marks for the quality of the acting. You are being assessed on your film production skills and cannot be assessed on the acting. You will be judged on composition, costume and framing, however, so you do need to think carefully about these elements.

CASE STUDY: A FILM TRAILER

One good option for film production at A2 Level is a film trailer. A film trailer is a marketing device for a new release with certain clearly defined conventions. It provides plenty of opportunities to produce something dynamic and visually gripping that is designed to really sell a film.

There are basically two types of film trailer – **teaser** trailers, which are usually about one minute long and full trailers, which are usually two minutes long. A teaser trailer is released some time before the actual release of the film, whereas a full trailer is released fairly close to the film première to heighten interest and excitement. Film distribution companies usually produce a range of trailers for different placements and different audiences. The trailer shown at the multiplex will probably differ from the trailer shown on the front of a video release and may be different to the trailer used on television. Most companies produce different trailers for different international markets and may use varying trailers on mirror websites for different countries. If the film is marketed on the back of other genre films, there may even be more versions of the trailer cut to match these different audiences.

Preliminary tasks

There are two primary decisions that you need to make at the very beginning of your film trailer project. You need to decide what film genre you will be working within and then to consider whether you will be producing a teaser trailer or a full trailer. Your identification of the target audience, genre codes and conventions to use, likely institution and placement will follow from these decisions.

A single teaser trailer would be appropriate as an individual project, but for a group project a series of teasers or a full trailer would be sufficiently substantial.

Questions to ask before you begin

- **What genre is the trailer?**
- **What sort of trailer will it be?**
- **Where will it be shown?**
- **What is the target audience for this trailer?**
- **How does this relate to the target audience for the film itself?**
- **What key genre elements will be employed?**
- **What will be the key point for the trailer?**
- **What studio/film company will you assign the film to?**
- **What will be the marketing points for the film (e.g. stars, director, themes)?**

Identifying the film

Having identified the context for the film and the relevant constructs, you should think about the film itself. You do not need to complete a detailed screenplay – a 500-word plot synopsis and some basic institutional information such as that identified above will enable you to create and target your trailer effectively. You should plan:

- **a title**
- **a 500-word plot synopsis**
- **a detailed statement of genre and target audience**
- **institutional information, i.e. the name of the studio, distribution company and release dates**
- **the key actors and personnel (NB do not use star names, but either invent names or use the names of your group members)**
- **the themes employed in the film**
- **the context for distribution of the trailer (e.g. will it be shown at the multiplex prior to similar films, or is it to be shown in a different context? Is it a national or international trailer?).**

Remember that many British films have different titles when they are marketed in the USA. For example, *Harry Potter and the Philosopher's Stone* (2001) was renamed *Harry Potter and the Sorcerer's Stone* for American audiences.

ACTIVITIES

Use one of the websites http://www.movie-list.com or http://www.apple.com/trailers to look at film trailers. Identify a range of four recent releases within your chosen genre and deconstruct the trailers in relation to the questions below.

- Identify the institution for each of these trailers and the institutional codes employed by the institution.
- What are the key selling points of each trailer?
- How does each trailer establish the genre, mood and expectations of the film?
- Which of these trailers is more or less successful for you? Can you identify which elements are more or less successful?
- What appear to be the target audiences for the films?
- How is the audience explicitly targeted in each trailer?
- Is there an identifiable format across these trailers? Does this apply for other trailers? Is it successful?
- Why are trailers constructed in this way?

When researching film production to prepare for the Critical Evaluation for your artefact, it can help to undertake some more theoretical research in advance. Consider the following:

- Are trailers a good way to market films?
- Why are trailers so popular?
- Do successful trailers depend on **enigma** codes?
- What influence does the institution have on the style and format of a trailer?
- To what extent must a trailer conform to audience expectations if it is to be successful?
- How many trailers are in a typical marketing package at a cinema? Are there institutional controls on these packages? Who decides which films to advertise and where?

Constructing the trailer

Planning

Having identified the institutional context, film and target audience for your trailer, you can begin to plan the trailer itself. You will need to complete a detailed storyboard for the trailer, part of which could be included as an appendix to your Critical Evaluation. You must also provide evidence of comparative study of commercial trailers and theoretical grounding for your trailer. You should make sure you justify each of the following decisions in the evaluation:

- where in the trailer you wish the title of the film to appear
- how the title should appear – font, colour, position, duration, effects, etc.
- what the opening and closing screen of the trailer should be
- what the soundtrack will be – for example, will it involve a voice-over (male/female? age? accent?) and dialogue for 'extracts' from the film, or will it be mostly musical?
- whether you are using 'extracts' from the film that you will need to script, storyboard and film first to incorporate during editing
- what special effects or graphics are required
- where the institutional information will appear, such as the name of the distribution company and release dates
- the ways in which the trailer targets the audience
- how the trailer matches audience expectations and relates to the film itself.

Recommended content for Production Log

- Storyboard, shooting script and continuity sheets.
- Annotated deconstruction of contemporary trailers.
- Drafts for graphics, fonts, etc., and sample screens from trailer.
- Logging sheets and notes, for example, if working with a non-linear system.
- Production Log and individual accountability information.
- Personal schedules and project timeline.

It is the producer's responsibility to ensure that all the necessary equipment is ready and that material is edited on time. This does not mean that the producer does all these jobs, just that he or she supervises them.

Titles

You will probably need to use a titling program to overlay the necessary institutional information for your trailer. If you are working with a linear system, you will probably have access to a titler, which will allow a degree of creative freedom when constructing the titles. However, if you are restricted in titling you can indicate this in your evaluation. If effective use is made of the available technology, this will be rewarded more highly than work that does not make creative and appropriate use of opportunities, but you must show evidence for this in your evaluation.

Still images

Still images can be an effective device in a trailer – they can be shown on their own or as part of a larger montage to highlight key points in the film or to signal a star presence, for example. They are used cautiously in many genres, but where used effectively, a series of still images with a powerful soundtrack can successfully establish expectations and excitement for a film.

Action sequences

One of the most common devices in trailers is the use of brief clips from the film, interspersed with the voice-over. These clips can be very short to create enigma, or they can be longer, with interaction between characters that creates **disequilibrium**, only restored and resolved by the film itself. It is sometimes said that the most effective trailers give enigmatic moments from a powerful idea and plot to attract the audience, but that less successful trailers reveal too much of the plot and show how the disequilibrium will be resolved, making it almost unnecessary to see the film.

Sample trailer decisions

If you were creating a trailer for a new *James Bond* movie, for example, you might decide to follow the traditional format for a Bond trailer, but using original images and constructed graphics.

This is a useful example because there are certain key images and sounds which an audience would expect to see in a trailer for a new Bond film; thus the trailer has to be sufficiently formulaic to satisfy audience expectations. Each new actor playing Bond causes disruption for the audience and it is interesting to note that the formula is becoming more rigid and is almost a genre in itself in order to ensure a degree of continuity. The Bond genre has become so precisely defined throughout the globe, it is unlikely that you would wish to tamper with the formula without a very good reason.

This is a typical poster for a recent Bond film, using many of the codes and conventions that have become typical. It would not be difficult to set up and shoot a similar image – it could be manipulated in a graphics program if necessary. Of course, you could extend this to become a cross-media project, by combining a trailer, two posters and a radio advert for a new Bond film, for example.

There are plenty of ways to demonstrate ownership of the trailer. You could construct your own title overlays and import these into your editing program at the appropriate points. You could set up still images of many of the set-piece graphics of a Bond trailer, such as the MCU (medium close-up) with the gun. Use an actor dressed appropriately – some of the most successful examples have commented upon the genre and ideology by employing a female Bond.

In this instance, try hard not to use any found material, for example, material copied from existing trailers, since you cannot be given credit for found material. The exception is probably the Bond theme, which appears at some point in all Bond trailers and movies. Consider where it appears in the trailers and why.

Again, you are unlikely to be able to recreate one of the standard Bond set pieces of destruction, but an effective substitute can be made with some simple shots and some manipulation – for example, some shots taken from a moving car, with a gun appearing in the viewfinder, used when editing with sound effects of bullets being fired or maybe with the footage speeded up to suggest that the car was moving very fast. You may be able to use a non-linear editing suite to merge some live-action shooting with separate shots of fires to create the trailer.

Part Two ■■■

Television Production

Television broadcasting is continuing to develop and remains, arguably, the most dominant form of global mass media. Current studies suggest that the average adult in Britain watches over three hours of television every day. Given that most of this viewing takes place after 7 p.m., it is clear that watching television is the principal leisure activity for many people. The proportion of active compared to passive viewing is debatable, yet *The Royle Family* would seem to be a credible exaggeration of many households at this time. There are important debates about the future of television and these include:

- the impact of digital broadcasting and the extension to the range of channels available
- the balance of **Public Service Broadcasting** (PSB) and commercial television.

Production facilities

It is also important to remember that you should not attempt a production in this medium unless you are competent with your available equipment.

Research activities

You will probably have studied television in some form at AS Level and may be studying television in some way for the other A2 units. There is so much information available about television and so many programmes to view, that you cannot expect to cover everything. You will need to decide very quickly what genre you will be working within for your television production and structure your research in relation to that genre.

CASE STUDY: EXTRACT OR PACKAGE FOR A REGIONAL NEWS PROGRAMME

This option requires competence with producing a news programme extract. It involves the very particular demands of working with an explicit target audience. No media text can be created in isolation, without direct address to the target audience, but in some cases, such as here, the relationship between form and content must be more carefully analysed and constructed to ensure that the text is accessible and appeals to the target audience. Regional programming depends on a good understanding of the relationship between content and audience expectations.

Preliminary tasks

Planning

You should think carefully about the structure and placement of your text before you begin. You may decide to create a news package, for example, an evening news update. Or you may simply choose to provide an extract from a longer news programme, perhaps with an introduction from a presenter and two items from the programme. Remember that you do not need to produce the whole programme. Five minutes is the maximum length needed.

In terms of institutional context, you will need to identify a region and a channel and thus an identity at the very beginning. You might choose to present a local package as part of a special report on the regional environment, for example, or 'local heroes'. If you choose to present an extract as part of a late evening programme on a local BBC channel, or on a new local cable channel, keen to carve an identity, the institutional context, and thus your text, will be very different.

Questions to ask before you begin

- **Are you producing an extract or a package?**
- **Which station will your programme be shown on?**
- **What is your target audience?**
- **What devices will you employ to ensure you target this audience directly?**
- **What stories will you want to include?**
- **If you are constructing a presenter for your programme, what image will they present? In what ways will this reflect the character of your chosen channel and identify your programme?**
- **If you are using reporters, how will they visually and aurally reflect the channel and programme identity?**
- **What stories will be appropriate for your given context?**
- **What *mise-en-scène* will you use? How will this create your context?**
- **Will your presentation be formal (presenter in a studio with a blue projection screen behind, for example) or more informal and chatty?**
- **How many items will be in your extract/package?**

- **Will you be using devices such as musical links between items or overlays to communicate with the viewers? Will you need supporting graphics (for instance, when presenting an item about local involvement in overseas conflicts, you may feel a graphic to demonstrate the process would be valuable) or interviews with particular people?**

You may wish to create the title sequence for the programme as well, although that would probably become a different project. However, you may want to use a presenter to open the programme, in which case you need to plan and construct an effective 'lead in' to the programme.

As with print production, it is strongly recommended that your reporters source, research and construct their own stories, rather than depend on found material. It is surprisingly difficult to 'own' found material sufficiently securely to be able to manipulate it effectively into a new format. A news item that is regurgitated from another channel and simply re-badged for a different context is likely to be fairly awkward in approach, insubstantial and is rarely successful. If the item is heavily dependent on a previous report with the use of found graphics and so forth, it is unlikely that you would be able to display sufficient skills with media construction to merit a high mark at A2.

Although the stimulus for a story may come from a found source, your reporters should ensure that they conduct their own primary research and locate their own interviewees and images. This level of engagement will enable them to produce a far more structured item, showing clear regard for institutional context, news values and choice of material.

DISCUSSION

As part of your planning, it can help to undertake some more theoretical research in advance, to prepare for the Critical Evaluation for your artefact. Consider the following:

- Why are there so many regional news programmes?

- Identify and justify a list of news values to be applied when compiling a regional news programme.

- Does television news sensationalise events?

- Why is television news important?

- The BBC was first created to fulfil the Reithian vision of broadcasting to 'entertain and educate', and PSB broadcasting has continued this vision. Do the contemporary news programmes on the BBC perpetuate this vision or is the news becoming entertainment-led?

- Should regional news and current affairs programmes be presented regionally or can this area be covered adequately in national bulletins?

News values of the institution and the role of the journalist

News values are the ideological backbone of the journalist and news editor. The most familiar identification of these news values came from Johan Galtung and Marie Holmboe Ruge. Although their research was conducted in 1965, virtually any media analyst's discussion of news values will refer to their list, despite the fact that initially it was intended to cover only international events. The values they identified were:

- *Frequency*: The time-span of an event and the extent to which it 'fits' the frequency of the schedule. On this basis, motorway pile-ups, murders and plane crashes will qualify, as they are all of short duration and therefore nearly always fit into the schedule.
- *Threshold*: How big is an event? Is it big enough to make it into the news? A fire in the city may be reported on the local news but is unlikely to be reported on the national news unless it becomes more of an event.
- *Unambiguity*: The mass media generally want closure. With an event such as a murder, its meaning is immediately grasped, so it is likely to make it into the news. A more complicated story may not be used, as it cannot be addressed sufficiently quickly.
- *Meaningfulness*: Stories tend to be judged in terms of how they relate to the viewers. The closer to home the events, the more likely they are to be reported. A train crash in Outer Mongolia which killed 300 people is likely to be of less interest to the viewers than a car accident on the M25 which caused a 10-mile tailback.
- *Consonance*: The audience – and the journalist – has expectations about how a story should unfold. To make the news immediately accessible, journalists tend to present stories very simply and rarely offer more than one perspective on events.
- *Unexpectedness*: Some events are more predictable than others – parliamentary campaigns may not be reported in any detail because they are not 'exciting'. A walkabout by a parliamentary candidate becomes a lot more exciting if they are attacked by a group of protesters who cover the candidate in baked beans, for example.
- *Continuity*: Audiences quickly come to expect continuation of running stories.
- *Composition*: There is usually a balance of stories in a bulletin.
- *Reference to elite nations*: Cultural proximity is an important factor for journalists – the less cultural proximity for the audience with the events, the less importance will be attached to them.
- *Reference to elite persons*: Some people are more newsworthy than others.
- *Personalisation*: The more human interest in a story, the more likely it is to be heard.
- *Negativity*: Most reported news tends to be bad news.

Role of the journalist

There are also differences between the neutral and participant roles of journalists. Neutral is associated with the idea of press as channel of information; participant is where the journalist behaves as a representative of the public. Most see themselves as neutral, but many political journalists deliberately have an adversarial role. Weaver and Wilhoit (1986) further qualified this:

- interpreter – analyses events and raises questions
- disseminator – the journalist as servant, providing information to the public
- adversary – the journalist as challenger, forcing individuals and institutions to answer to the public.

Would you say that Galtung and Ruge's news values are applied in the same way for regional news programmes as for national programmes?

ACTIVITIES

Watch your regional news on two different channels for a week and consider the following questions:

- How long is each bulletin? When is it shown? Why is it scheduled here?
- How many stories are there each day? From the observation of a week, what conclusions can you draw about the balance of stories to be used each day?
- In what ways do the presenters of the programme define the identity of the programme (consider clothes, interaction, studio background, register and image as a starting point). In what ways do they show themselves to be 'regional'?
- Compare and contrast the presentation of two stories on your two chosen channels. What similarities and differences in presentation can you observe? What does this reveal about the role and function of these two programmes?
- What is the target audience for each of your regional news programmes?
- What is the institutional context (i.e. which channel and at what time)?
- What is the format of the programmes? What similarities and differences can you observe?

See if you can identify two stories which are reported on the national news and in the regional bulletins.

- How are these stories re-presented for a regional audience?
- What differences in camera angles, interviews, graphics, etc., do you observe? What does this tell you about the different regional approach?
- How does a regional broadcast attempt to 'own' a national story?

CASE STUDY   (continued)

Audience research

Once you have analysed a range of regional programmes in this way, you should think carefully about the target audience for each programme.

- **What is the target audience for each programme?**
- **Is the target audience similar for all these programmes?**
- **Is the audience the same for the channel itself?**
- **Can you account for these similarities and differences?**
- **How do the programmes 'brand' their identity for their audience?**

- **Do these programmes have an audience or a community?**

Once you have completed this research, you should be able to plan your programme more effectively, using the appropriate and successful elements that you have identified in the activity above.

BBC Spotlight South West

BBC South West news has been running since 1961 and has been rebranded many times since then, in keeping with contemporary trends and overarching national BBC identity and expectations. There is a very useful website tracking this development that gives an insight into how BBC South West News has retained its particular identity at:
http://www.tv-ark.org.uk/bbcsouthwest/bbcsouthwestnews.html

The site features a series of clips from programmes over the decades that show how the graphics, presenters, style, theme music and logos have all changed. It also gives you some useful insights into how much news bulletins have been shaped by the available technology of the day and how important presenters (and their visual style) remain to the identity and shaping of a news bulletin.

Look at some of the clips on the site and notice when the programme has been forced to change in line with national BBC expectations, for example, the clip from 11 May 2004. This shows how the set has been rebuilt to more closely resemble that in use on national bulletins and also how the format of the opening section of the programme now models the structure of the national programme. It's also interesting to look at the clips recounting the start of BBC Channel Islands Spotlight news in 2003, to see a new programme establishing a regional identity and hopefully attracting a regional audience.

Constructing the news programme

Administration
Once you have the concept of your programme you need to think about the logistics, such as allocating responsibility for each of the bulletin items or casting presenters. You should plan each story carefully, with a lead reporter and a director for each bulletin, so that one person can be responsible for content and one for form. You will need plenty of planning meetings to ensure that there is consistency of form and style across each of your stories. All your material must conform to the 'house style' that you designate and must reflect an appropriate institution.

If you are working in a group it is fairly easy to allocate a range of responsibilities to each of the group members and to change roles between stories. This allows for greater diversity of experience and research and, if properly managed, should strengthen Critical Evaluation opportunities.

Editing
Unless you are severely limited by the quality of your editing equipment, you should try to complete each story separately and only combine the sections during editing. It is easier to control shot choice, rhythm, length and focus across all your stories in this way. Complete the

filming of each section (which should be substantially longer than the final time available) and structure the rough cut before editing begins. Look for consistency and finalise the house style for reports, graphics, and so forth, before you begin editing. You should ensure appropriate time for each story, consistency of overlays and graphics, natural links (if appropriate) and similarity of shot across stories, if possible, to sustain your bulletin. Assess the relevance to the target audience and the institutional factors during editing.

Framing

When you are filming interviewees, it is usually most effective to allow them to face a reporter standing next to the camera, allowing them to look to the side of the camera.

It is intimidating for an interviewee to be expected to stare straight into a camera, and full frontal shots of most people are unflattering. By allowing a person to look to the side, their face will gain perspective and depth and they will feel more secure looking at the interviewer during their responses. If you are using a formal studio, remember that the presenters are usually positioned slightly to the side of the frame as well, to ensure eye-line matches on the pivot points. In a formal studio situation, there may well be a blue-screen behind the presenter where the videos can be shown (you can show an opening graphic for a story as a still image in the blue-screen space). Use the **chromakey** option, or other transparency filter in your editing program, to make the graphic appear on the page. Then use a zoom transition to move to a full-screen version of the story.

If you are using a less formal studio set, it may be easier to lead in to the various stories. However, you should make sure that there is still plenty of space in the frame for the presenter to look into as they look off-screen to lead off the story. You should also try to use audio lead-ins to make the bulletin more cohesive. An audio lead-in means that the audio track for the new clip starts slightly before the previous visual image has disappeared so that it is already playing when the relevant clip begins.

Part Three ■■■

Print Production

Despite the **digital** revolution, print artefacts are still a fundamental mass media form. Newspapers are currently reviewing their online provision, after discovering that even the most techno-literate of their audience have yet to make a full transition to on-screen editions of the daily papers. Readers still prefer to retain the traditional print product and use the on-screen versions as searchable archives, responding most favourably to a 'daily digest approach'. At the time of writing, the introduction of e-books has not remotely affected the global sales of books. Book production figures are increasing in fact. Readers do not seem ready to give up the physical sensation of holding and opening a book or the tactile appeal of a glossy magazine or the expectations raised by the visual construct which is a broadsheet front page. The *Financial Times* would not be differentiated and elevated in the same way by an online version using black text on a pink background, yet the newspaper is instantly recognised and situates its entire ideology in its format.

The range of possible options for print production work is as varied as the print media themselves, including newspapers, magazines, adverts, pamphlets, leaflets, comics and posters.

Each medium within the production context involves different production skills and different research expectations and so it is logical to consider two case studies individually rather than apply generic principles across such widely divergent media forms.

Production facilities

It would be unwise to embark on print production work unless you feel that you have access to appropriate technologies.

It is assumed at A2 Level that you will have access to computers that have desktop publishing (DTP) and image-editing software available on them, just as at AS Level. Again, the industry standards in terms of software are usually InDesign® for DTP work and Photoshop® for image editing (both made by Adobe). There are, however, many cheaper (and less complex) alternatives available, such as Green Street Publisher™ and Paint Shop Pro™. Without access to such software you will be unable to draft and compose your print artefacts with enough flexibility. DTP software allows a greater degree of adaptability by treating form and content as different units, allowing you to isolate either for redrafting without affecting the other.

The artefacts should be shown in their real size and they should be carefully presented and labelled. Laminating the work is often a good way of preventing wear and tear. Hand-drawn artefacts are unlikely to be successful at this level, even if well presented. It is also unlikely that work dependent on found images would be successful, even if the images were significantly manipulated. You need to remember the stipulations in the Specification about use of found images and the requirement to use a minimum number of original images.

It is useful to have access to an A3 full-colour printer. This allows better printing options and credible presentation of film posters or **broadsheet** newspapers. At this level, broadsheet newspapers are not expected to be presented on a single sheet of A4 because proportions of the font sizes, balance and image sizes would be totally inappropriate. Although most professional products are produced 'full page' without borders, it is not necessary to replicate this with print artefacts when using a printer that does not allow full-bleed printing. The only exception to this would be artefacts made to suit a particular context, such as a CD sleeve and insert, where the artefact is smaller than A4, so can be printed onto A4 and then trimmed to size.

CASE STUDY: A NEW TABLOID NEWSPAPER

You should aim to produce about six pages from a new **tabloid** newspaper, in line with the expectations for other print-based projects. Remember that you will be expected to present your tabloid in a professional way and at an appropriate size.

Beware of designing your tabloid at A4 size and blowing up to A3 size. If your fonts are appropriate on your A4 version or you have carefully managed the quantity of white space visible on your page, remember that the fonts will be too large and the white spaces seem empty when this is blown up to A3 size.

- Research the current tabloids available in your area, both national and local. Identify the institution, target audience, approach and circulation figures for each one.
- What are the key signifiers of the local tabloids in your area?
- Write a detailed deconstruction of the front page of three different tabloids. Try to compare one national and two local tabloids if you can, and look for editions which focus on the same stories.
- Complete an analysis of the audience for each of these publications and explain how they are directly targeted by the publication.
- What are the key features of the local and national tabloids? How do they differ?
- What is the balance of visual against text in your chosen publications? Does this vary for different sections of the newspapers?
- How is colour used (or not used) in these titles? Why is this?
- Which do you feel is most successful and why?

Preliminary tasks

Detailed analysis

Select fairly recent editions of three different tabloids (ideally from the same day or at least the same week). Try to choose examples from different cultural or ideological backgrounds, for example a right-wing national tabloid, a daily local news-orientated title and a niche title such as a specialist publication.

Use the following questions to structure your analysis:

- **How many similarities are there in the choice of stories?**
- **How does the language and tone differ in each?**
- **How important are photographs to the text?**
- **What is the proportion of text to graphics on the pages?**
- **What representations are operating in the texts?**
- **What is the target audience for each text? How are they directly targeted by the publication?**
- **What are the institutional codes operating in the texts? (You may need to look at different examples from each of the relevant institutions to draw clear conclusions.)**
- **Why have you chosen to research these three texts in detail?**

When researching print production, it can help to undertake some more theoretical research in advance, to prepare for the Critical Evaluation for your artefact.

- What is a tabloid newspaper?
- What differences in role and function are there for gatekeepers on local and national papers?
- Do newspapers report the news or present an interpretation of the news?
- Should journalists operate as interpreters of news or disseminators of news?
- Are the tabloids ever too hungry for 'human interest'? Are we, as readers?
- Why are dramatic and disastrous occurrences such a powerful draw, and why do we not see more good news in the media?

Constructing the extract

Planning

Once you have completed the above tasks, you are ready to begin to plan your newspaper extract.

You should start with detailed research to discover an appropriate market for your new tabloid and define your target audience carefully.

You may prefer to construct a local paper. Since it is expected that you will source and research all your stories directly, a local focus will simplify the logistics of production. Remember to allow a substantial amount of time for **newsgathering** and research for your newspaper, as well as for the basic construction.

Assembling material

Identify likely local stories, think of an appropriate angle and prepare material, for example, photographs and background research.

If you are working in a group, it may be useful at this stage to delegate responsibility for different stories to different members of the group. One group member could act as editor to oversee the process and take primary charge of the final production. This allows a fair degree of autonomy for group members and ensures direct involvement in the newsgathering, photography, research, organisation and writing and editing of articles.

Source material

You should endeavour to source all your stories directly. Although your interest in a story may be triggered from another news source, you should follow normal journalistic practice and create your story from scratch. There are some very good reasons for doing this.

The most important reason is that you cannot 'own' the material sufficiently and construct and edit it appropriately for your particular publication if you are dependent on the words, images and research from a different journalist or publication. Having defined the niche and target audience for your tabloid, you are expected to construct a newspaper that relates to this position. There is also great danger if you try to manipulate material intended for different publications because it can become distorted or unfocused – it is far better to use this kind of material as a stimulus. Undertake your own research and take your own photographs to construct the exact image you wish to present in your publication, and write your own copy which directly relates to your audience.

Photographs

Original images are required. The process of constructing and editing your photographs reveals much about the decision making involved in constructing your text and allows far more sophisticated targeting of graphics to audience. If you have simply copied images from a different publication they are unlikely to fit well (physically or as **representations**) and may constrain the production process unnecessarily as you attempt to assimilate them.

Interviews

Most local public figures are happy to cooperate with media students if approached in the right way. You should make a polite request, for example, a letter to a local politician asking for an interview in relation to one of the stories you are researching. You should ensure you appear professional on the day (for instance, your tape recorder has fully charged batteries, the photographer has the camera ready, the list of questions is already prepared and you are punctual). It is far easier to add credibility to your stories if you have quotes or interviews from relevant people.

Register

Newspapers have a particular register that their journalists employ. For example, the style of *The Sun* is very different to that of *The Times*. It is important that you think carefully about the register you use for your newspaper and how this will be reflected in the language of each story. Your register should reflect the institution and audience that you have defined for your newspaper.

Advertising

You may wish to construct some suitable advertisements for inclusion in your paper. This gives you more opportunity to ensure that appropriate products and adverts are placed. The adverts are not usually controlled by the news or editing teams in a real publication, although the advertising and editorial departments of the newspaper coordinate layout and proportion of advertisements to **editorial** copy.

Page content

It is likely that you will produce the front page for your newspaper and a range of inside pages. These may be news-based or in-depth interviews or articles (for example, a newspaper targeting local clubbers may have a double-page spread story about gang warfare outside local clubs at closing time, or an interview with a bouncer at a local club). Avoid filler pages, such as the horoscope pages or letters pages – these are difficult to achieve effectively and provide little opportunity to demonstrate your understanding of the processes of newspaper production. Tempting as it may be to construct the range of letters for inclusion in your paper, it is likely to be more entertaining for you than for your proposed audience.

Flat-plan

One important aspect of your research will be to analyse the layout of comparable publications and use this analysis to inform your flat-plan for your newspaper:

- **What proportion of text to graphic might be appropriate on the front page?**
- **What type of story and image is appropriate for the front page?**
- **Are you going to use colour in your newspaper? If so, where and why?**
- **What fonts and point size are appropriate for the front page?**
- **How will you construct the masthead for your newspaper?**
- **What institutional codes will you use on your pages?**
- **What fonts and point size will you use inside your paper?**
- **How are the columns, titles, images, pull quotes, captions, and so on, organised on the page in your newspaper? Can you justify these decisions in light of your institutional context and target audience?**
- **How do your images reflect the ideology of the stories they are supporting?**
- **What use will you make of additional material like advertising?**

Compare and contrast these newspaper front pages to see how certain conventions are employed globally.

- How readily can you identify the target audience for each newspaper?
- How is the combination of text and images used to create meaning?
- How effectively do these front pages communicate?

A2 MEDIA STUDIES FOR OCR

THE TIMES

No. 68468 ■ WEDNESDAY AUGUST 17 2005 ■ www.timesonline.co.uk ■ 55p

WAYNE & WARNE

EXCLUSIVE IN THEIR OWN WORDS SPORT

Police 'errors' in killing Brazilian

Scotland Yard was accused in a series of leaked witness statements of "catastrophic errors" which led to officers hunting the July 21 bombers killing a Brazilian electrician.
NEWS page 4

Gaza deadline

Israeli soldiers entered Gaza's main Gush Katif settlement bloc just after dark to prepare forcibly to remove their fellow Jews as the midnight deadline passed for settlers to leave.
NEWS pages 2, 3

Schools admission

Independent schools admitted that there was no evidence that leading universities snub their students. In fact, they continue to win a larger share of places at top universities.
NEWS pages 12, 13

SU DOKU
WIN CHAMPAGNE
T2

Passage to Oz

Australia is to mount a new raid on the British labour market in an attempt to attract more chefs, bricklayers and motor mechanics.
NEWS page 25

Inflation jumps

Soaring oil prices and less than generous summer sales drove inflation to an eight-year high, dealing a new blow to hopes for more interest rate cuts.
BUSINESS page 39

'Great culture – with added envy, politics and speculation'
MAGNUS LINKLATER page 16

COMMENT	14	WEATHER	51
BUSINESS	32	TELEVISION	
REGISTER	47	AND RADIO	T2

Buying The Times overseas: Austria €4.20, Belgium €3.00, Toronto $4.20, outside Toronto $4.95, Cyprus €5.00, Cyprus £0.90, Denmark Dkr 26.00, Finland €4.00, France €3.00, Germany €3.00, Gibraltar £0.70, Greece €3.00, Italy €3.00, Luxembourg €3.00, Malta Lm 0.50, Morocco Dir 36.00, Netherlands €3.00, Norway Nkr 31.00, Portugal €3.00 (cont.), south Africa Rand 29, Spain €3.00, Sweden Skr 31.75, Switzerland S Frs 6.00, Tunisia Din 5.25, Turkey TL 8,000,000, VTL & USA $3.60. Periodicals Postage Paid at Rahway NJ Postmaster Send address corrections to: The Times c/o Mercury International 365 Blair Road Avenel NJ 07001.

Couples to choose sex of baby to 'balance' family

By Mark Henderson
Science Correspondent

COUPLES could choose the sex of their children to balance their families under a radical overhaul of fertility laws being considered by the Government.

Families with a number of sons or daughters may get the right to select an embryo of the opposite sex in the first review of assisted reproduction for 15 years, ministers said yesterday.

The major U-turn by the Government has reignited controversy over sex selection. Critics fear that sons may be favoured over daughters and predict that the move will make it harder to prevent the selection of traits such as looks or intelligence, should the technology become available.

The proposal to allow "family balancing" is part of a public consultation on fertility legislation, which was framed in 1990 and is considered out of date.

The review asks whether the ban on sex selection should be lifted for families who want a boy or girl, and how many children of one gender they must have to be allowed to go ahead.

Sex selection was outlawed except for medical reasons less than two years ago. The Human Fertilisation and Embryology Authority (HFEA) ruled against it in November 2003 after its consultation found 80 per cent public disapproval.

Sex can be chosen only to prevent diseases such as muscular dystrophy and haemophilia that are inherited only by boys.

Ministers have decided to think again after a report from the Commons Science and Technology Committee, which called the ban groundless.

"We are asking the ques-

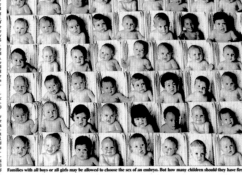

Families with all boys or all girls may be allowed to choose the sex of an embryo. But how many children should they have first?

tion," Caroline Flint, the Health Minister, said. "I think there are very good reasons why sex selection has been allowed on medical grounds rather than non-medical grounds, but these are important and complex questions."

The decision astonished fertility specialists. Professor Peter Braude, of King's College London, said: "This is quite extraordinary so short a time after the HFEA consultation. It does rather smack of 'you'll keep doing it until you give the answer we want'."

Mohammed Taranissi, of the Assisted Gynaecology and Reproduction Centre in London,

said: "These technologies are for helping people with medical conditions. If you accept family balancing you will have to accept a lot of other things that might come later."

John Harris, Professor of Bioethics at the University of Manchester, disagreed. "If it's not wrong to wish for a bonny,

bouncing baby girl, how can it be wrong to use technology to play fairy godmother to ourselves?" he said. "Unless palpable harm can be demonstrated, people should be free to make their own choices."

Fertility, pages 6, 7
Leading article, page 15

After A levels
Your essential guide to clearing and universities

IN THE TIMES TOMORROW

Fashion
Lisa Armstrong spots the trends for next season

T2 pages 12, 13

Part Four

Radio Production

Radio production is changing in many ways as stations are becoming more audience-aware and audiences are expanding as digital radio increases listening areas. The range of stations and content is growing all the time. A recent estimate is that there are currently over 50,000 web-only radio stations.

Audience and institution

You may have studied digital radio and changing technologies as part of your AS study on New Technologies and so you may have experienced some of this variety already. This gives you a strong background for the Critical Evaluation for a radio project.

If you are creating a radio text using some of these digital stations as your context, we recommend that you choose a station where the relationship between institution, text, audience and society allows you to demonstrate your synoptic understanding of the context and practice of production. In the same way, a campus or school radio station would not fulfil the criteria, since, by definition, the audience is far too limited.

Production facilities

It is also important to remember that you should not attempt a production in this medium unless you are competent with the equipment. While it is relatively easy to produce a simple radio production using a single-track recording system, it would be difficult to create a production to a higher standard without access to some form of multi-tracking or mixing facility. This may be software- or hardware-based, but production values for A2 work should demonstrate this level of competence.

Research activities

Radio is often overlooked as a media form, with many students and centres concentrating on TV, film and print forms. Yet radio is the earliest of the broadcast forms of mass media, preceding television by many years. In this country, radio broadcasting began with the BBC, but has now broadened into a range of national and local BBC and commercial stations as well as global stations and web-only stations.

ACTIVITIES

- Which radio stations are available on FM, MW and LW in your region?
- Identify the institution for each of these stations.
- Which are commercial stations and which are run by the BBC?
- Are there any pirate stations or other stations that do not fit either of these profiles? What is the remit of these stations? Are they successful?
- Identify at least five features of each of the major stations that make it easy for a listener

to tune in without knowing the frequency. How important are these features for the stations?

- Identify five major differences between the BBC stations and national commercial stations.
- Identify at least five similarities and differences between the national and local commercial stations.
- Are there any stations that are badged for your region? If so, try to listen to equivalent broadcasts from a different region and compare how they are mediated for the different audiences. For example, the GWR group re-badges stations for different regions, using the same format and style but different presenters, with an emphasis on local competitions.
- Research the **demographics** of the audience for a national and local BBC Radio station and for a national and local commercial station. What conclusions can you draw about these four audiences?
- The demographic of a radio audience changes at different times of the day – in what ways do the morning/daytime/teatime and evening audiences change for your chosen stations? Can you account for these changes?

ACTIVITIES

At some time in the day, most of us will turn on a radio. But do we really listen to the radio, or is it just on in the background? Write a short account of the role of radio in your own life, reflecting on the following issues:

- How often do you listen to the radio and where do you listen?
- When you do listen do you usually switch on to listen to a specific programme or do you simply use radio as background noise – and what programmes (if any) do you concentrate on?
- Why do you choose these programmes?
- Why do these programmes make you want to concentrate?
- What audience '**hooks**' do they use?
- How far do you fit the audience demographic for these programmes?

DISCUSSION

When researching radio production, it can help to undertake some more theoretical research in advance, to prepare for the Critical Evaluation for your artefact. Consider the following:

- Is advertising the best way to fund commercial radio?
- Based on your earlier research, what conclusions can you draw about the audiences for local and national and for PSB and commercial radio? What is the significance of these differences?
- It has been said that the presenters of a radio programme are the personification of the station and its listeners. Discuss this point of view with reference to the presenters of at least three programmes of your choice.

- It can be argued that the trend from broadcasting to **narrowcasting** has transformed radio speech into an agent and reflection of anti-standard social and intellectual currents. Do you agree?

- Many 'shock jocks' assert that they are the 'voice of truth' in radio, operating against the hegemonic function of talk-based radio. Is this the case or are they merely sensationalist?

- Why does pirate radio continue?

- 'It is listeners who decide the content of the airwaves, by listening to certain stations and not to others.' Do you agree with this statement, or are there other factors that control the output of the radio stations?

Practical exercise 1 – Radio drama

When creating video productions, you will frequently run into logistical problems. Even apparently simple shots, such as an actor being chased along a road, can be hampered by bad weather or too much traffic. If your production requires more visual support, for example, if you were trying to film a spaceship landing in the middle of the local shopping centre, you would rapidly enter the realms of special effects and laborious production. However, on radio, these problems are easily overcome. Just listen to the Radio 4 afternoon play or any episode of *The Archers* to hear how effective sound effects can be in creating a sense of time and place. It is easy to tell when scenes in *The Archers* are set in a pub or in a field by the different background sound effects that are used. It is far easier to establish a change of location than when working with visual material.

Below is a short script for two people. You should record this script three times, each in a different location. You will need to think about the sound effects and possibly the music that will create the right atmosphere for each of the locations. You will also have to consider how the lines will be spoken.

The scene

Opening music and/or sound effects.
Enter J

J:	Are you there? I can't see a thing at the moment. (Shouting) Are you there?

Enter P

P:	I'm right next to you. Keep your hair on!
J:	OK. Let's get this thing open and see what's inside.
P:	There isn't much time left. You know what might happen. So, you go down that end, and when I say 'now', lift.
J:	Right. On the count of three: one, two, three…
P:	Now!
TOGETHER:	What is that?

This is a very short scene but you can make it as long as you wish with sound effects and additional music.

Location

So, where will this be? You must choose three from the following list:

- A graveyard at midnight.
- A main road during the morning. Two workers looking at a manhole cover.
- Two archaeologists in an ancient Egyptian tomb.
- Two space explorers on Mars.
- Two people mending a lavatory cistern at home.
- Two surgeons in an operating theatre.

There are obviously a number of decisions to be made with each of the locations.

You will need to think about:

- what is being opened
- what music to use to set the mood at the beginning
- what other background noises or music to use in order to keep the mood going
- what opening or use of presenter's voice you will use at the beginning and end to open and close your piece.

When you have finished this production, test-market it on an appropriate audience.

- Can they identify the locations and atmosphere you created?
- Which elements of the recording did they consider most effective? Why?

Practical exercise 2 – Jingles

There are now many more radio stations and so it is important for each one to make sure that its audience can identify the station as quickly as possible. One way we identify stations is by the regular jingles which tell us that we are listening to 'Wonderful Radio Whatever'. The jingle must reflect not only the station but also the particular programme or item about to come on the air. A jingle for the news would be very different to a jingle for a 'Top 20' music programme. You should tune in to as many stations as possible, listen to their jingles and try to work out the images projected for both the stations and the programmes.

Now compose jingles for the following programmes on the following types of station. You have been given a brief profile of the station and the type of audience it hopes to attract.

Radio Oldie

This station plays nothing but records from the 1960s, 1970s and 1980s. It has a profile audience of 30-year-olds plus, although it is discovering that more and more teenagers are tuning in. You must compose the following:

- A station jingle for Radio Oldie.
- A jingle for the news.

- A jingle for the '20 Year Top 20'. This is a daily programme immediately following the breakfast programme, which plays the Top 20 from this day 20 years ago.

Radio Nose Stud

This dance station broadcasts to the local area. It is heavily alternative in approach, with an audience profile comprising young people, aged 16–21, who like the club focus and local dance scene information available on the station. Compose jingles for the following:

- The station.
- The local traffic bulletin.
- The local club update programme.

Classics Radio

A classical music station, aimed at a sophisticated A/B audience with an age profile of 25–50. A national station, it plays classical music, with the occasional programme which reviews new releases and gives background information on different composers. Compose jingles for the following:

- The station.
- 'Composer of the Week' – a look at the music of one individual composer.
- A programme that reviews new CDs.

CASE STUDY: DOCUMENTARY PROGRAMME FOR A RADIO STATION

If you choose to create a documentary programme, you should aim to produce a maximum of five minutes of material. You do not have to produce the whole programme so you may choose to do the beginning, middle or end. In five minutes you cannot hope to produce a whole programme. You may wish to include some of the following:

- **the opening link and opening sequence**
- **the opening monologue**
- **jingles**
- **a discussion**
- **narrative**
- **interviews**
- **the closing sequence and lead-out.**

Most documentary programmes are pre-recorded, giving you plenty of opportunities to get the sections right. However, it is important to make sure that you have pre-prepared some elements before recording the main **narrative** or discussion sections so that you can add them during editing. Do not try to assemble everything at once. For example, interviews should be pre-recorded and edited to fit your script before you record the main narrative sections. Jingles obviously need to be pre-prepared. Ensure these are pre-recorded and lined up ready to play, with no delays or confusion during the recording of the programme, or slot them in during the edit process.

Alternatively, there is no reason why you cannot pre-record the entire programme and then edit it as required, if that is more convenient. You should also experiment with the sound quality available for your programme. In particular, when recording interviews or **vox pops** you will need to be careful with sound quality – especially if you are recording outside on a windy day.

Recommended content for Production Log

- **A script outline and studio time-plan. In addition you should ensure you have a detailed production schedule. Remember to allow time for elements that need preparation. It is no good turning up in the sound studio to record the final version of the programme, only to realise that the jingles have not yet been recorded and edited for inclusion!**

- **It is a good idea to construct a script so that you know what information will be available in each section. You may prefer to use memo cards to prevent your presenters and callers from sounding as if they are simply reading aloud. This is especially worthwhile if you are doing a phone-in, to help achieve a sense of spontaneity. It is also good to put timings on the script so you know how quickly or slowly you are going. Clearly, if you are producing a radio play, you need a full script with sound effects, additionals and timings annotated clearly, so that it can be adhered to during production.**

- **Make sure there is a large clock which can be seen by all the members of the group so everyone is aware of timing.**

- **If you are using pre-recorded sound effects, make sure you have clearance to use them – just as you do with music tracks.**

- **A Production Log is necessary to keep track of the creation of elements such as station idents and to keep research information that may be useful to the project. A Production Log allows you to keep detailed records of objectives for meetings and rehearsals and problems to be sorted out. It also allows you to allocate responsibilities and schedules clearly.**

It is the producer's responsibility to ensure that all the necessary equipment is ready and that material is edited on time. This does not mean that the producer does all these jobs, just that they supervise them.

As part of your planning, it can help to undertake some more theoretical research in advance, to prepare for the Critical Evaluation for your artefact. Consider the following:

- Do you feel radio documentary is a popular and/or successful format?
- Select three documentary programmes to research as part of the project. BBC Radio 4, Five Live and local BBC stations are good potential sources. For each one consider the following:

1. What is the institutional context (i.e. which station and at what time)?
2. What context is constructed for the programmes? How does this affect the style of the programme?
3. What is the format of the programmes? What similarities and differences can you observe?
4. Are the programmes successful? Can you account for this?
5. Why do these three programmes make/not make successful radio?
6. What is the cultural and social context for each programme? How does this affect form and style as well as content?

Constructing the radio programme

The construction process will vary, depending on the software and hardware you have available for the programme. This will be determined by your centre and by your previous experience. Allow enough time for testing and re-recording your programme. It is easy to assume that a programme will be successful when the recording quality is actually too low.

When creating your programme, it is strongly recommended that you have access to either a multi-track recording system with effects units, or that you access sound-recording software and hardware that allows you to record each track and edit or add effects before mixing for airplay.

You should use as many microphones as you have speakers and ideally these should all be good quality unidirectional microphones to avoid picking up background sound. A unidirectional mike only records in one direction; in other words, it only picks up the sound aimed directly at it. An omnidirectional mike picks up sound from all round. This is good for background or blanket sound but not so good for a single sound source such as a voice. The microphones on a video camera are usually omnidirectional, which is why the sound recorded by these mikes during filming is unclear and unbalanced; the microphone cannot sort out the sounds to hear only the important sounds. You may need access to one omnidirectional mike to record sound effects or 'studio noise' during the show.

It is very difficult to get good quality radio work at this level if you are working by crash editing onto a single-track recording device like a cassette player or CD player, where multi-track is not possible. It is possible to use two cassette players and a basic mixing facility, but the reproduction of sound is likely to be weaker, even with first-generation multi-tracking. However, as mentioned below, you may be able to record a radio play using a single recording source, although you are strongly advised to test your recording beforehand. You may discover that recording from a single microphone detracts from your production because the sound quality is so poor that it cannot be easily evaluated. It is plausible to record a live performance of a radio play using live or canned sound effects, providing you have access to a multi-tracking recording system. You can use more than one microphone and take a direct feed into the mixing desk if you are using canned sound effects.

Whatever method you use you will still need a substantial amount of rehearsal time to make sure that you know what you are doing and to synchronise all the various activities.

Audience research

Once you have analysed a range of documentary programmes in this way, you should think carefully about the target audience for each programme.

- **What is the target audience for each programme?**
- **Is the target audience similar for all these programmes?**
- **Is this the same audience as the audience for the station itself?**
- **Can you account for these similarities and differences?**
- **How do the programmes 'brand' their identity for their audience?**

Once you have completed this research, you should be able to plan your programme more effectively, using the appropriate and successful elements that you have identified above.

Constructing the radio documentary

Opening the programme

Remember that the opening sequence of a radio documentary must paint a picture for the audience about the subject being explored and enable them to relate to it and empathise. Sometimes this is done with a dramatic opening – possibly even a short dramatic scene or simply an opening monologue with sound effects and background music – but whatever you choose, this is vital for the listeners. Equally, each section of the programme will need contextualisation – 'We are now on the factory floor about to interview some of the workers'. This is another vital difference which you do not need to provide in a television documentary as this is communicated to the audience visually.

When you are constructing the programme, the content will be far easier to author if you spend some time at the beginning of the project constructing the format. For example, you should define:

- **what station the programme is for and the time of day of transmission**
- **the target audience profile**
- **what hooks are given in the programme for the audience**
- **the theme and context of the programme**
- **the motivation for making the documentary**
- **the factual content of the programme (i.e. what the programme is about)**
- **the attitudes and opinions of the presenter(s) and how these will be revealed**
- **the interviews, vox pops or other inserts which you may use**
- **the outcome (which may not be a conclusion) to the discussion.**

Concluding the programme

Any documentary, whether television or radio, needs to have a beginning, a middle and an end. Of course the 'end' of the documentary may be an enigma (what will happen to the place now?), but it should clearly be a conclusion.

Documentary style

It is also important to think about the style of your documentary before you begin. Different types of documentary will require different approaches. In general, radio documentaries offer the same range of possibilities as television documentaries, although investigative programmes can be harder to do. Investigative television documentaries often make use of secret camera filming, for example – depending on the visuals for effect. A key element in many investigative documentaries is also the doorstop confrontation with an antagonist – again, this is harder to convey on radio. However, this is not to say that it cannot be done, just that you need to have thought it through before you begin.

Part Five ■■■

ICT/New Media Production

There are a variety of options available within this area. You might choose to create a website for a new online edition of a local film, a new computer game, a Dorling Kindersley presentation on CD-ROM about *film noir* or a short animation for the web.

Production facilities

It is important to remember that you should not attempt a production in this medium unless you are competent with the chosen software. While it is relatively easy to transfer skills between different video editing programs, for example, it can be far harder to transfer skills between multimedia software – not least because the programs are intended to achieve very different outcomes.

Your project should be presented in the format in which it is intended to appear. Thus a website must be accessible online. You should also provide a hard copy of the basics of each page.

CASE STUDY: CREATE A WEBSITE FOR A NEW FILM

A common feature of cinema marketing now is a promotional website for the film, with a range of information and content, generally starting some time before the first release date for the film itself. Blockbuster movies in particular are supported by high-profile, high-concept sites with information, interactive content, freebies and downloads, all designed to sell the brand of the film prior to release and during first release.

You should aim to produce the homepage and at least eight other pages for this site, with accompanying media files. For example, you might want to include stills from the film, downloadable files, poster images and maybe even trailers or 'interviews' with people involved in the film. You may even wish to include streaming video trailers from the film, a game related to the film, wallpaper and screen savers for download, or other elements. If you integrate many of these elements, you may need to reassign your project to 'cross-media', but this should not be a problem. However, you cannot work in the same medium as you chose at AS Level. Remember too that you should produce an official site, not a fan site, in order to adequately research and evidence the institutional determinants on production.

For the purposes of this project example, we will focus on the website itself and not on these associated media. Nonetheless, there will be some suggestions about more complex technologies involved, like streaming media.

ACTIVITIES

Identify a range of contemporary film releases that have associated websites. Identify three different studios (ideally two mainstream and one independent).

What similarities and differences can you see between the sites?

Now find sites for at least two other films produced by the same studios (or equivalent independent production companies).

What common elements can you identify between the sites? Can you identify a corporate identity for the studios? To what extent are the sites formulaic?

Now complete the same exercises for at least three different genres of film. Analyse the elements of these sites to identify common elements – is the layout or the style of the sites similar, for example?

Do sites within a genre tend to rely on similar selling points, such as freebies and downloads, for example? What methods do they use to hook the audience? How do they communicate about the film? How do they establish a sense of 'community'?

You may find the sites make use of bulletin boards or chat relays. How popular are these? Do they affect the success of the film in any way? Why are they used?

DISCUSSION

When researching film website creation, it can help to undertake some more theoretical research in advance, to prepare for the Critical Evaluation for your artefact. Consider the following:

- Which comes first – the trailer or the website?

- How much money do studios invest in websites for new releases? What evidence is there that this results in increased revenues? If websites are seen as loss leaders, are they important? Why?

- Some sites are more substantial than others. Is there any evidence that these sites have a different purpose? What examples of substantial or insubstantial sites can you find? Do they affect your responses to their films at all?

- What trends can you identify in film websites? Can you account for these trends?

- Do you prefer to visit official film sites or fan sites? Why is this?
- David Gauntlett, in his book *Web.Studies,* dismisses film sites as largely irrelevant to cinema and to film marketing. Do you agree with him? Why do you think the studios consider it important to create sites for new releases?

Planning the website

Once you have completed the above tasks, you are ready to begin to plan your site. You should start by thinking about the film that you wish to promote.

What genre is the film?

Just as there are generic elements and conventions for a film poster, you will see the same conventions reflected in a website for a film. A studio is likely to ensure consistency across a campaign and establish a 'look' for the site in order to identify the film and establish familiarity.

Who produces it?

Just as there are key genre elements, there are institutionally driven elements in the promotional campaign for any film. A website dedicated to a new release will make use of the elements of colour, layout, fonts and logos of the company producing or distributing it. If you are creating a website for a new film, it is made within an institutional context and the institutional codes and conventions should be defined at the beginning of the project.

What is the target audience for the film?

There are two important elements when identifying the audience: you need to identify the audience of the film and then the sub-audience for whom the website is likely to be an attractive marketing tool. It may be that the site can also extend the initial audience – perhaps by promoting the film or creating a cult identity or a community or fan group for the film. For instance, the target audience subsection who access the site may be keen to find out about the film prior to release or to gain access to images to use as wallpaper or screen savers, to reflect their enthusiasm for the film. A successful site will create a strong identity for the film and this can become a very successful marketing ploy. A good example is the now infamous *The Blair Witch Project* site, which acquired a cult following.

Elements of a site which entice surfers to revisit the site or engage them for some time – perhaps by offering games based around the film – can act both to heighten interest in the film among the target sub-set, and to extend this across a wider community. This is usually achieved by 'word of mouth' (usually via email) and establishes a sense of belonging and involvement which may cause more people to feel familiar with the film and choose to go to see it.

Choosing the film

Once the broader context for the site has been established, you should spend some time thinking about the particular film. Unless you have thought about the film in detail, you are unlikely to be able to isolate it and establish a strong site branding.

You may wish to create your own film and write a short treatment, define stars and select a studio, and so forth, as you would do when creating film posters and video covers. You need to have the basic packages constructed before you can begin to plan the site. Much of web design work consists of creating a basic design and using it as a casing for other media elements, for example, stills of the cast, extracts from the storyboard, trailers and copies of posters.

Designing the website

Once you have defined the film and thought about the target audience, institution and genre of the film, as suggested above, you can begin to design the website, knowing what you are seeking to achieve and why.

Remember to allow enough time to complete the site and test it before submission – especially if you are constructing posters or trailers that will be available on the site. If you do decide to create these artefacts rather than just using mock-ups to indicate how and why they would function, you should be prepared for the substantial amount of additional work that this is likely to entail.

ACTIVITIES

Identify at least five film promotion websites that already exist on the web. Try to choose a variety of mainstream or blockbuster films and more independent or less well-known ones – make sure you include a non-Hollywood example.

For each site, audit the content information available:

- How many pages?
- How many sections?
- What are the key section headings?
- How much emphasis is placed on hearing the soundtrack?
- How much emphasis is placed on stills?
- How much emphasis is placed on video material?

Now analyse the design of each of the sites:

- Does the site suggest the USP of the film is the story, the stars, the director or some other factor? How can you tell?
- Does the site provide background to the film, such as interviews with stars or location information?
- Are there opportunities to be interactive, by joining a web community to talk with other fans or by sending in images, for example?
- How effective are these opportunities? How well designed are they?
- What is the basic design of each site?
- How does this relate to the genre/style of the film?
- Why have they designed the site this way?
- How successful do you feel this design is?

- What fonts and colours are used? Are these successful?
- Do you feel the sites match the films?
- What differences can you observe between sites for blockbuster films and those for smaller, more independent films?
- Do you feel the site is an appropriate marketing tool for the film?

Once you have analysed a range of similar sites in this way, you should think carefully about the target audience for each site:

- What is the target audience for each site?
- Is the target audience similar for all these sites?
- If there are differences in the target audience, (for example, the target audience for the website may be a subset of the main audience) how does this manifest itself?
- How do the sites brand the film for their audience?
- What elements on the sites establish the **USP** of the film?

Once you have identified and differentiated the target audiences in this way, you should select three sites that you feel are successful and test them on members of the target audience.

- What responses do you get?
- Do they feel part of the target audience?
- Do the sites appeal to them?
- Which site is the most/least successful for them? Why?
- Do they respond to the music, the film or the site? Does this matter?

Once you have completed this research, you should be able to plan your site more effectively, using the appropriate and successful elements that you have identified above.

Producing a site map

When planning the site, the place to start is with a site map. Depending on the film you are working with and the proposed target audience, you may choose to structure the site differently.

- **A linear structure may be appropriate for a simple site – perhaps a site for a new children's film.**

- **A hierarchical structure may be more appropriate for a film in a series – another _Star Wars_ film, for example, where the principal part of the site may relate to the new film, but other site sections may cover the previous films.**

- **A mesh structure would suit many high-budget blockbusters because it allows for freedom of navigation. Each page is linked to all the other pages – perhaps with a navigation bar as a fixed element – making navigation more flexible. Users can easily access trailers, downloads, stills, inteviews with the cast, background information, game and/or community pages, and so on.**

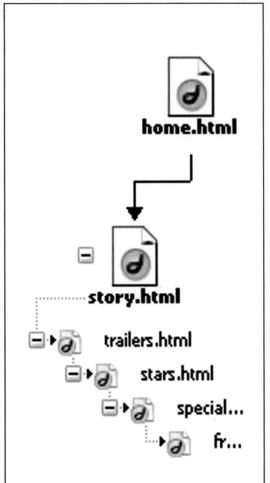

Consider these examples of how each type of site might be laid out. The imaginary new film being promoted here is called *Galaxies*. What does each design layout suggest about the genre and target audience?

home.html

story.html

trailers.html

stars.html

special...

fr...

Linear structure for *Galaxies* site.

Hierarchical structure as an alternative.

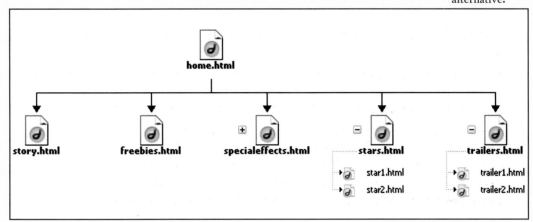

home.html

story.html   freebies.html   specialeffects.html   stars.html   trailers.html

star1.html   trailer1.html
star2.html   trailer2.html

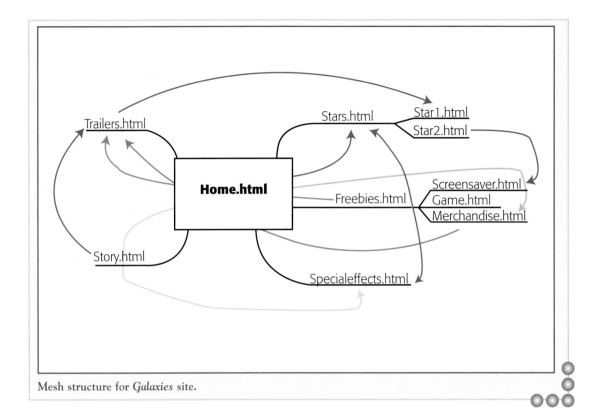

Mesh structure for *Galaxies* site.

Below are six possible site designs for *Galaxies*. Each of these is produced as a different 'theme' in Microsoft FrontPage®. These themes are an easy way to brand a site and can be tweaked to suit your film. However, you should be aware that many people are familiar with them, so they may not seem as unique and dynamic as you would wish. It is also important to remember that using these FrontPage® themes can make it difficult to upload your site onto a live server once it is complete.

Sites made with Microsoft FrontPage® will usually only display correctly on servers that use the 'FrontPage Extensions' provided by Microsoft®. If you want to look at the site you have designed on the web, you should check that the ISP you intend to use to host your site has these extensions. Remember, of course, that you only have to produce a CD-ROM version of your site for the A2 practical unit.

Site design

Having planned the basic structure of the site, you need to design the site appearance. How are you going to use visual codes to reflect and present the film? As starting points, you should think about the choices of background, which fonts to use, type and placement of graphics (including the possible use of a background image), use of design elements such as frames, focus points on the page, possible placement of adverts and balance of information/space. From there you need to work on creating an online identity for the film. Effective sites reflect the image of the film and highly successful sites identify this almost before a viewer even knows who the site belongs to.

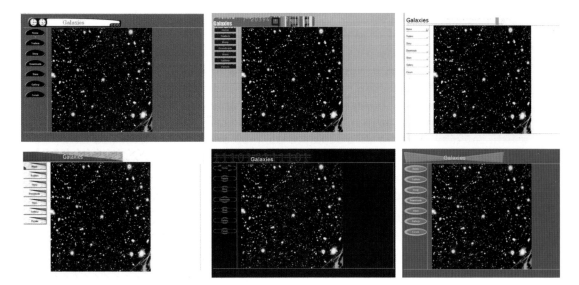

Six possible site designs for *Galaxies*.

ACTIVITIES

Look at each of the possible site designs for *Galaxies*. What is the impact of each design? What expectations does each design create about the film? Is a different genre created by each different scheme for *Galaxies*?

For each of these designs, make notes about the following:

- The colours used and their impact.
- The fonts used and their impact.
- The effect of the colour scheme and style on the image constructed.
- Your personal response to this design scheme.
- Your opinion about whether elements of this scheme would be suitable for your artefact.

There are no graphics on these design samples. Why is this? What would be a suitable image for the main page? How would that affect our assumptions about the film?

Developing the pages

If you are working in a group, you may decide to make each person responsible for a group of pages, or perhaps one group member could take charge of creating a series of images of the stars and preparing them for web use. One member of your group should also undertake the responsibility of project management and make sure that all the required elements are prepared and assembled on time.

It is sensible to have a range of paper-based planning materials. Not only will these help you to prepare the site, but they will also provide the necessary evidence for your written work to illustrate *how* you planned and prepared the site.

Recommended content for Production Log

- **A storyboard or site map. This may include a site map along the lines of the examples shown above, or you may map out your site differently. Once you have designed the basic site map, it is a good idea to construct the storyboard so that you know what information will be available on each page. You can use a simple arrow with a page number above to indicate which pages link to which. You may prefer to do a separate site map and storyboard or you may prefer to combine the two in one planning document.**

- **Draft layouts for at least three pages from the site so that you can analyse the design process and explain how you reached a design consensus.**

- **Original copies of stills used on the pages, annotated to show how and why you selected and manipulated images.**

- **An asset sheet for each page so that you know what elements need to be inserted into each page and who is responsible for them. An asset sheet can be laid out in various ways, but one example is given below.**

Constructing the site

You should construct each page of your site in line with your production schedule and allow enough time to create each of the required elements well in advance of their insertion into the relevant page. It is usually a good idea to assign a group member to be responsible for each type of asset here. In this way, one group member is responsible for taking and editing the pictures, another group member researches stories and writes the content, a third group member puts the pages together and the last group member films a couple of interviews or edits a trailer to include as streaming video files, for example.

The construction process will vary, depending on the software you have chosen to use. This will depend on what is available at your centre and your previous experience. Remember to allow enough time for testing your site. It is easy to assume that a site will be successful, but you may experience technical problems with your site. You will provide a hard copy of the site, but you should also try to test your completed site in a different browser before submission. If you are working on a PC, the browser which you are using and familiar with is likely to be Internet Explorer™. However, Macs can use different browsers and there are different browsers available for PCs as well. You are strongly recommended to test your site in Netscape Navigator™ or Mozilla Firefox™, as well as in Internet Explorer™. If your site displays correctly in these browsers, it is reasonable to assume it will display correctly in all browsers.

It is strongly recommended that you create your site with a web-editing package. Many word-processing packages (e.g. Microsoft® Word) or DTP packages (e.g. Microsoft® Publisher) have a 'Save as web page' option, which can make site production seem quite straightforward. Unfortunately, the output from these packages does not always work and in extreme cases may be impossible to save properly.

Lastly, do not forget that you need to put a copy of any file that you insert into your pages on the CD along with the pages themselves. The professional way to ensure that all the images,

Title _____ Frame No _____
Due Date _____

Basic layout of page drawn here

	Name and location of file	Description of media e.g. duration/file size/placement or timing
Image		
Video		
Music		
Text		
Background		
Links		
Web elements e.g. buttons		

Example of an asset sheet listing all of the files required for each page when constructing a website.

video, music tracks, and so on, are safely copied for assessment and moderation is to copy them all onto the CD which you will be submitting before you start designing the site. You can then tell the web-editing program to look at the copy of each file that is already on the CD, as required.

Part Six ■■■

Music Video and Animation

Music video is likely to be a popular choice for many students, but animation is offered as an alternative so that you can choose to work in this medium if you wish. You should, however, remember that animation is extremely time-consuming and requires painstaking attention to detail in order to be successful. If you already have experience and interest in animation, you would be in a position to offer an animated text at A2 Level.

Music video

If you are going to make a music video, you need to begin by deciding what sort of music video you wish to make and decide on your purpose. Some possible examples of music video are:

- a video for a new release composed and performed within school or college
- an animated video for an older track, re-badging it for a new audience
- a video for a re-release of a track not previously released as a video.

While it is not essential to compose and perform an original track for this project, it is often highly successful. It is far easier to integrate sound and vision when the composer, performers and video director can combine as a team. In the event that an original piece is presented in this way, the music is not assessed, but the freedom of control allowed is usually very beneficial. In many centres, there has been an opportunity for work across departments, with music technology students composing and performing the track and media students constructing the video.

It is generally accepted that pop music began in 1950s America with the birth of rock 'n' roll. In the last 50 years pop music has developed into a global economy, going far beyond the expectations of those early performers and audiences. The extensive range of musical types and styles in the contemporary scene presumes a sophisticated and experienced audience that is readily able to identify and analyse music.

Music video is a far more recent phenomenon. The fusion of image and sound in a video adds a further layer of complexity and creativity beyond that of the music itself. Early music videos were little more than edited 'live' recordings, which progressed from live cuts to multiple performances spliced together, or a combination of live and rehearsal shots. Later, videos added a narrative sequence as well as the performance, usually closely related to the lyrics. From this came the complex narratives and abstract interpretations that now define music video as a genre in its own right, leading to the multilayered representations that comprise contemporary music video.

Each new popular music style and genre is a development of the early rebellion that was rock 'n' roll and it is perhaps for this reason that the music video has developed into such a complex and varied media text. The forms and conventions of moving-image text are challenged and manipulated endlessly in music video and it has clearly transmogrified into a complex form in its own right. The combination of live performance, narrative, computer graphics and animation within a single video is both the epitomy of a **postmodern** text and a rejection of the realist conventions.

Indeed, music videos may be more appropriately defined as 'spectacle' than narrative. This presumes the different modes of address and representations that operate within a music video. The videos operate both as fantasies constructed around the music embodied within the text and as definition and limitation for the music presented. The visual construct extends and defines the reception of the musical track that is presented as spectacle in this way.

Video style now tends to be related to the genre of the music embodied in the video. A hip-hop video is likely to be different in form and convention to a rock video, a punk video or a lyrical ballad. We readily identify different visual codes with different musical genres. The target audience for any video identifies with the video very quickly because of this use of visual conventions. The vast sums of money spent on videos by artists such as Bjork or Madonna suggest the importance of the video in the lexicon of the artist's work. Indeed it has been suggested that the visual has been more influential for some artists such as Madonna (who reinvents her image with each new video) than the music they promote.

CASE STUDY: A VIDEO FOR A RE-RELEASE OF A TRACK NOT PREVIOUSLY RELEASED AS A VIDEO

Preliminary tasks

Research

Trace the career of a particular star through their videos (for example, Michael Jackson, or Madonna). In what ways does their image change through the videos? Why is this? Which comes first, the video or the image changes?

Select four music videos for different musical styles which you think are especially influential. Provide a detailed reading of each video, justifying your choices. Identify the specific target audiences for each of these texts. In what ways do the music videos target their audiences?

DISCUSSION

As part of your planning, it can help to undertake some more theoretical research in advance, to prepare for the Critical Evaluation for your artefact. Consider the following:

• With the increase in digital channels and more demand globally for video material for these channels, will music videos become such significant promotional tools that there will no longer be a CD release for many tracks?

• Has the rise of the music video changed the artists who produce the music in any way?

Deconstruction
When deconstructing the four videos, or your own video after production, you may find the following list of prompts helpful.

- **What representations are set up by the visual image?**
- **What media forms are used within the video?**
- **Does the video depend on the music for its context or does it define the context for the music? Why is this?**
- **What themes are set up within the video?**
- **In what ways are colour/style/fashion and make-up used to define this image or contextualise it?**
- **What are the social, economic and cultural contexts being employed in this video?**
- **What narrative is being constructed for the audience? In what ways is it constructed?**

- **What image is constructed for the artist?**
- **Are there other texts referenced within the video? What is the effect of this referencing? To what extent does it presume a knowledgeable audience?**

Planning

When planning your video production, probably the most important decision to make is how much live performance to include. This is crucial to the structure of your video but may be determined by the technology available at your centre.

When shooting the live action strands to the narrative, you should apply the theory and knowledge of video production that you learnt earlier in the course. This basic knowledge will not be repeated here.

Your planning should include:

- **a complete copy of the lyrics of the track and detailed timings**
- **identified target audience (with research notes and evidence)**
- **narrative breakdown for the composition of the video**
- **themes which need to be incorporated into the video**
- **storyboard for the video**
- **detailed breakdown of the visual codes to be constructed**
- **props list and shooting schedule**
- **equipment list.**

Constructing the music video

Live performance and sound recording

Most contemporary videos utilise a multilayered approach, combining live performance and other elements to construct a narrative. However, although there may be four or five different strands to the narrative constructed, the soundtrack is usually singular and consistent. In many cases, the narrative comprises a live performance supplemented by other narratives. The soundtrack will usually be taken from the live performance, with other narrative strands used as cutaways. This creates a complex and sophisticated structure for the video. Clearly, if constructing a video for a re-release of a track, you would not want to use pre-recorded commercial material (even if it were available) as extensive use of found material is always discouraged. Therefore, to lay down this kind of visual structure for your video and soundtrack you would require access to a group who could perform the track (copyright permitting) and the equipment to film the performance from at least three angles, while playing a CD for the group to mime to.

Once you have decided how you are going to produce the soundtrack to be laid down, there may be no need to record audio for the filming that you undertake, which obviates the need for microphones and sound equipment.

Choice of music and performers

As suggested above, the ideal arrangement for your video is to work with an entirely original track from an original source, such as a track from a local up-and-coming band or the music technology students at your centre. Remember that just as with actors, the video performance of your musicians and the musical performance are not assessed as part of your project. However, clearly the fusion of sound and vision is so important that a lacklustre performance is unlikely to help your project. If your musicians are not performers, you may wish to consider actors, but remember that this complicates the logistics of your project planning.

Pre-released material

If you have decided to go with a pre-recorded track, you should think carefully about the choice of track. You need first to decide upon genre, style and target audience and then find a suitable track, simply to narrow down the choices. You may prefer to work with a track that inspires you, but you must think about a wider target audience than just you and consider carefully whether the track is a good choice for visual representation. Some heavily sampled dance tracks would present immense problems for a video and may require full animation if a video is to be constructed at all, simply because of the way the images need to link with the sound. Equally, you should try to choose a fairly unknown track – it might be very difficult to create a new video for Michael Jackson's 'Thriller' or Pink Floyd's 'Another Brick in the Wall'. If you choose a track that is too well known (especially if the video is also very well known), you may find that your target audience responds less positively to your video.

Mise-en-scène

If you are using a set for one element of your narrative, you should try to film all those clips at the same time so the set can be dismantled as soon as that shoot is complete. This eliminates most continuity problems with the set – and probably with costume for that strand as well. You may not have the facilities available to shoot a performance against a blue-screen (for example, to supplant the screen with images from a desert island), or indeed to shoot on location in Barbados to begin with, so you need to choose a *mise-en-scène* that you can credibly create and work with. The videos produced by artists such as Travis may provide some examples and inspiration for possible formats.

Live action filming

If you are filming a live performance, you should try to use three cameras and shoot from different angles. If you try to film the performance three times from different angles you may run into substantial continuity problems when editing.

As far as possible, it is probably best to try to shoot each strand of the narrative as a batch, possibly even in one go. If you are constructing a conventional narrative as one of the strands of the video, you may find it helpful to treat this as a mini-production and plan it separately to the live performance filming. You may even be able to distribute responsibilities among your group for the different sections to ensure that everyone is fully integrated.

Clearly this does not apply to any computer graphics material or animated material that you are integrating.

Miming

If your video is going to include footage of the band miming to the music, you need to establish the context of this fairly quickly. Is this to be obvious miming (such as the band performing in a strange location with bizarre representations of instruments), or is it going to be presented as live action? If you are filming the former, you should work from the same copy of the track that you will be using for the soundtrack and record the music playing as you film.

Editing

This is likely to be the most complex and challenging aspect of the production. If you have prepared your storyboard well and shot the required material with a range of shots and pacing as required, the assembly should not be too painful. You may find with a complex narrative that it is a good idea to shoot a couple of different versions of many shots to allow for 'matching up' with the soundtrack. It is usually not a good idea to change the speed of a clip to make it fit a particular space, unless this is done specifically for a purpose and the change is explicit. Usually you will need to cut clips carefully to fit the soundtrack. You have more licence with a music video than with conventional narrative material, so you can repeat clips or use longer transitions than normal.

Some editing packages allow you to see the audio waveform while you are editing and enable you to match sound and vision more carefully. In Adobe Premiere® you can do this by clicking on the triangle to the side of the name of the audio track to reveal the waveform. Remember that you can layer up the soundtracks as well as layering the video (such as when adding titles).

Titles

These can also be created elsewhere or within your video-editing program. They can be integrated into your project and layered up as conventional titles at the beginning of the video, or may be more restrained as simple overlays. You may prefer to place the titles before the video itself, either against a black background or against one or more stills, so that the titles do not interfere with the video. If your video text is complex, the latter approach might be preferable, so that your audience can concentrate on the narrative strands presented to them.

Computer graphics

Many contemporary music videos make use of computer graphics, either to create a narrative strand or within the narrative of the video itself. These can be effective and are easily integrated into the project. They can be made in 3D software applications such as Lightwave 3D® or 3D Studio Max™, which can be very expensive. A more budget solution is software like Poser™ (which creates figures and creatures that can be animated fairly simply). Computer graphics can also be made as cartoon sequences, either as animations (which would probably result in a project too complex and time-consuming for the requirements of A2) or as narratives in 2D software such as Flash™ or Animator:Master™.

Shapes, text, colours, and so forth can be animated easily to provide abstract strands in a music video. This is sometimes used for the big-screen videos shown on video walls at outside events. The shapes and colours are animated to the music to create an abstract narrative in its own right. This can be effective but usually requires skills beyond those you are expected to develop at A2 for competent results. However, the integration of some animation in this form, for example, animated shapes or images of the group members, using software such as Adobe After Effects®, can be readily integrated and highly successful. Simple text and graphics effects of this kind can also be established in most video-editing software (such as Premiere®), where a combination of movement, distortion and fading text and shapes in and out can create a surprisingly effective animation for your video without being too time-consuming.

Animation

There are many different forms of animation that you might choose to work with for your practical project. Generally, these fall into the following distinct categories:

- Claymation (*Wallace and Gromit, Morph, The Plonsters*)
- 3D animation (*Cyberworld*)
- **Manga** cartoons (*Armageddon, Ninja Scroll, Angel Copy, Bubble Gum Crash*)
- Animated cartoons (Disney/Pixar animations, *Pokèmon, Scooby Doo, Tom and Jerry*).

If you are going to make an animated film, you need to start by deciding what sort of animation you wish to make and decide on your purpose. For example:

- an animated trailer for a new animation release
- an animated Public Information Film.

DISCUSSION

As part of your planning, it can help to undertake some more theoretical research in advance, to prepare for the Critical Evaluation for your artefact. Consider the following:

- What is the difference between an animation and a cartoon?

- Watch at least four television animations and deconstruct them in detail. What differences and similarities can you find between the animations?

- Identify the specific target audiences for each of these texts. In what ways do the animations target their audiences?

- Use the internet to research examples of children's animations from other cultures. What differences and similarities can you see between these and those you have already studied?

- From your study of these animations, would you say that visuals or sound are more significant when constructing an animation? Why is this?

Preliminary tasks

Planning

Having researched similar products and constructed a theoretical scaffold for your product, you can now begin to plan properly.

Animation is very time-consuming. It is usually shot at 24 frames per second and each of those 24 shots is constructed and shot individually. So, a one-minute film comprises 24 x 60 shots, that is, 1440 different shots! Animators generally try to shoot 'in twos'; that is, to film just 12 frames for each second of video, which cuts the work in half. If you were creating a very fast action piece you might find that this would be too slow, but for most animation work this is more than adequate. Almost all of *Wallace and Gromit* was filmed in twos.

Your planning should include:

- an outline of the entire series
- identified target audience (with research notes and evidence)
- treatment for the first episode
- hooks/themes which need to be incorporated into the opening sequence
- storyboard for the opening sequence (which will probably last no more than one minute)
- props list and design schedule
- equipment list.

You may want to use a shooting script, as you would for live action work, to ensure, for example, that you shoot all the shots against a particular background at the same time. However, most animators find that the **dope sheets** can be used as a shooting script as well.

Software

A range of dedicated software packages is available for creating animations, some better for stop-motion work and some better for drawn animation. However, these can be expensive and time-consuming to learn. For Windows PC users, the best option is probably to use Adobe Premiere® if you do not have access to the Lego® animation system (see page 52). As explained below, Premiere® will allow you to import single frames at a time from a camera, using the stop-motion facility. It is then easy to edit the material on the timeline, as with live action clips, and even to combine live action and animated footage with graphics overlays.

Mac users also have another option, with a simple, easy-to-use software package called iStopMotion, available from Boinx software (www.boinx.com). This package is simple and allows easy capture from a camera attached to the Mac and simple editing of the images into motion sequences, with blurring and onion skinning as additional effects, for example. Once edited together, sequences can be exported easily to iMovie for graphics, further editing and tweaking, or exported directly from iStopMotion as QuickTime or DV. The availability of an educational licence also makes it less expensive.

Constructing the animation
Using a blue-screen

It is often effective to shoot a claymation scene against a blue-screen or a single-colour background, which can then be 'keyed out' in your video-editing software and a more appropriate background added. This technique takes practice but does allow for more choices.

If you have to design and build a fully realised set for your claymation action, this can be extremely time-consuming. It can be very simple to draw or design a background and simply superimpose your figures over this background. For example, the children's programme *Blues Clues* makes extensive use of blue-screen techniques to combine the live presenter with the cartoon graphics to create the interaction. The presenter is filmed against a blue-screen and this film is layered above the background information using a post-production editing package with the background keyed out to create the final action.

This effect can be achieved with most video-editing software, using an 'effects' option and choosing either the chromakey option or image control effect and then selecting a colour to be transparent. The most important factor for success here is to ensure that the background is as solid and flat a colour as possible. The more variations in colour in the background (even those caused by the effect of light and shadow on the screen), the more difficult it will be to key it out accurately, without unwanted distortions. A suitable blue card is available from most theatrical and film suppliers and can be bought in sheets suitable for small-scale animation work, but also in rolls suitable for full-size studio backgrounds.

This technique has been used to great effect in many other films and television programmes. Another very famous example which merges live action and cartoon graphics is *Who Framed Roger Rabbit?*, where Bob Hoskins interacts with the very glamorous cartoon figure of Jessica Rabbit throughout the film.

Audio

If you are using characters in your animation, you should try to avoid using dialogue. To create effective lip-synch is very difficult and can involve 30 or more different mouths for a character to create the sound shapes. It is better to add a simple audio track to your animation – perhaps a piece of original music you have created on a keyboard. It is often easier to create a piece of music which matches your action than to try to edit your animation to match the music. Unlike most live filming, you are unlikely to have extensive choices as to which shots you use in your final animation. Although for a conventional film you would probably shoot at least three times as much material as you might need, to do that for an animation would triple your workload!

Sets

If you are using a set behind your characters, you should aim to keep it fairly small (a set built on a tabletop is useful as it is easy to film from different directions). Make sure you stick everything down very firmly. Putting something back even slightly misplaced because it was knocked over can look very clumsy on film. If you are constructing a room, leave at least one wall missing and try to ensure that one of the other walls can be removed if necessary, to allow for different **camera angles**.

Camera

Your camera must be on a tripod and you need to think about the camera angles very carefully. If you shoot a scene over several days, make sure that you mark the position of the tripod, just in case. If it is moved even a fraction, this can affect the final result quite dramatically. You can use a video camera set to single-frame recording (if your camera can do this), manually controlled or controlled by the editing software. If you do not have access to this kind of video camera, you can use a digital stills camera instead and upload your images to the computer more frequently.

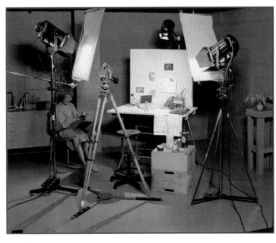

The set for *Morph*. Notice the storyboard attached out of line of the camera! Taken from *Cracking Animation: the Aardman book of 3D Animation.*

Lighting

You cannot create an effective claymation without lighting your set properly. You will need several lights to ensure you only get the shadows you want. Desk lamps are usually fine – try experimenting with different wattage bulbs, different colour bulbs, filters over the lamps and different positions to create the effects you want. Do not forget, however, that if you are using clay models they will melt if they get too hot!

Models

You can create a relatively sophisticated animation with models that do not move, for example, Lego® characters or small dolls/animals. Alternatively, you can build your models using plasticine or modelling clay. Make sure that you use a modelling material that does not dry out too quickly and try not to handle your models too much once you have made them. It is usually better to have five heads showing different expressions that you can swap between frames, than to try to mould your figures between frames. Make sure your hands are clean and dry when working with the modelling material (you can even wear gloves to be sure) and use some talcum powder if the modelling material becomes too oily. You can build small models successfully without a frame, but larger models will benefit from a frame. You can buy specialist 'armatures' or frames or simply make a basic shape from chicken wire to build around. Glass eyes and bits of bead are useful to give substance to your figures.

Lego™® kits

There are kits available now which allow you to make a simple animation using proprietary software and models such as the Lego® Studios kits. These can be just as effective for creating a set, lighting it and creating models as more traditional methods. You might choose to use proprietary kits like this to build your animation, but use more sophisticated cameras and editing to create a very strong animation.

Even if you do not have access to the complete Lego® animation kits, Lego® figures can be excellent for animation work. You can find a wide range of Lego® 'characters' and these are easy to use for stop-motion photography, being easy to manipulate and staying far cleaner than Plasticine™ models. It does not matter that their faces do not move at this level (indeed, it makes things a lot easier for you).

Editing

When you import your frames into your video-editing program to create your animation, it is important to check the default values for still images imported into a project. This varies depending on the software program, but most programs assume that if a still image is imported into the project, it should be visible on the screen for at least one second. This would make for a very slow animation and needs to be changed before the frames are imported.

In Adobe Premiere®, the standard default is for still images to span 150 frames when they are imported (1 second at 15fps). This must be changed before the frames are imported so that they import correctly. This can be done by going to: Edit – Preferences – General and Still Image, then changing the default duration from 150 frames to 2 frames if you are working in twos. Although you can change the duration of each frame manually on the timeline, this might take quite a while if you have imported 500 images.

Stop-motion capture

Another way to import your footage into Adobe Premiere® is to use the Stop-Motion Capture facility within Premiere®, if you have a compatible video recorder. This will allow you to operate your video camera through Premiere®, shooting single frames and importing them directly into your project. This can be a very quick way of working as you do not need to spend time uploading your images from your camera to the computer and then importing them into Premiere®. It also makes it quicker to see if a shot is wrong and to correct it.

Backgrounds

If you have not created a fully realised set for your animation, or if you have only created the foreground set, you will need to design a background for your animation. This could be hand-drawn, scanned in and then put into the animation as a layer behind the action (make sure you import it and put it into a lower level on the timeline or it will appear in front of the action). Alternatively, it could be created in Photoshop® or with a drawing program. Some animators make an animated background using software such as Macromedia Flash™ and import that behind the models to create a multilayered piece.

Titles

These can be created elsewhere or within your video-editing program. They can be integrated into your project and provide an easy way of extending your project by some seconds without needing to shoot so many model frames. If you are fortunate enough to have access to more sophisticated software such as Adobe After Effects®, you can create some good special effects to support your animation. However you make the titles, they are a vital element of an opening sequence and should be created with as much care as your claymation.

SECTION 2
CRITICAL RESEARCH STUDY

Introduction

The Critical Research Study is an exciting area of the course because it allows you to independently research and analyse an area of the media that you find particularly interesting. You should view your study as an opportunity to use the research skills and critical abilities you have gained so far within your Media Studies A Level course in order to produce a comprehensive and challenging piece of work. This section aims to define what is expected from you within a Critical Research Study and to give you guidance on how to research and present your chosen area in the most effective way possible.

To help you produce a detailed, wide-referencing, organised and challenging study, this section provides:

- a description of the exam
- a description of the nine areas of investigation that have been specified by OCR
- an explanation of the areas of investigation that need to be discussed within your study
- detailed guidance notes on how to approach the unit
- guidance on research methodology
- case study examples from the eight areas of investigation
- examiner hints.

The exam is two hours long and breaks the unit down into two areas. You will have to answer two questions on your chosen topic. The first area is research and you will be asked to give an account of the research you have undertaken, commenting on a range of primary and secondary research. You will need to demonstrate your ability to reflect on your methodology, clearly reference materials and explain your research process.

The second part of the exam asks you to analyse and present your research. You will need to comment on:

- your research findings
- the creation and development of your thesis (with reference to research and textual evidence, where appropriate)
- your conclusions.

The nine set topics

Below is a list of the nine topics of study, as set out in the OCR Specification. Later in this section we will look closely at each of these topics in turn and consider a selection of more specific study areas.

55

1. Women and Film
2. Advertising
3. Politics and the Media
4. Children and the Media
5. Crime and the Media
6. Sport and the Media
7. Community Radio
8. TV Drama
9. World Cinema

Areas of investigation

As with any independent academic study, your research needs to be active and rigorous. Your set topic will be chosen from the nine offered within the OCR Specification, but the specific area of study will be chosen by you. The Critical Research unit asks you to create an investigative area and you must choose something that you feel you have the enthusiasm to research and analyse in detail.

Once you have chosen your topic and specific area of investigation, you need to make sure that your research includes audience, institutional and critical perspectives. Remember, however, that one of the most important aspects of the study is that you should try to formulate your own critical thoughts. Your research findings should be used to lead you towards independent analysis. Your own thoughts rather than those of established critics should be the focus of conclusions about your chosen area.

When looking at the issue of audience within your study, try to consider not only the profile of the audience you have defined, but also how they reacted to the media texts they were offered. You could bring in theories of audience consumption here, but use them sparingly.

Make sure that if you discuss theories you make your comments directly relevant to the topic, research area and media texts you have chosen. Your own audience surveys could be as relevant to this unit as established theories and can be an invaluable element of research. You should also recognise that you are an audience member yourself and that your own readings of media texts are important points of reference.

Institution is the second area which needs to be covered and should be considered in terms of the people who have a role in the production process of media texts, the companies and organisations they represent, and the processes of production, distribution and marketing in which both are involved. The institutional research which you carry out will provide information on attitudes towards your chosen topic area and the ideological and historical contexts in which texts were produced.

As we have already identified, perhaps the most important critical perspective that you will discuss in your study is your own. This should be informed by other critical thoughts and frameworks and you should make sure that you include analysis of both academic and popular criticism. You will need to research existing academic critical work, but you should also look out for discussions within the press, TV programmes and sites on the internet that may be relevant to your chosen area.

Guidance notes on approaching the unit

As you can see from the outline of the exam, the Critical Research Study needs to be detailed and organised in a way which allows you to easily access relevant information. Later in this section you will look at case studies that discuss not only the possible content of your chosen area, but give you additional areas to consider and a way of working which will cover the requirements of the exam. These areas are outlined below and should provide guidance for your investigative work.

Generating the research title

Once you have chosen your topic, you should then brainstorm areas that may be of interest to research. Make sure that you choose an area you will be able to explore fully, that you will be interested in and around which you can build a compelling thesis. It might be useful to create a more specific research area under one of the following general headings:

- Issues of representation (linked to institution and context)
- The relationship between product and audience
- The individual producer's relationship with the industry in which they are working
- Historical changes within the chosen area
- Conflicts or controversial issues within the topic area.

Within your preparation, it is essential that you cover a complete range of research methodologies. Your examiner will look specifically for examples of both primary and secondary analysis within your exam answer.

Primary research

Questionnaires

Questionnaires can be a very effective way of gathering primary information and data for your project. In order to be most effective, each questionnaire will need to be carefully planned. You will need to define clearly how many individuals you want to complete your questionnaire and be able to explain why you targeted these people. Did you choose these individuals because of their age, gender, interests or some other defining factor?

The questions you use within your questionnaire must be very carefully thought out. Do you want to use open questions, which allow the individual to offer their own opinion of/response to a particular topic; closed questions, which will generate a more defined response, or do you think a mixture of both types of questions will generate more useful results?

Interviews

Interviews can be conducted in two ways: on an individual basis or in groups. As with questionnaires, the questions that you ask will need to be planned carefully before you conduct the interview. You should create questions with your interview subject in mind. If you are interviewing members of your peer group, for example, the questions will probably be very different from those you might ask an individual who works within an organisation. You might decide to conduct both individual and group interviews, in which case the different dynamic which exists within a group and a one-to-one interview scenario will need to be discussed within your project. It is always a very good idea to record any interview you conduct, as this will allow you to scrutinise your findings more closely. You could video the interview, but equally a tape recording of the process would be very helpful to your research.

Questions on internet message boards

Internet message boards on sites which have relevance to your topic can provide another useful means of research. As with the previous two primary methods, you will need to think very carefully about the questions that you post, considering both the audience for the questions and what the aim of your questioning is.

Own textual analysis

If your project includes study of media texts, then your own analysis will constitute a part of your primary research. Your response to the style or messages and values within a media text and the similarities/ differences between your response and that of others could provide a very useful discussion point within your exam answer.

Secondary research

There are three main sources that you can access when searching for references and materials: the internet, print publications and visual materials. The internet can be used to find reviews, critical writing, popular criticism, surveys and institutional information. Make a note of the websites that you use and the authors behind the materials so that you can reference them correctly in the exam. Print publications may be books of media criticism, media-related magazines, biographies of particular individuals, newspapers or guides relating to specific texts. You may need to photocopy the particular materials you wish to use, and you must note the author's name, the title of the publication and the date of publication. Visual materials do not have to include texts only related to individual or institutional producers; they could include TV programmes that discuss an issue concerning your chosen area. DVDs of films frequently have very useful documentary material as 'extras'.

Keeping organised notes and using reference materials effectively

You will need to organise your notes and materials in such a way that allows information to be easily accessible to you. You should use sectioned folders to store your findings, but you also need to break these down into particular areas. Below are some headings that might help you to organise your Critical Research Study.

Primary research

Once you have chosen a topic, you should look at all the sources you have located and create your own means of finding appropriate information. You should create questionnaires and sets of interview questions for target audiences and consumers, try to contact people within the industry, post questions on websites for people to comment on or answer and note your own responses to texts which are associated with your chosen topic area.

Secondary research

- Secondary textual analysis – notes on academic and popular criticism that have been written on texts related to your chosen area.

- Biographical information – information concerning particular individuals who are significant within your chosen area.

- Contextual information – information on the social, political and ideological context relevant to your area. You may have looked at, for example, the impact of political shifts on your chosen topic area, the role and perception of producers or texts in a particular period, or controversial issues which may be relevant to institutions or textual production.

- Institutional detail – your notes will include details of the companies and organisations that are significant within your research area. You may have information concerning their attitudes to and intentions behind the media texts produced, their role within new developments (either technical or ideological) or their attitudes to certain groups of people who work within them.

- Audience-related research – you should have information concerning the audience for the texts related to your particular area in terms of their profile, expectations, modes of consumption and contexts. This section should include any academic research that you think is relevant concerning audience reception, as well as details of audience research that you have carried out.

Finding and applying critical frameworks

Remember that this unit has been designed to enable you to use the materials you have created during your research in order to develop an independent critical response. Whichever idea and framework you use from established critical work should be incorporated into your own arguments. However, established theorists can be challenged and your study should include discussion of the relevance and the pros and cons of using certain critical frameworks. The case studies featured later in this section will give you more specific ideas concerning critics and critiques that may be appropriate to the set topics.

Creating your own critical response

Your own ideas and responses should always be systematically argued and fully substantiated, using examples from your primary research. Your ideas may challenge much of the existing criticism you have read and this can provide a thought-provoking study if your argument is supported by specific examples. Remember to refer directly to your area of research when you are creating your own response and not to formulate ideas that are not relevant to your title.

Notes for the exam

You will be allowed to take four A4 sides of notes into the examination and some of these should be selected so that you will be able to show evidence of the following:

- your reasons for identifying your topic of study
- your chosen topic has been thoroughly and appropriately researched
- you have made relevant use of existing criticism
- you have considered the profile, expectations and text reception of your identified audience
- you have understood the nature and impact of institutional questions
- you have considered historical and social context as factors which influence your topic area.

Research methodology

The exam asks you to comment on the investigative findings and process of your research. You should make sure, therefore, that you adopt a systematic approach to this study in order to gain the most effective results and be able to discuss your methodology clearly in the exam.

Your research will be mainly qualitative, in that it will consist of active investigation, analysis and evaluation of texts and institutions. Below is a possible model of the different stages that may occur during your project; this should be used in conjunction with the guidance notes on approaching the project to ensure that both content and process are thorough.

Research methodology model

You could use this section as a tick list of areas to cover while you are involved in your research.

Define your sub-topic clearly

You need to do this both for yourself and for the examiner when you take the exam. What kinds of areas will need to be discussed within your sub-topic? What kinds of information do you predict that you might find? You could create a spider diagram, outlining the ideas you think will be pertinent to your study. The contents of this diagram will of course be added to or amended by the end of your study, but the comparison and contrast in itself will provide you with possible developments within your investigation.

Identify the breadth of the topic

Even sub-topics have huge investigative potential and you need to create some limits for yourself in order that the project is manageable. It is much better to research a specific area thoroughly than to offer a vague, overly broad and therefore insubstantial account in the exam. In your planning you need to describe the limits of your project. They may change slightly as the research progresses, but in your final account make sure that your project and findings address one specific aspect of the sub-topic thoroughly.

Be realistic with the secondary information you collect

When you are browsing the internet, searching through libraries or reading through back issues of magazines, always keep your specified topic area in mind. It is very tempting to download everything you find connected with the general topic or to read through every piece of critical work that refers to it. However, you have set yourself limits for your research area and you should stick to these. You may have chosen to research 'Children and the Media', but only a small percentage of the information concerned with this massive topic area may be relevant to you. You may have been more specific and have begun to research the impact of video game play on children, but even within this narrower sub-topic there is still an overwhelming amount of information. However, if you have already decided to limit yourself to violence in video games and have defined the exact age group of children you are going to be studying, then the information available to you will be that much smaller and your study will have more investigative weight.

Evaluation of information

As we have already discussed, it is essential within this study that you develop an informed, personal response to the sub-topic you have chosen. Part of the process of doing this is to evaluate the information you have collected. Try to comment on the advantages and disadvantages of certain pieces of information for your study. If you have found some connected data or critical responses, try to evaluate their usefulness. They may be biased in some way, out of date or reflect differing views on your topic. Evaluation is an extremely useful critical procedure, because it allows you to prove to an examiner that you have not merely absorbed and regurgitated secondary critical thinking.

The process of evaluation must also extend to the whole project when you are near completion. Read back through your notes and comment on what you find. Do you think you have created a comprehensive project? Are there any questions that you feel have been left unanswered? What kind of conclusions have you come to through your study and do these challenge or confirm established critical positions?

Providing accurate references and organising your project

For any piece of information or secondary source you gather, make sure that you have logged the source, the author and date of publication. If you note down a quotation for your project, also give its originator and source.

When you come to write your project, it needs to be developmental and systematic. Make sure that you refer back to the section on 'Keeping organised notes' in order to do this.

Case studies

This part of Section 2 provides examples of materials which would be appropriate for the study of particular sub-topics. The examples given do not indicate an exhaustive list and you should use the sections to guide you in the creation of your own research topic and set of comprehensive notes.

Part One ■■■

Women and Film

The topic Women and Film allows for many areas of study connected to the varying roles that women can occupy within the film industry. You may decide to look at issues connected with just one film-maker or to consider a group of female film-makers and the issues raised by their work or their position in the industry. There are many areas of study on which you could focus within the general heading of Women and Film. Below is a selection of possibilities.

Gender issues within the film industry

You could take a historical perspective and trace the position of and attitude to women in the film industry. What developments can you see? What difficulties and restrictions have meant that women still occupy a minority percentage, especially within the realm of directing?

Issues of gender representation in films

This section considers the interior world of films, rather than being a direct analysis of female personnel, and so you could study texts by both male and female directors. You could analyse a group of similar texts (the group could be constituted by nationality, genre or historical period) and research the different representations of women offered. You could look at the developments and shifts within the representations of certain female character types or investigate what expectations audiences have concerning the women they see on the screen.

Jodie Foster

Jodie Foster and co-star from *Little Man Tate*.

Feminist or other critical perspectives

An analysis under this heading might consider the approaches and theories of different feminist critics or look at how feminist criticism approaches certain groups of films. You could take a more contextually driven approach and discuss the dynamic between feminist criticism and films produced within a particular decade.

Audience reception of films by female film-makers

The first stage of a study under this heading would be to choose a female film-maker. You do not have to limit yourself to directors, but could look at female producers, actors and editors as well. If the films you have chosen are not explicitly female-driven in some way (i.e. they do not have central female characters, discuss a female agenda or are from a female film director), then your analysis will be more difficult because audience reception will not be of the film as a piece of female film-making. It would be more straightforward to choose films that the audience will recognise as being 'female' in some way. Once you have your film group choice, try to gather a range of critical responses, from academic to popular. You then need to pose yourself some questions that can be answered from the criticism you find.

- Are these films targeted at female audiences?
- Are these films from a particular genre?
- Are they successful?
- Are there expectations involved in the audience's viewing of a film by a female film-maker?

Female film-makers within Hollywood or the independent system

Within this area, you could study the different ways in which female film-makers are treated within Hollywood and the independent system (remember to avoid any literal preconceptions about one system being the polar opposite of the other). How have female film-makers risen within both systems? Is there any crossover between the two? Remember that you do not have to limit yourself to American or British female film-makers.

Whichever sub-topic you decide on, it is important to remember that the research project needs to include at least the majority of the areas outlined in the guidance notes section. You should not limit yourself to providing points of textual analysis, but also extend your research to include institutional and contextual information.

CASE STUDY

Gurinder Chadha

With an individual film-maker, it is probably best to begin with research into their filmography. This will give you an immediate sense of the genres of film produced, the period in which the film-maker was or is working, and their range of talents. Gurinder Chadha, for example, has directing, acting and production credits.

Director

I Dream of Jeannie (2006) (in production)
The Closet (2006) (announced)
My Sassy Girl (2006) (announced)

Bride & Prejudice (2004) ... aka *Bride and Prejudice: The Bollywood Musical* (International: English title: promotional title)
Bend It Like Beckham (2002) ... aka *Kick It Like Beckham* (Germany)
What's Cooking? (2000)
Rich Deceiver (1995) (TV)
A Nice Arrangement (1994)
What Do You Call an Indian Woman Who's Funny (1994)
Bhaji on the Beach (1993)
Acting Our Age (1992)
Pain, Passion and Profit (1992) (TV)
I'm British But ... (1990) (TV)

Writer

The Closet (2006) (announced)
My Sassy Girl (2006) (announced) (screenplay)
Mistress of Spices (2005)
Bride & Prejudice (2004) ... aka *Bride and Prejudice: The Bollywood Musical* (International: English title: promotional title)
Bend It Like Beckham (2002) ... aka *Kick It Like Beckham* (Germany)
What's Cooking? (2000)
A Nice Arrangement (1994) (also story)
Bhaji on the Beach (1993) (story)
I'm British But ... (1990) (TV)

Producer

Mistress of Spices (2005)
Bride & Prejudice (2004) ... aka *Bride and Prejudice: The Bollywood Musical* (International: English title: promotional title)
Bend It Like Beckham (2002) ... aka Kick It Like Beckham (Germany)
What's Cooking? (2000) (associate producer)
What Do You Call an Indian Woman Who's Funny (1994) (from www.imdb.com)

For any project under the heading of Women and Film that considers a particular female film-maker, it will be very useful to consider the critical reception of her work. A review, such as the one for Chadha's *Bride and Prejudice* below, can indicate critical response to the film-maker and the representations she includes within her work. The opinions expressed in this type of review can then be evaluated against your own response to the film text and the film-maker.

Gurinder Chadhra

A still from *Bhaji on the Beach* (1993).

Review by Philip French

Bride & Prejudice (112 mins, PG)

Directed by Gurinder Chadha; starring Aishwarya Rai, Martin Henderson, Naveen Andrews

Comic transpositions are nothing new in the cinema – the 1940 Cary Grant classic *My Favourite Wife* was inspired by Tennyson's *Enoch Arden* and Jacques Tourneur's 1943 horror movie, *I Walked with a Zombie*, is a version of *Jane Eyre*, but there has been quite a spate of them these past few years. We've seen *The Taming of the Shrew*, *Les Liaisons Dangereuses* and *Emma* relocated to American high schools, and now Gurinder Chadha's *Bride and Prejudice* re-creates Jane Austen's *Pride and Prejudice* as a Bollywood musical.

Of course, borrowing plots from anything fashionable in world cinema is standard practice in Bombay, and there have been stage musicals of *Pride and Prejudice* – I saw one at the Birmingham Rep some years ago, starring Patricia Routledge as Mrs Bennet. What is new is having a Bollywood musical conceived in the West and co-produced by Miramax, whose boss, Harvey Weinstein, makes a jolly appearance on the streets of India during *Bride and Prejudice*'s final credits.

Chadha, as she has shown in her previous pictures – *Bhaji on the Beach*, *What's Cooking?*, *Bend It Like Beckham* – is a crowd-pleaser, and the chief characteristics of her new film are populist cheek and cosmopolitan chic rather than subtle social observation. The film establishes its tone from the start. Jane Austen begins her novel with one of the most famous lines in English literature – 'It is a truth universally acknowledged, that a single man in possession of a good fortune must be in want of a wife.' This becomes, in the mouth of the incredibly beautiful Aishwarya Rai (playing Lalita Bakshi, the film's version of Elizabeth Bennet) 'Anyone who's got big bucks is shopping for a wife.'

Austen's little England, around which people take long journeys by coach, is replaced by the global village of the Indian diaspora, where well-off Indians travel by plane. Longbourne, Hertfordshire becomes Amritsar, Punjab, the 'Hicksville, India' hometown of Mr Bakshi and his outrageously vulgar wife (who have one daughter less to dispose of than Austen's Bennets), and the action spreads out to Goa, London and Los Angeles.

The American hotel magnate Will Darcy (Martin Henderson) comes to Amritsar with his friend, the handsome London-based lawyer Balraj (Naveen Andrews) and Balraj's snooty sister, and begins his complex romance with the headstrong, outspoken Lalita. There is, however, so little chemistry between the two that this encounter between East and West fulfils Kipling's claim that never the twain shall meet.

Lalita's suitor, Chadha's substitute for the insensitive vicar William Collins, is Mr Kholi (Nitin Ganatra), a ludicrous Ali G figure. The film's principal comic butt, Kholi is a successful accountant in Los Angeles who has come home to find a wife. He considers that Indian girls who have grown up in California 'have lost their roots and are clueless'. This refers, presumably, to *Clueless*, Amy Heckerling's brilliant Beverly Hills version of *Emma*. The picture's chief attraction, apart from its gorgeous leading actress, is the ingenuity of the transposition. Particularly amusing is the way the military cad George Wickham becomes a backpacking bounder. Prior to seduction he takes Lalita's sister Lucky (i.e. Lydia) on the London Eye, and is then pursued into the National Film Theatre by Darcy, where they have a fight on stage while a Bombay musical featuring a melodramatic seducer is projected behind them. But the movie is ultimately trite and banal rather than poised, and this comes from its chosen form. Are we watching a parody of a Bollywood musical, or a pastiche? Are we intended to find the broad effects, the musical routines, the crude acting funny because they're so naive?

In simultaneously sending up and celebrating Bombay cinema, Chadha is trying to have her chapati and eat it. Satyajit Ray, India's only great movie director, has often and rightly been compared with Chekhov. *Bride and Prejudice* is not even a baby Austen. It's Mills and Boon, which we know to have been the favourite reading of Ray's friend Indira Gandhi.

Source: *The Observer*, 10 October 2004

Part Two ■■■

Advertising

There are lots of possibilities for effective projects under this heading and you can choose adverts from any medium. As with any of the other topic areas, however, you must not rely entirely on textual analysis within your research. Any study you carry out concerning advertising will need to consider institution and audience, as well as the adverts themselves.

The nature and purpose of advertising

If you choose to create a project under this subheading you will need to consider in detail what is being sold, why and to whom. Consider what strategies are being used in order to sell the 'product' within the advert. These strategies will include textual features, such as the particular use of sound, *mise en scène*, and so on, but you will need to extend your analysis beyond these features to include consideration of what is being implicitly sold by the advert. Is the purpose of your chosen advert to sell an aspiration, an image or a lifestyle? What value is the product attributed in the advert and how is this being used to engage the target audience?

For this particular sub-topic, you could also create a research project which looks into the different purposes of advertising. Not all adverts are created in order to sell a particular product. Some advertising aims to inform, to educate or to raise public awareness about particular issues. You might consider a campaign which promotes a set of ideas or values, rather than one in which a tangible product is being marketed. Whether the strategies used for the promotion of an idea/ideology/issue are the same as those used to sell products to particular audiences would be a key question for you to consider within this type of research project.

Ideological issues: messages and values

This sub-topic does have an element of crossover with the previous one in that you will need to consider what it is that is being sold. However, the focus here would be different in that you will need to discuss the relationship between the messages and values generated within the advert and those which exist within its context.

In order to evaluate what kinds of messages and values are being generated in the adverts you have chosen, you will need to begin with textual analysis. However, as has already been mentioned, this should not become the dominant focus within your study. Use your analysis of the text to create comments concerning the representation of particular social groups, places, events or institutions. Once you have identified the representations you think are evident within your chosen adverts, you will then need to address the following questions:

1. How is representation being used to sell the product to its target audience?
2. Why has the company/organisation behind the advert used this/these particular representation(s)?
3. To what extent does the representation within the advert confirm/challenge attitudes held within the target market?

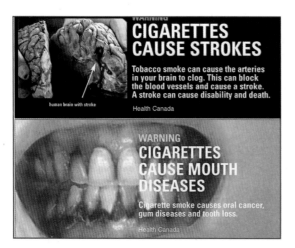

Product placement

As you are probably extremely aware, product placement is evident within many media texts today. For the advertising industry, product placement can provide a means of exposing either a product or the brand name itself to an extremely wide audience. Although product placement is not such explicit advertising as print or TV campaigns, it is often not that subtle either. Companies will pay a vast amount of money, for example, to have the hero of a particular film drive a particular car, thus associating in the minds of the audience for that film the positive attributes of the film's hero with the car.

You might look at a case study of a particular company and the media texts in which it has placed products. You would then need to consider why these particular texts have been chosen. Breadth of potential market might be one reason for using a film or TV programme, for example, to sell a product. The media text may have particular values attached to it which the makers of the product want audiences to also attach to their product. The company might be aiming to expand their market and chose a particular text in order to target a new audience.

Niche and mass markets

A niche market traditionally is one which is small and has specific interests. A mass market is made up of a broad range of individuals and has a diversity of interests. These types of markets are different, but they are not fixed, in the sense that for certain products an individual might be part of a niche market, and for other products that person will be targeted within a mass market. The niche markets for magazine publications, for example, will not necessarily be the same as those for food items.

Your project under this subheading has many possible directions for study. You could research into whether the strategies for advertising to mass and niche audiences were similar or markedly different. However, this kind of project would need to have a clear focus on one particular medium in order for it not to become too broad and vague. You could restrict yourself to a particular niche market and investigate what products are being targeted at them and the strategies being used to advertise. For any project under this subheading, remember that the relationship between the product and the potential consumer is a dynamic one. Potential consumers have expectations and demands which need to be catered for in order for the product to be successful. Do not assume the target market you have identified passively consumes; the relationship between company, product and consumer is much more complicated than that.

CASE STUDY

Adverts that have generated controversy

A project which focused on the nature and purpose of advertising, with particular focus on adverts which have generated controversy, would do well to look at the Advertising Standards Authority's website, which gives clear case studies of discussions and adjudications connected with specific adverts. This type of case study can be used to evaluate both viewer and institutional reactions to particular adverts or series of adverts.

A Frog's Tale that spawned viewer outrage

Like the last song on the radio or a tune you hear someone repetitively humming, some things enter into your subconscious and won't get out of your head. In the competitive world of advertising, where grabbing consumers' attention is paramount, advertisers are acutely aware of the importance of making their advertisements distinctive and memorable.

This is exactly what the marketers of a mobile ring tone, screensaver and mobile video managed to achieve by promoting their product using their advertising creation, 'Crazy Frog'. However, it stuck in some viewers' minds for all the wrong reasons.

Crazy Frog, a computer generated, animated amphibian clad in a leather motorcycle cap and goggles was used to sell the advertiser's mobile jingle. The ring tone consisted of Crazy Frog pretending to be on a motorbike. In the commercial he stood making revving noises which became increasingly noisy until reaching a crescendo. Innocent enough, you might have thought.

Not to some viewers. It wasn't long before complaints were flooding into the Advertising Standards Authority (ASA). Some viewers complained that the commercial was annoying and broadcast far too frequently. However, the main crux of the complaints related to a far more unusual and surprising subject matter: frog genitalia.

Viewers had noticed that Crazy Frog was very definitely male due to a protrusion that stuck out from his cartoon body. The complainants found this inappropriate. Some were worried about children seeing this kind of advertising material whilst a few parents had felt embarrassed by some of the questions their children had asked them. The ASA decided to formally investigate the complaints.

Though the ASA takes all complaints about offensive advertisements very seriously, this certainly ranked as one of the more unusual investigations it had ever launched. However, despite the high volume of complaints, 60 in total, the complaints were not upheld.

Because the commercial prompted viewers to order the ring tone via text it had been given an ex-kids restriction and automatically moved away from being shown around programmes specifically made for children. With regards to the anatomical anomaly, whilst acknowledging it was surprising for genitalia to be shown on an animated frog, the ASA found that there were no sexual or inappropriate references made about it. Furthermore, whilst it appreciated adults were concerned about the frog, it noted that none of the complaints reported children being upset. As an ex-kids restriction was already in place the ASA did not consider the genitalia to be a problem. Lastly, though the ASA accepted that advertisements which are broadcast frequently can rankle with some viewers, it didn't uphold the complaints as it is the advertiser and broadcaster who decide how often they show a commercial.

Source: ASA website, 26 August 2005

ASA takes the fizz out of Tango ad

Tango is renowned for its bizarre style of advertisements, however its latest offering – entitled Pipes – was deemed to have gone one step too far by some viewers.

The TV commercial for the soft drink showed a young man wrapped in a carpet filled with oranges that lay on top of a pyramid of concrete construction pipes. The pyramid was held together with a rope, one end of which was attached to a goat. As the goat moved away, the pyramid collapsed and the man tumbled uncontrollably fast down a steep hill. He then crashed into a tree and two pipes hit him consecutively. The man emerged from the carpet, drenched in juice but completely unharmed and smiling. 'You know when you've been Tango'd', announces the voice-over.

The viewers who were particularly upset by the ad complained that it trivialised and condoned a harmful situation, and could even encourage children to play with potentially lethal construction materials.

In fact, one of the four complaints to the ASA – which took over the regulation of broadcast advertisements from Ofcom in November 2004 – came from relatives of a boy who was killed in an accident involving concrete pipework. Another complainant pointed out that the TV commercial could jeopardise the construction industry's current efforts to discourage children from playing with construction materials.

Because of the dangerous nature of the ad's potential effects, Lord Borrie, the ASA Chairman, took the unprecedented decision to ban the advert with immediate effect, ahead of a formal investigation.

Both the advertiser and advertising agency defended the Tango ad by saying they believed the public would recognise it as pure fantasy and entertainment. Nevertheless, they fully accepted the complaints and Tango owner Britvic agreed to withdraw it, offering genuine apologies for any offence caused.

The Broadcast Advertising Clearance Centre, which is responsible for pre-clearing TV commercials before they are aired, defended their decision to give the ad clearance. The BACC believed the ad was obviously surreal and the very fact that it wasn't set in a building site – or indeed anywhere realistic – suggested that the stunt could not be copied and the behaviour was not condoned. Only the very young wouldn't appreciate the fantastic content of the ad, it said, and with this in mind it had decided to allow it to be shown only after the 9pm watershed.

Although the ASA agreed that viewers might be familiar with the Tango style, it judged that previous commercials were far harder to copy. Those ads required equipment that was not readily available or accessible and children were unlikely to perceive the scenarios as at all realistic.

The new commercial, however, showed someone rolling down a hill – an activity appealing to many children. This in itself could cause serious injury if copied and if pipes – which are found near many road works and building sites – were involved, the danger would be greater still.

Above all, the ASA concluded that the impression given by the ad was that construction materials are fun to play with and that there are no consequences to that dangerous activity, except perhaps having fun.

Because this is in breach of rules relating to both the health and safety and physical harm of children in the CAP (broadcast) TV Code, the complaints by viewers were upheld and the advertisement will not be shown again.

Source: ASA website, 26 August 2005

Part Three ■■■

Politics and the Media

Initially this topic can seem quite daunting. You might think that you know relatively little about contemporary politics. However, look carefully at the potential sub-topics below and you will probably find areas about which you already know a substantial amount.

Party political broadcasts, campaigns, photo opportunities and lobbying

General elections will have been part of your media experience over the last few years. You may not have studied them closely at the time, but you may have seen the party political broadcasts or passed an advertising hoarding of the poster campaigns. As a media student in your second year of study, you are already something of an expert on the effects of visual campaigns on an audience.

You will have studied the ways in which colour, iconography, representation, framing, language and cultural signifiers are used to attract an audience and you will be able to discuss the ways in which the audience consumes what they see. Why not transfer this knowledge to the study of a political campaign?

You could look at a poster campaign, political broadcast and series of photo opportunities connected with a particular party during the last election and evaluate both the messages they are trying to deliver and the effectiveness of that delivery. You could compare and contrast two campaigns, broadcasts and photojournalistic treatments, evaluating the relative success of each one. You could compare and contrast a particular party's campaigns over two or three elections, noting the changes in cultural signifiers, target audiences and even media technologies.

You do not necessarily have to base your work on general elections. You may prefer to concentrate on local or regional elections. If you choose to base your research project on lobbying, you could examine the media products attached to an interest group and how they have been used to try to influence political action. Greenpeace campaigns on posters and television could provide an interesting debate. What do the campaigns include? How do they attempt to influence public and political opinion? Are they successful?

Government press secretaries, public relations managers, spin doctors and the media

This could be a fascinating area of investigative research because it asks you to consider how the political 'personality' of both party and individual is constructed. An evaluation of the role of press secretaries and public relations managers could consider press releases, for example, offering an analysis of the content and the desired effects. The role of spin doctors can be assessed in relation to how particular political events or incidents concerning individual politicians are reworked in order to either confirm positive readings or attempt to avoid negative readings. You could analyse the press reports around a particular politician's actions and try to identify how, through TV interviews and comment from other politicians, the incident was 'spun'. It would be essential for you to assess the effectiveness of the 'spinning'. Did John Prescott ever detach himself from the press reports that labelled him a 'bruiser' for hitting the demonstrator who threw an egg at him?

Media commentators

This is an extremely broad area to contend with and it would be useful at the beginning to identify the particular area of media commentating that you are going to investigate. You may wish to limit yourself to analysing press political commentary, possibly looking at the differences between broadsheet and tabloid coverage of a particular political event. You could investigate the stories themselves or comment on how the editorials of certain papers respond. You may decide to concentrate on photojournalistic commentaries and investigate the differing representations of politicians and political events delivered to the reader through the photographs chosen by different newspapers. You could compare and contrast the various newspaper cartoonists' readings of politicians and events. For all these areas you will need to employ your knowledge of both intent and consumption. What is the ideological and political stance implied through the cartoons? Are they supposed to confirm the target audience's thoughts or introduce new arguments? What impact do the cartoons have on the political landscape? Are they influential?

Television and radio are the other main outlets for media commentators on politics. Your study may identify the programmes that aim to deliver political discussion and comment and assess them for format, delivery, target viewer and political comment. You would not need to restrict yourself to terrestrial channels if studying television and it would be interesting to investigate the different kinds of programmes available within both satellite and digital channels. As for press analysis, you should consider content, format, delivery and target audience and assess the effectiveness of the programme against what it assumes it is delivering. You could even compare and contrast programmes from different mediums, which may bring up issues of audience response to differing consumption formats.

The media commentators you choose do not have to be of the 'traditional' variety and political satire is a particularly fertile area of study. You may like to look at one political event or a political party and investigate how it satirised. The scope for this sub-topic is huge and the texts available to you are probably ones that you have encountered already. Rory Bremner's brand of satire through impersonation could provide the basis for a research project, as could Chris Morris' shows *The Day Today* or *Brasseye*. *2DTV*, which delivers its brand of the satirical through television cartoon, would also provide rich comment, as would an investigation into the purpose and impact of the satirical magazine *Private Eye*. There is a great tradition of satirists offering a counterpoint to 'straight' political commentary and as well as focusing on content, format, target audience and impact, you could extend your analysis by noting the ways in which the current crop of satirical texts are treated by those they satirise. Are they deemed to be useful or obstructive by those who act as satire's 'targets'?

Impartiality versus editorial or owner's values

A study within this sub-topic would consider the issue of whether or not a media text and its content can be independent of the value system and the beliefs of its owner or editor. Within a study of the press, both the editor and owner would need to be considered in terms of their influence. Where there is a high-profile owner – for instance Sky/News International and Rupert Murdoch – first you would have to identify the political stance and value system of the owner and the mission statement of the company, and then look at the extent to which this influence permeates programme type, article content and scheduling. Does owner influence affect the type of political coverage offered or the format in which it is delivered? How much influence is the owner legally allowed to have? In the case of less conspicuous individuals, you could evaluate the role of the editor of a newspaper in shaping comment and bias. Does the comment you read at the beginning of a paper provide an ideological or political model for how the articles are written (and by extension how they are supposed to be consumed)?

The relationship between media owners and government legislation

This area of study asks you to consider the relationship between those who own media companies and the government legislation that is in operation around them. You will need to assess whether you think that legislation is helpful or restrictive to the production of media texts and describe the changes in various pieces of legislation attached to different media areas. Also consider the shifts in type of legislation that occur from one government to the next. It may not be that a new government party wants to legislate differently. The same party might change particular laws, either because of a shift in ideological climate or, to give a more cynical reading, because of political expediency. You could look at the laws that inform censorship in the media, for example, those that have informed the shifts in assessment criteria for the **BBFC** (British Board of Film Classification). You could look at the 1990 Broadcasting Act and identify not only what it specified and how this was a change from what had gone before, but also the changes in programming it caused and any resistance there was to it.

Public Service Broadcasting and politics

A research project on this area would need to go much further than a basic definition of Public Service Broadcasting (PSB). The BBC should not be seen as the sole provider of PSB. The original Reithian view of PSB as completely separate from commercial interests should be examined thoughtfully. Although the BBC, and to a lesser extent ITV, remain constitutionally independent from the state, they have both been subject to regulation and organisation by public bodies. Your study could identify the regulatory bodies that have been connected to the BBC (as an example of PSB) and assess the extent of their influence. You could examine the political programming available within the BBC and discuss how this might be considered public service. You could look at how the idea of Public Service Broadcasting has been influenced by the advent of new technologies, both in terms of production and consumption.

CASE STUDY

Evaluating different press representations

Looking at a specific event can be a very effective way of focusing your study. If, for example, you were evaluating press representation of the Iraq war, then consideration of the varying reports that presented events to readers would be essential. Your research would need to discuss the ways in which events, political leaders and the nations involved were represented by different sections of the press. Below, for example, are two articles which both look at Tony Blair's decision to enter Britain into the Iraq conflict. They express differing attitudes to events.

Blair backs Bush over Iraq threat

Iraq's development of weapons of mass destruction posed a threat to world stability, Tony Blair said today.

The Prime Minister said he agreed with the "sentiment" behind US president George Bush's description of Iraq belonging to an "axis of evil", in what appeared to be his strongest support yet for action against Saddam Hussein.

Mr Blair is reported to be holding talks with President Bush in Washington in April to finalise what action should be taken against Iraq as part of a "second phase" in the war against terrorism.

"I certainly agree with him (President Bush) very strongly that weapons of mass destruction represent a real threat to world stability," Mr Blair said in an interview with the Australian Broadcasting Corporation.

In a statement to the House of Commons in the immediate aftermath of September 11 he had said the next issue to be tackled after international terrorism was the issue of weapons of mass destruction, the premier added.

The spread of weapons of mass destruction were "a real threat", he said, adding: "George Bush is right to draw attention to that … It is important that we act against them."

Mr Blair, who was travelling to Australia for the Commonwealth Heads of Government Meeting (CHOGM) later today, added: "It is an issue that those who are engaged in spreading weapons of mass destruction are engaged in an evil trade and it is important that we make sure that we take action in respect of it.

"I think that George Bush has shown tremendous leadership since September 11. I think he has acted always in a very measured way, in a calm way, but he is right to raise these issues and certainly he has our support in doing so."

He and President Bush were in constant contact and agreed on the "general issues".

Mr Blair added: "We do constantly look at Iraq … Saddam Hussein's regime is a regime that is deeply repressive to its people and is a real danger to the region.

"Heavens above, he used chemical weapons against his own people, so it is an issue and we

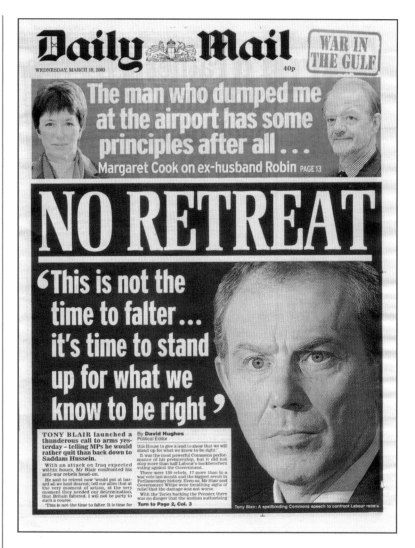

have got to look at it, but we will look at it in a rational and calm way, as we have for the other issues.

"The accumulation of weapons of mass destruction by Iraq poses a threat, a threat not just to the region but to the wider world, and I think George Bush was absolutely right to raise it. Now what action we take in respect of that, that is an open matter for discussion.

"Since September 11 we have proceeded in a calm, measured, sensible way, by discussion and we will carry on doing so, but when we are ready to take action then we will announce it."

Mr Blair said Britain was "in discussion" with the US about the status of British prisoners held by the US at Camp X-Ray, adding it was a "tricky issue".

"This is a unique situation because what you have in Afghanistan are certain members of the terrorist network, the al-Qaida network, some have been detained, some people obviously are part of the Taliban regime, they were effectively prisoners of war.

"Now we are in discussion with the Americans about the status of these prisoners, when those discussions are over we will establish properly exactly how they should be treated."

Asked whether he would like to see the British detainees return home to face trial, he said: "We have just got to see about that … The best thing when there are ongoing discussions that are taking place in detail is to let the discussions take place."

Mr Blair said he would like to be remembered as a prime minister who "brought in a revolution in economic management for economic stability, rebuilt our public services, particularly education, and who gave Britain a sense of its place in the world."

Asked if that meant with the euro, he replied: "Well it is the economic test, isn't it?"

Source: *Daily Mail* website, 28 February 2002

Blair's black day

Bombs, demos and serious mid-term drift – and all the direct result of the prime minister's own decisions

Polly Toynbee

The prime minister has waited for months now with a deadly certainty that the terror attacks would come. "When, not if," he warned spine-chillingly about the threat to Britain. Once he had decided to take the country to war, terrorist retaliation was certain and if ever there was a prime time to expect it, then it was now, during George Bush's state visit. The wonder is only that Britain has escaped for so long. London was fortified beyond endurance this week, but there will always be soft underbellies exposed to Islamist extremist fury. There is no defence against terror.

So now Turkey has become another case of collateral damage in the spreading calamity of the Iraq war. It is tragic that it should be Turkey of all places to take the brunt of this revenge; Turkey, the actual existing model of moderate Islam. In their game of fantasy Middle East politics, how often Bush and Blair boasted they would turn Iraq into a "beacon" of democracy that would shine its light into every dark, feudal, corrupt and theocratic state across the region. What an irony if, instead, the Iraq war has dragged Turkey, a true beacon of modern Islam, down.

Turkey tried to protect itself from contamination with the war by denying US troops access through its land to northern Iraq. But it was a natural target for al-Qaida fundamentalists attempting to turn back the clock to an Islamic dark age. To them, Turkey's ever strengthening democracy is a western abomination.

Visiting Istanbul this year to interview all parties and religious groups united in Turkey's determination to qualify for EU membership, I walked through the gates of the British consulate and met the consul general, Roger Short, who was, sadly, among the dead yesterday. It was well guarded but relaxed, without any sense that Istanbul was a dangerous place.

Tayyip Erdogan's new government aims to take the country into Europe as a "synthesis" between east and west. With threatening neighbours – Iran, Iraq, Syria and Russia – it is hardly surprising Turkey seeks to turn towards Europe. So these bombs in Istanbul serve a sinister dual purpose for the Islamist fundamentalists – to attack Britain, but also to blow up Turkey's ever-closer European ties and haul it back into the morass of Islamist extremism.

These bombs made yesterday one of the darkest days of Tony Blair's prime ministership. As if that horror were not enough, too many other disparate pigeons came fluttering home to roost at once. Whichever way he turned, things looked black. They were no mere accidents, for everything that happened came as a direct result of his own decisions, all of them taken against the better instincts of most of his party.

While the colossal anti-Bush demonstration swirled through the capital, and central London ground to a halt due to the visit of this unpopular president, inside beleaguered Westminster two bills ricocheted between the Lords and the Commons in a near-meaningless battle. The unimportant substance of these bills had long become irrelevant.

That a handful of complex fraud trials might be conducted without juries was, frankly, nothing that mattered much despite great protestations on both sides. Nor was the watered-down foundation hospital bill critical to either improving or destroying the NHS. But these issues had become totemic simply because Tony Blair wrongly attached too much symbolism to them, forcing them through without listening. The trouncing he got in the Commons was deserved. Although the Lords finally gave way to the superior right of the Commons on foundation hospitals, it was nonetheless a sharp reminder both of disquiet within his party and the constitutional mess in which he has left the House of Lords.

Bombs in Istanbul are the only outcome from this presidential visit. George Bush brought no gifts to thank his ally for taking so much damage to support this politically alien president. Nothing has been gained on US illegal trade tariffs: a promise to obey the WTO might have given Blair something to show the Europeans the value of engaging with America. No sign was given of serious intent to intervene in the Israel/Palestine conflict. The president leaves unabated alarm that the US will cut and run from Iraq to suit the presidential election timetable and not the needs of Iraqis. This visit has been all downside for our prime minister.

All these woes were avoidable. But there is something in the set of Tony Blair's jaw these days that suggests he feels most sure of his own convictions when facing down the faint hearts on his own side, instead of stopping to listen to them. No turning back. Sounds faintly familiar? There's a hint of Thatcherite hubris after six-and-half years in office.

Yet, curiously, the other blow to strike him leaves him dumbstruck and devoid of defiance. This week Rupert Murdoch menacingly rattled the prime minister's cage with a bullying warning that he might shift the allegiance of his mighty newspapers to Michael Howard – and disgracefully Tony Blair said nothing. If ever there was a time for all that jaw-jutting pugnacity, this was it. But he said not a word in protest at the arrogance of the man. Here is a clear and present threat to democracy itself, when one magnate controlling 40% of Britain's newspaper readership and an ever greater slice of television plays cat-and-mouse with our elected government. He is a terrorist, too, operating by striking terror into the heart of politicians, forcing them all into craven subservience to his whims.

Another unsavoury media rogue tumbles, caught in financially questionable circumstances after we have endured his aggressive free-market sermonising all these years. Conrad Black's ignominy should have prompted the prime minister to get brave with these strutting brigands. Downing Street worries about public cynicism and how to get its message out beyond the distorting megaphones of the Tory press. But they never consider the valiant David and Goliath path. If he dared risk his political life by standing up to media baron bullies, that would reach the ears of the voters as a moment of truthfulness and bravery. But no. It will be backroom sycophancy again.

Ahead lies nothing but more trouble. Tony Blair has little to look forward to in the Hutton report. If the centrepiece of the Queen's speech is only university top-up fees, that is another fight that may not be worth the candle by the time it has been softened round the edges.

Even if technically the right approach, it is well nigh impossible to sell to those it affects most, raising not enough to make much difference to the universities.

So where is the lantern to light us through the mid-term winter? Where has the vision thing gone? Alas, the sense of drift is yet more collateral damage from the Iraq war which seems to sap too much energy and strength from the government. Bombers must be defied, but who is tackling the global causes of bombing? And will the agenda for the next session set a new course with some clarity of purpose? No sign of that yet.

Source: *The Guardian*, 21 November 2003

Part Four ■■■

Children and the Media

This topic is usually extremely popular because it describes an area that we have all experienced at some time in our lives. With Children and the Media you need to be careful because unless your sub-topic is clearly defined, the research projects produced can be vague and insubstantial. Having direct personal experience of a topic does not necessarily make it easier or a better subject for close critical scrutiny. Although this may seem to be a warning, you should not be put off studying this area if you have a clearly defined topic that you are prepared to research in depth.

Broadly speaking, this topic asks you to research the relationship between children as subjects of media representation and as consumers of the media. This topic used to be confined to the relationship between children and television, but has now been broadened to include film, radio, magazines, comics, newspapers, video games and the internet. There are many potential sub-topics that could provide the focus of study, with examples shown below and explanations of the possible content.

Representations of childhood and gender

For this sub-topic, you will need to look at the representation of childhood and gender within particular media texts, considering both why the producers of the text might have used this particular representation and how it is received by the text's target audience. You should begin a project on childhood and gender by describing the limits of your study. The first stage is to collect texts that include representations relevant to your study. If you were focusing on the representation of childhood and gender in television, for example, you could look at programmes that are aimed at children and also those that are aimed at adults, but that include specific representations of children. You could look at a TV guide in order to find examples, but make sure that the examples you choose include enough variety. If your chosen medium is film, you might consider the representation of gender and childhood in films produced for children by a particular company, such as Disney or Pixar. You could select video games which have child characters and research both the impact of these representations on the video game consumer and the reasons why you think these particular representations have been used by the game's producers.

Blue Peter

The Tweenies

The media as educative

Whether your focus is television, the internet, radio, film or the press, your aim for a project under this subheading will be to discuss whether you consider the media to be educative, and if your answer to this question is yes, *who* is being educated and about *what*? You could look at specific examples of media texts which have an explicitly educational aim. You could then look at what strategies are being used by these texts to engage the child in the education process.

The other option with this kind of project is to focus on media texts which do not have an explicitly educational remit, but which you consider to have an educational and instructive impact on the child consumer. For example, your study might discuss whether you think that all TV programmes aimed at children of a certain age have an educational value, regardless of whether this is implicit or explicit. You would then discuss a few key examples of programmes and the impact they have on the child viewer. You might evaluate internet sites aimed at children which claim to have an educative aim, and consider how effective you think these are at educating children about certain subjects.

Children as participants in media productions

There are many ways in which children can be said to participate in media productions. Children might be used as actors, competitors, presenters or even producers of a media text. There are many TV programmes, for example, that use children as participants, not all of which are aimed at children. You may even argue that there are programmes that use children *in absentia* as participants, for example, *You've Been Framed*, which has many examples of children doing apparently funny things. You could equally consider the contributions made by children to magazines aimed at particular age groups and discuss the impact of a child 'producer' on a child audience.

Pre-teen girls' magazine

Views of parents, teachers and children on the media and childhood

This sub-topic focuses on your evaluation of, and discussions around, responses which you collate from parents, teachers and children regarding the relationship between the media and childhood. This is a wide topic and you will need to establish the parameters of your research project very clearly before you begin. Selecting particular media texts, whether these are films, TV programmes, magazines or a combination of these, to use as a prompt within parts of your research is essential. Your primary research will need to be very specific too. Try to avoid questions that are too wide ranging. For example, 'Do you think the media damages children?' is the type of question which will receive very limited responses. Questions such as, 'Do you think Hollywood cinema has a tendency to romanticise childhood in films for under 12s?' would be a much more specific question.

CASE STUDY

Media products and preschool children

It is essential within your study that you bring together a wide range of resources. For example, if you were researching a project which considered media products aimed at preschool children, you might look at articles such as this one from *The Guardian*.

Is television destroying our children's minds?

Stuart Jeffries examines the evidence

Stuart Jeffries

Should parents worry about what television is doing to their children? Is it making them fatter, stupider, more violent? After all, TV has changed since today's parents were children. It's bigger, brasher and on all the time. There used to be something called the "toddlers' truce" when TV went off air between six and seven o'clock so parents could put their children to bed; now kids' cable networks broadcast 24 hours a day. In the old days, too, there was a kids' slot called *Watch with Mother*; today there are fears that television is watched too much without mother, that the goggle box is being used disastrously as a virtual babysitter.

TV has moved on from the innocent world of *Camberwick Green* to become a fearful source of seemingly imponderable questions. Should parents be limiting the time children spend in front of the television? Does it matter what they watch? Parents' fears are fuelled by surveys purporting to demonstrate that TV viewing is harmful. Last week, a report in the *Lancet* warned parents of a link between children's excessive viewing habits and long-term health problems such as poor fitness and raised cholesterol. It also claimed that youthful TV addicts were more likely to smoke.

One study has linked television viewing to obesity and another to aggressiveness. Earlier this year, an American survey claimed to have found an association between TV viewing among toddlers and attention deficit and hyperactivity disorder (ADHD) at school age. On a positive note, you might think that the hyperactivity would help to cancel out the obesity, and that the consequences of aggressiveness might well be ameliorated by wandering attention (they

---

might forget who to hit), but researchers at the Children's Hospital and Regional Medical Center in Seattle don't seem to have considered these possibilities. They were concerned to show that the hard-wiring of toddlers' brains can be detrimentally affected by the unrealistic visual stimuli that television allegedly sends pinging all over toddlers' synapses. Not only are kids destined to become fat and thuggish, it seems, but early exposure to TV is going to make them prone to concentration problems at school.

"We all know that the brains of newborns continue to develop rapidly, that the final tuning is done, as it were, outside the womb. The rapid pace of TV may not help," Dr Dimitri Christakis, who led the research, tells the *Guardian*. "The idea came to me when I was at home with my three-month-old son. If he saw a television he was mesmerised by it. He had no idea of what the content was. I was curious what the effect of that degree of stimulation would be."

His hypothesis was that very early exposure to television during critical periods of synaptic development would be associated with subsequent attention problems. "In contrast to the pace with which real life unfolds and is experienced by young children, television can portray rapidly changing images, scenery, and events," says Christakis's paper. "It can be overstimulating and yet extremely interesting. This has led some to theorize that television may shorten children's attention spans."

We cannot deny a proliferation of programmes and videos aimed at pre-school children, and even at the under-twos including *Teletubbies*, *Fimbles* and *Tweenies*. The Disney Corporation bought up a company called Baby Einstein which allegedly helps in the educational development of small children and is exploiting its new acquisition assiduously here and in the US. If Christakis's theory holds, all these programmes and videos are going to create not a generation of Baby Einsteins, but hordes of unprecedentedly dim children.

The content of the programmes and videos that children watch must be significant. After all, some programmes targeted at under-twos – *Teletubbies*, for instance – unfold in a very slow manner. Furthermore, great claims are made by some TV programmes and videos targeted at pre-school age children, claiming to assist small children's intellectual development rather than retard it. We also need to give consideration to the notion of "watching television", which might well be qualitatively very different for different children. Some might be gormlessly staring at nothing very much; others making important visual judgments about Tinky Winky's bottom, for example. "What is a one-year-old doing when it watches television, and how does this compare to how other ages watch television?" asks David Buckingham, professor of education at the University of London and a long-time critic of anti-TV polemicists. "These sorts of questions get lost and yet they are fundamental to any decent research."

The anti-TV groups' critique of the medium is not that the stuff children watch is rubbish, but that TV viewing itself is a catastrophic lifestyle option that parents have inflicted on their children. Jean Lotus of the anti-TV group White Dot, who is currently writing a book about raising her four children without a TV in her family home in Oak Park, Illinois, says: "Television is displacing learning activity during early years." But aren't some programmes designed to educate children? "Yeah, right. All those make-your-baby-smarter videos are doing is creating a docile drug addict in front of the screen. I have encouraged my children to climb and be physical. Surely that's better than letting them sit in front of the telly."

But are the two mutually exclusive in a child's early years? I recall watching *Bill and Ben* and falling out of trees on a regular basis before I went to school and I suspect the former was less harmful than the latter.

"We have found doctors very reluctant to say there is a link between TV viewing and attention deficit", says Lotus. "Doctors are keen to say it's genetic or behavioural. You should talk to teachers who are at the brunt of it. They will say that your mind works differently if you watch TV when you're very young."

In the US, especially, there has been a glut of books claiming that television is responsible for many ills. Such books include Neil Postman's *The Disappearance of Childhood: How TV is changing Children's lives, The Plug-In Drug* by Marie Winn and T*he Collapse of Literacy and the Rise of Violence in an Electronic Age* by Barry Sanders. These books were joined on the shelves earlier this year by a volume with possibly the best subtitle ever, namely *The Epidemic: The Rot of American Culture, Absentee and Permissive Parenting, and the Resultant Plague of Joyless, Selfish Children* by Californian doctor Robert Shaw – a book that worries about the revolting consumerism, obesity, illiteracy, sleeplessness associated with watching television, and yet suggests, rather more modestly, that under-fives should be allowed to watch television in moderation but never unattended.

These polemics are all similar, argues David Buckingham, in that children are not seen as differentiated as TV viewers. In his book *After the Death of Childhood*, Buckingham writes: "Children, in particular, are implicitly seen to be passive and defenceless in the face of media manipulation ... Television, because of its inherently 'visual' nature (one wonders what happened to the soundtrack), is effectively seen to bypass cognition entirely. It requires no intellectual, emotional or imaginative investment, but simply imprints itself on the child's consciousness. Again, no empirical basis is offered for these assertions."

Buckingham adds that what makes all these polemics questionable is the one-dimensional analysis of the electronic media as causes of terrible tendencies among children. Excessive TV viewing could, for instance, be symptomatic of, rather than a cause of, sociopathic behaviour among children.

The crucial issue here, arguably, is the notion of "excessive". The American Academy of Pediatrics (AAP) does not make it clear: "Too much television can negatively affect early brain development. This is especially true at younger ages, when learning to talk and play with others is so important. Until more research is done about the effects of TV on very young children, the American Academy of Pediatrics does not recommend television for children aged two or younger."

Buckingham also has a problem with the very notion of ADHD. "Ten years ago this label didn't exist. What used to be called 'bloody annoying children' has had a label put on it, and this has consequences. Drug companies are making big money out of making tranquillisers like Ritalin for children and there are whole industries in medical research working to construct this way of defining children's behaviour."

Buckingham adds that parents' fears about the possible deleterious consequences of children watching television is exploited by politicians. "When one thinks of how TV viewing is associated with violence among children, this is used by politicians as a way of displacing attention away from other causes of violence in society that are difficult to eradicate – such as racism, poverty, gun control. I'm by no means saying that there aren't associations, just that it is too easy to blame one thing for children's problems. We're dealing with really complicated matters here that readily get over-simplified."

So is watching TV a bad thing for under-twos? The research suggests no more than that it could be, while never really tackling the issue of how much TV viewing among toddlers would be regarded as excessive. Ten hours a day might be too much, but what about one hour of *Teletubbies* watched, in the traditional manner, with mother? Would that be a bad thing? As far as I could discover, there seems to be an inverse relationship between the anti-TV rhetoric and the plausibility of the data upon which it is based. What is also certain is that any such research is going to get a great deal of attention because so many people stand to make a lot of money out of children – programme-makers, soft-toy producers and Ritalin manufacturers among them. Not to mention all those people writing apocalyptic texts that pander to the panic of parents worried that they are raising goggle-eyed sociopaths, thanks to the chattering cyclops.

Robert Shaw, the hard-boiled critic of today's allegedly joyless kids, suggests that children aged five and under should not watch TV unattended at all and that, when you do watch TV with your very young child, you ought to talk to them about the programme and the issues it raises. "Explain the meaning and motivation behind commercials and programming", urges Shaw. "Help her to understand fantasy and reality, the difference between a sales pitch and an honest evaluation."

The main things, I would argue, are not to blame television for all the modern child's ills, nor to panic – after all, there are plenty of other people who will do those things for you.

Source: *Guardian Unlimited*, 21 July 2004

Part Five ■■■

Crime and the Media

The focus of this particular topic is the representation of crime across a range of media, and as with the other topics, you do not need to restrict yourself to British media products. However, your study will need to consider not just how representation is generated and what this indicates about the messages and values of the text you have chosen to study, but also the context of the text and how it is received by its target audience. Below are areas of study which you might wish to consider when creating your research title.

Crime films/TV crime series

An increasing number of crime films and TV crime series are available to the viewing public, so you will have no difficulty finding case studies on which to base your project. In order for your project to be manageable and effective, however, you will need to have a clear focus within your question. Try to avoid restricting your consideration to genre analysis or any other text-only type of focus. Your project should consider context and audience, too.

If you chose to concentrate on crime films, you could consider the ways in which particular crimes are represented and then compare this representation to that which occurs within news reports. You could extend this type of study to an analysis of viewer expectations of crime films and the types of crime which appear in them. The numerous films which present a serial killer narrative, for example, will have been produced in order to try to secure big box-office returns. You might question why producers are prepared to invest in this kind of film and what kind of demand there has been within cinema/video/DVD audiences. Have these kinds of films been successful because they reflect a prevalent contemporary fear? You might also define any study of crime films by nation in order to give your project clear focus. British crime films, for example, could be discussed in terms of how they either do or do not reflect British attitudes to crime (and punishment). You could create a project which discusses the representation of criminals, the police or the judicial system in a particular country and consider the extent to which this might influence public perceptions.

If you prefer to focus on TV crime shows, then your projects could have similar types of focus to those outlined above for crime films. You could also consider the phenomenon of long-running TV crime

Still from *Silent Witness* (UK TV series).

Still from *CSI: Crime Scene Investigation* (US TV series)

Section 2. Critical Research Study

series and investigate what it is about these shows that sustains audience interest. Is it the characters, the way in which crime and criminality is represented or some other factor? Studies that look at the ways in which crime shows are viewed would also prove interesting. Do audiences build up a loyalty to particular shows and not watch others, or do they watch crime series in a less selective manner?

True crime magazines

As with the ever-increasing number of crime films and TV crime series, true crime magazines have become very popular and have a significant readership. These magazines offer a particular representation of crime, criminals and criminality, and you will need to consider the relationship between how crime is presented in these publications and how readers receive this presentation. You might consider whether the focus of a particular magazine series is crime or the criminals who perpetrate the crimes. The question in this instance might be related to the 'celebrity' attached to particular criminals. If you think this might be the case, then you will need to analyse the ways in which the criminals are represented within the magazine (both visual and in terms of language), discuss why the magazine has chosen to represent its subject in this particular way and what expectations the magazine's readership has for content.

Your study might focus on the relationship between the 'true' crime presented within this type of magazine and news reporting of the actual crimes or crimes similar to those presented in the magazine. Your question here might concern the motivations of audiences for true crime publications. Do readers want or expect accurate crime reporting or do they read these magazines for very different reasons?

Front cover of *True Crime* magazine

News reporting of crime/press representations of crime and criminality

This sub-topic encompasses newspaper, TV and radio reporting of crime. You could even consider internet-based crime reporting. You could choose one particular TV channel, newspaper or radio station and consider what the conventions for news reporting might be. These conventions may include everything from *mise en scène* to the running order of news stories in TV news, photo captions to choice of adjectives in newspaper reporting, and news theme music to use of interviews in radio reporting. What you will then need to do with this textual analysis is discuss what this indicates about the ideological stance of the newspaper, TV or radio show. The last stage for this type of analysis will be to relate the institutional values you have deduced to those of the news report's target audience.

One of the other possibilities for research under this sub-topic would be to use one particular crime and then research the ways in which the details of this crime have been presented across a range of media, discussing the relationship between the style of presentation of events and the target audience for the different news reports you are discussing.

Trial by the media

This sub-topic would provide you with the opportunity to research one particular crime-related event in detail. There have been many instances, even within your memories, of cases that have gained almost saturation news coverage. These types of cases receive a high profile in the media usually because the case itself is sensational or the individual(s) involved in the case is (are) high profile. The extent to which the media becomes judge and jury, either mirroring or provoking public responses, would provide the main question within your study. You might consider the breadth of media coverage attached to a particular crime-related event and discuss whether or not there existed a consistency of coverage between the different media. You should also investigate the impact of any 'trial by media' that you study on the case itself. Your own opinions concerning the role and responsibilities of the media would, of course, be important within this sub-topic.

CASE STUDY

New bill offers pets protection

Matthew Tempest, political correspondent

Pet owners who fail to care for their animals will face heavy fines or up to a year in prison under a new animal welfare bill published today.

For the first time animal owners will have a duty of care for pets in their possession, in what the government is calling the biggest shake-up in animal welfare in a century.

Those causing unnecessary suffering to an animal will face up to 51 weeks in prison, a fine of up to £20,000 or both.

Animal welfare minister Ben Bradshaw said: "Once the legislation is enacted our law will be worthy of our reputation as a nation of animal lovers."

Section 2. Critical Research Study

The bill applies to all vertebrates owned by people, except farmed animals and animals used for scientific experimentation, and imposes responsibility for looking after animals by providing a suitable environment, a suitable diet, the ability to express normal behaviour, and freedom from pain, suffering, injury and disease.

Mr Bradshaw said: "The vast majority of pet owners and others involved with the care of animals have nothing to fear from this legislation. This bill is aimed at those few who do not properly fulfil their responsibilities for the animals in their charge."

The RSPCA, which has campaigned for such legislation for years, today welcomed the bill. Jackie Ballard, RSPCA director general, and a former Liberal Democrat MP, said the bill would be "the most far-reaching improvement to the welfare of companion animals for almost a century – and for that we are absolutely delighted.

"A new welfare offence will, for the first time, protect thousands of pets from enduring serious neglect each year, by legally obliging owners to care for them properly – something the RSPCA has been campaigning on for many, many years."

The bill also simplifies animal welfare legislation by bringing more than 20 pieces of legislation into one.

The Liberal Democrats also welcomed the bill, but their spokesman Norman Baker complained that it failed to ban animals other than horses and dogs from being used in circuses, and did not cover animals bred for experimentation.

He said: "We will be pushing for changes to the bill so that the welfare of all animals is protected."

The bill also bans the giving of animals as prizes at fairs to children under 16.

Source: *Guardian Unlimited*, 14 October 2005

Government plans new rights for pets

LONDON (Reuters) – The government launched a new bill to protect animals on Friday with measures that included banning children from buying pets.

Ministers described the Animal Welfare Bill, which applies to England and Wales, as the most significant such legislation for nearly a century.

It would make it an offence to sell an animal to a child under 16, raising the age from 12, and would also ban animals being given to youngsters as prizes.

"Once this legislation is enacted, our law will be worthy of our reputation as a nation of animal lovers," said Animal Welfare Minister Ben Bradshaw.

"Anyone who is responsible for an animal will have to do all that is reasonable to meet the needs of their animal."

The bill, which would replace laws from 1911, proposes raising the maximum penalty for animal cruelty to 51 weeks' imprisonment from six months, with fines up to 20,000 pounds from 5,000.

Owners will have to ensure their pets have a suitable diet and are kept free from pain, suffering, injury and disease.

"This bill will make a real difference to the lives of domestic and kept animals," Bradshaw said.

The RSPCA animal charity welcomed the move which it said it had been demanding for years.

"A new welfare offence will, for the first time, protect thousands of pets from enduring serious neglect each year, by legally obliging owners to care for them properly," said Jackie Ballard, the RSPCA's director general.

Source: *Mirror*, 14 October 2005

Pets may get 'Bill of Rights'

Pet owners would be forced to treat their animals well. Pets would get the legal right to a minimum quality of life under plans the RSPCA has put forward to the UK Government.

Ministers are expected to unveil proposals later this week which would mean pet owners facing prosecution if they failed to provide enough food and water or space in their cages.

The move would extend the same standards that apply to the care of laboratory animals to farm animals and pets in the home.

But the RSPCA (Royal Society for the Prevention of Cruelty to Animals) wants the government to go even further by making pet owners have a legal "duty of care" to their animals.

'Normal behaviour'

This would allow the RSPCA to take steps to prevent cruelty rather than waiting until there is evidence of harm before acting. The charity wants "five freedoms" for animals enshrined in what would be a "Bill of Rights" for pets.

Freedom from hunger and thirst – enough good food and water to keep them healthy

Freedom from discomfort – comfortable cages or resting areas

Freedom from pain, injury and disease – and rapid veterinary treatment if they are ill

Freedom to express normal behaviour – so they have enough space and company

Freedom from fear and distress

The charity claims it is hampered under current animal cruelty laws because pets have to be actually suffering before any action can be taken against owners.

It wants animal welfare officers to have a similar role to social workers, educating owners on how to better treat pets if legal obligations are not being met.

"It would put the 'P' of prevention back into the RSPCA," a spokeswoman said.

'Suffering'

"We are saying that every owner should have a duty of care to every animal. This is to ensure that the animal will be looked after. Most people look after animals very well. But there are a percentage who don't."

She added: "If owners were bound by law by a duty of care they would need to ensure that their animals have been fed and given water. At the moment, legislation does not enable us to do anything with animals unless they are already suffering."

'Vermin'

The concept of a bill of rights for animals is hotly contested in academic circles.

Professor Michael Reiss, a bio-ethicist at London University, said: "This is a very contentious issue. If pet rats and mice have rights then it raises the question of the way we treat farm animals, vermin and fish. Once you start down that road it is hard to know where to stop," he told The Sunday Times.

The government's rural affairs department, DEFRA, is consulting on the possibility of modernising animal welfare law. The RSPCA has made its own submission to that.

A DEFRA spokesman said: "This is a sensitive area of legislation and the Protection of Animals Act dates back to 1911 so what we need to have in place is legislation that not only protects animals against physical abuse but recognises quality of life."

Source: BBC Website, 29 April, 2002 (*http://news.bbc.co.uk/1/hi/uk_politics/1957455.stm*)

Part Six

Sport and the Media

The aim of any project under this topic heading is to investigate the relationships between sport agencies and the media. Below are some of the sub-topic areas that could be investigated.

Sky Sports

The attraction and retention of audiences via sport in order to promote other products

The popularity of sporting events to many groups within a television audience means that these are often used by television companies to entice new viewers or retain audiences. Digital television operators and companies such as Sky promote the sports content of their programming vigorously. Exclusive coverage of events or new ways of watching events, for example, through interactive technologies, often encourage viewers to pay for access to certain channels or to move away from standard, terrestrial reception modes. The possibility of watching exclusive coverage of a boxing match or being able to decide which camera angle you desire at any given point in a football match is often a heavy incentive to buy a particular package of services or access to a particular channel.

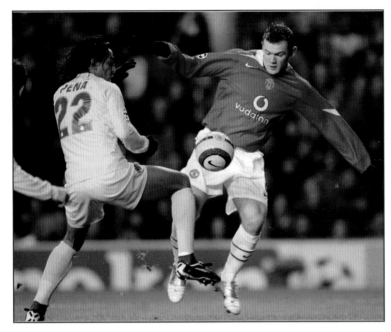
Football

If you choose to study this sub-topic, you need to investigate which channels offer such exclusive viewing and how this acts as an incentive, and also the profile of consumers who deem it attractive. Is the profile of audience members attracted or retained the same? Does the issue of monopoly arise within this kind of channel marketing? Are some sports given more coverage than others by particular channels in order to retain or attract viewers?

The representation of ideology such as global unity, nation and gender

Do not be put off by the term **ideology**. As a second-year student of Media Studies you will have encountered it many times before. In the context of this sub-topic, an investigation into ideology requires you to analyse what messages are being delivered to you through sporting events and types of coverage. For example, are we being encouraged to view the world as a unified place through the presentation of Olympic Games coverage? If the answer to this question is yes, then how are we being encouraged to do this? Is it through equal coverage of different nations' sporting achievements, through an equality of encouragement from commentators, or by the very fact that we are introduced to athletes from different nations who we have not seen before? If the answer to this type of question is no, then are we being encouraged to be nationalistic through the process of competition? Are the events selected for coverage chosen because of the involvement of a British athlete? Are these kinds of global events a unifying mechanism through which nations pride themselves in their national difference?

Minority interest sports

You do not have to concentrate on sports that have a massive following or are given huge exposure in order to create an effective Research Study. Minority sports, such as skateboarding or snowboarding, could provide an equally fertile area of study. You could begin by analysing the reasons why these sports are termed minority and even whether or not the term minority is accurate. Is a sport defined as minority because of the numbers of people who are interested in it or is it relegated to minority status in scheduling because of the profile of those who watch it? Gymnastics, for example, is a popular hobby and viewing preference for young girls, but it is not until the Olympics that this sport features prominently in the schedules.

You could then move on to ask yourself further specific questions concerning the minority sport you have chosen to analyse. For instance, what effect do new technologies have on the coverage of that sport? What effect does sponsorship (or the lack of it) have on the way the sport is perceived? Does sponsorship-associated advertising and merchandising contribute to the perception of your minority sport?

The use of new media technologies in sports coverage

There is a wide range of new media technology used within the coverage of sporting events, from new reception hardware, such as TV set-top decoders and hard-drive recorders, interactive digital programme types and internet fan sites, to new advances in 'capture' technologies, such as miniature cameras placed within the sporting event.

A study of this area would have to question whether these new technologies have affected the way that sport is consumed by its audience. Does the advent of an interactive digital consumption type

Snowboarding

mean that audiences are becoming more insular in their sports viewing? Do you think the new ways in which sport can be consumed will mean a decrease in attendance at live events? Do you think that these technologies provide greater potential for seeing a sporting event clearly and thus enhance viewing? In attempting to answer these types of questions you should use both your own response to sports that are affected by new media technologies and investigate the opinions of other target consumers.

CASE STUDY

Press representation of Britain's Olympic bid

As has been indicated, there are many possible topics to research under the main heading of Sport and the Media. One possible research route would be to focus on the press representation of a particular sporting event and comment on the different representations of this event. Below, for example, is one article concerning Britain's Olympic bid. This article could be compared with later ones in which the successful bid is discussed.

We must go for gold with London's Olympic bid

London's mayor says the whole country, not just the capital, would gain from the 2012 Games

Ken Livingstone

Those who argue that London couldn't possibly win the chance to host the 2012 Olympic Games because our city suffers from too much traffic, crime, overcrowding and pollution are missing the point.

New York and Paris are touted as London's biggest competitors, but suggest to natives of either of these cities that they live in a clean, peaceful and traffic-free urban paradise, and you would be met with derision.

But what both of these cities have recognised, and Britain's government has yet to decide, is that hosting the Olympic Games is not the crowning glory of a city's success, it's an opportunity for change.

Barcelona is testament to that: a depressed industrial city took a scrap of land on the edge of town and with the help of a £5 billion investment in infrastructure turned their city into a major tourist centre.

There is no reason why London cannot emulate that success. Yes, the site we're talking about for the main stadium and Olympic village is at the moment far from impressive, but in 10 years' time it could be a very different story.

But before readers outside London switch off, we need to be clear that a London bid is a British bid. The rest of the country will benefit, and many other cities and venues would share in the staging of many of the events. Furthermore, only London of our major cities has the existing facilities capable of forming the basis of a bid.

This is not surprising. London's main rivals for 2012, Paris and New York, are similarly huge urban centres, although only New York really compares in terms of size and population.

In 2012 the East End could be home to a state of the art stadium, and an Olympic village of 4,000 new homes. The area will be easily accessed by the new Stratford Channel Tunnel rail link and the planned Crossrail service will have the capacity to transport 150,000 people across the city during the weekday morning peak time.

Once the Games are over, there is little chance that these new amenities will gather dust. Premiership football sides have already expressed interest in the main stadium, and the other facilities and new housing will quickly be absorbed in a city that is expected to have gained 700,000 new residents by 2012, equivalent to the entire population of Leeds.

The Games' other great economic gift will be the benefits of tourism, an industry that has been seriously shaken by the double blows of foot and mouth and 11 September.

The pessimists say that the long-term benefits to Sydney's tourist industry are so far uncertain, that other Australian cities were denuded of visitors as a result of the 2000 Games. But this is hardly a strong comparison. Australia is an enormous country, and a gruelling flight away from the major tourist markets in Europe and North America. Visit London, an easy task for anyone in Europe, and you can be in Oxford or Edinburgh in just a couple of hours.

But if the East End needs regenerating anyway, and the UK's tourism industry obviously needs a shot in the arm, why should we do it with sport? The answer is that the Games represent a unique opportunity to combine the transformation of the East End's economy and physical environment with the transformation of the city's, and even the nation's social capital.

One Londoner who has been quick to recognise this is Jacqueline Valin, head of Southfields Community College, a specialist sports school in Wandsworth. Having seen the improvements that sport has brought about in her own students' self-esteem and academic achievement, she has started a letter-writing campaign among London head teachers to try to convince the Government to bid for the Games.

Ms Valin explains: 'For a few weeks, sport will be at the centre of most people's lives, and the home advantage will translate into lots of medals — look at how well our athletes did at the Commonwealth Games, or Japan and Korea did in the World Cup. London's school children will have the chance to see this at first hand. I'm sure that will have a lasting impact on their lives.'

Crucially, the Olympics will also bring much-needed new facilities: an Olympic-size swimming pool in a city that has just two Olympic pools to Berlin's 19, and a warm-up track that would be turned over to community use.

Apart from encouraging the nation's couch potatoes off their sofas, the Olympics will be one of those rare occasions that gives us a sense of a common enterprise. Thousands of people, young and old, will have the opportunity to work as volunteers and be part of one of the world's most exciting events.

There is no need to worry that Londoners' habitual cynicism will stop us from being every bit as welcoming a host city as Sydney or Manchester. Polls show that 75 per cent of Londoners back a bid. Our teenagers are engaged too: when Linford Christie came to the prize-giving at

Jacqueline Valin's school the first thing the students wanted to know was whether he'd be supporting a London Olympic bid.

Other cities will share in this enthusiasm by hosting the football tournament and the national training camps, which will also deliver significant amounts of cash into their local economies. We'll have the feel-good factor of the 2002 World Cup, but the influx of visitors will mean we won't need to worry that sport is keeping people out of the shops.

London can host a magnificent 2012 Olympics, a Games with the golden legacy of Barcelona. The lessons of the Dome, Wembley and Picketts Lock will serve as cautionary tales for whoever heads the team for the Olympic bid, but they cannot be used as an excuse for avoiding ambitious projects. Our competitor cities too will have learnt from previous failed sporting bids and less than successful projects.

The expected battle between New York, London, Paris and Moscow will be a clash of the titans. Hosting the 2012 Olympics is one of the most ambitious projects we will have seen in Britain for many years, but as any sportsperson will tell you, you don't get anywhere without ambition.

Source: *The Observer*, 12 January 2003

Part Seven ■■■

Community Radio

This topic asks you to investigate the relationship between radio stations and their communities. You could analyse commercially or publicly funded stations or niche programmes, and evaluate how they mirror the interests and tastes of their target consumers. There are many possible avenues you could explore as sub-topics within this area and below are some possibilities.

The nature and profile of radio communities

This sub-topic asks you to consider who the members of particular radio communities are, what their expectations might be and how their interests/lifestyles are reflected in programming. For example, you could compare two or three radio shows and consider the audience for each. As well as your own investigation, consider how the target audiences for these shows perceive themselves and their tastes; you could do this very effectively by interviewing members of the target audience. Are gender, age, race, geographical location and lifestyle common among those who listen to a particular show, or is the diversity of the listening audience greater than you would expect? Are listening audiences 'migratory'? Do they shift listening profile en masse or is there longevity of listening? To what extent do audiences have influence over the content and format of the programmes they listen to?

The formation of radio communities

In a research study under this heading you need to identify and assess the factors that are important in the formation of a radio community. Again, it would be much better to concentrate on two or three examples of radio programmes in order to make your comments comprehensive and specific, and to use interviews

Section 2. Critical Research Study

with focus groups of target audiences to gain information. Do the programmes you have chosen encourage a particular community identity? Do they use language or cultural references which are comprehensible to the target listener alone? Is any exclusivity set up by the content of the programme something that attracts the target audience? You could also consider how new radio programmes initially attract listeners. Is word of mouth a powerful publicity tool? Are new programmes advertised through other media or media products? Are radio personalities and individuals a factor in drawing in new listeners?

The role of community radio within community identity

You could choose a local radio station, a commercial station or one from Public Service Broadcasting in order to approach this sub-topic. This is an interesting area of investigation, because it encourages you to look at the influence and impact of community radio programmes. To what extent do the lifestyles, cultures and particular ideological positions presented through radio programmes galvanise, create or cement community identity? You could investigate whether or not the frames of cultural reference and language used within programmes, if adopted by the target listener, act to create a sense of shared community. Is the extent of potential influence affected by the profile of the audience member (i.e. their age or gender)? You could also analyse whether or not radio is an important and effective medium within community building.

Radio communities within Public Service Broadcasting

The case study below looks in more detail at how radio communities can be created within a PSB context, but here we will consider a general approach to this sub-topic. All the BBC stations are potential sites for examples of shows that have a particular community of listener. If one of the definitions of the term community is a group of people who have cultural, ethnic or religious 'interests' in common, then you could argue that programmes as diverse as Radio 4's *Women's Hour* and Radio 1's *Chris Moyles Show* have listeners who share commonalities. You need to identify what these particular commonalities are in relation to your chosen shows and what the dynamic is between the content and format of the show and the listening community to which it broadcasts. Is the relationship between show and community mutually sustaining, in that one feeds off the other, or is the balance slightly skewed, which suggests that one influences the other more? In other words, do listeners' lifestyles, expectations and interests influence the content of programmes or is it the programme that generates certain tastes in the listener?

You do not have to limit yourself to local radio stations within this topic area and you could analyse a national show that has a specific community as its target listeners.

CASE STUDY

Radio communities within Public Service Broadcasting

Westwood: The Radio 1 Rap Show

The real-life Ali G

Danny Leigh

He's a middle-class white man who's the face of hip-hop to faithful fans of his Radio 1 show. But not everyone loves Tim Westwood – last summer he was shot in a London street. Danny Leigh meets him.

Tim Westwood's bright red van is parked outside Radio 1. I know this because Tim Westwood's bright red van has his name painted on it in big white letters. Inside, a courier turns to a security guard. 'What the hell is that?' Another man walks in. 'Is that Tim Westwood's bloody van outside?'

Next comes the veteran DJ Simon Mayo. 'I see Tim Westwood's here.' The first guy shakes his head. 'I'll tell you what that's about, Simon. M-O-N-E-Y.'

'And the flava,' Mayo deadpans. 'Don't forget the flava.'

As if. Because Tim Westwood has flava to burn. Two decades after making his debut as a pirate DJ, he is doing what he loves, playing the latest in US rap. To the half million British fans who listen to his weekend shows on Radio 1, he is, quite simply, Westwood: the face of hip-hop.

The white face of hip-hop. Straight outta Lowestoft, son of Bill, the late Bishop of Peterborough. No, make that the white, faintly wrinkled face of hip-hop, complete with transatlantic intonation and studied lexicon of mad skills and hot goddamn beats. Better yet, the white, faintly wrinkled, public school-educated face of hip-hop, in his bright red van with his name painted on the side.

There. You've had the cheap shots. It's not rocket science. While he may be Westwood to his fans, to detractors he's merely the real-life Ali G, a gibberish-spouting embarrassment, guilty of being entirely the wrong colour and class for his chosen profession. To the BBC, however, he is a godsend, a proven draw for otherwise indifferent 'urban' (read black) listeners.

Which is why, alongside Radio 1 publicist Paul, he is here in spotless camouflage, talking up his employer's plans for a new 'urban' digital radio station.

'I believe in public service, man,' he declares. 'I believe in serving the audience that supports you.'

An admirably Reithian sentiment. Only I feel obliged to mention that, by fronting a project designed for, to quote the Radio 1 blurb, a black audience under 24, he (neither black, nor under 24) is playing into his critics' hands. He bristles, just slightly.

'I'm here as a DJ, man. And I really feel that I can make a strong and positive contribution to the running of the station.'

He sounds as if he is at a job interview, and that is before he gives an exhaustive rundown of his CV ('that's a lot of experience man'). Then he catches my eye. 'So…what would these criticisms be, man?'

There is no chance to reply before Paul reminds me that the Radio 1 Rap Show is the BBC's best-performing programme with a young black audience. 'Right,' Westwood nods emphatically. 'And I think I can offer experience on-air, in production, and also in management.'

Great. After all, no one would question his commitment. When he talks hip-hop, it's almost touching. For real. 'Come on, man. There's a multimillion dollar industry comin' outta hip-hop, man, outta people who would have had no choice but be sellin' drugs on the corner, man. Come on, man. That's a revolution, man. Respect it and be part of it, man.'

Except that, despite the enthusiasm, he seems wary. Defensive. Then again, you'd be touchy if you'd been shot at point-blank range at a set of south London traffic lights, as he was last July when two men fired repeatedly through his Range Rover window. The first bullet just missed his spine. Despite various conspiracy theories, no charges were brought. 'The police got a couple of people,' he shrugs. 'Lack of evidence let 'em go. Just one of those things, man.'

No, to Westwood, the bitterest legacy of the shooting was his sniggering appropriation by the media. 'I been around forever, workin' for the hip-hop community, but before I got blasted, the press wasn't bothered, man. Then everyone wanted to know me.'

And to make a joke of him. Unkind voices even suggested that, in terms of credibility, getting shot was the best move of his career. So why does he think he provokes such hostility? 'I don't, man. I get tremendous love out there, man. Tremendous love.'

But not from the media. 'What, do you hate me?'

No, I say. I don't hate him at all.

'Then some of the media's feelin' me, man…I don't know, man, some cats don't understand hip-hop, man. That's their issue, man.'

He's getting pricklier by the minute. Perhaps, like dogs smelling fear, the press have latched on to his reluctance to discuss his background. Take him at his word, and you would think he had come out of the womb spinning mad flavas.

'So? I'm a DJ, man. Talk to me about music, man. That's who I am, man. I'm not a '– he spits the word – 'personality.'

But he has got a van outside with his name on it in 3ft-high letters. He hesitates. 'That's just a hot truck, man. Come on man. That's a lot of flava, man. A lot of flava. Paul? Are you feelin' me, Paul?'

Paul seems ambivalent. Anyway, that doesn't explain why he won't acknowledge his early life. 'OK, man. What d'you want to know, man?'

Regrettably, I ask about his first childhood memory. Five minutes later, he's still fuming. 'Childhood memory? How is that relevant to hip-hop, man? Damn, man. My first childhood memory isn't relevant, man. Come on, man. Ask me another.'

OK. 'How old are you?'

There is a very long silence. It seems a fair point. After the shooting, his age was given as everything from 30 to 42. 'So, how old are you?'

'I'm 27.'

'Tim, you're not. How old are you?' 'I just told you my age, man. My age, right...I'm going to tell you about my age. I don't want to be saying my age, man. My age, right...it depends what paper you read. HAHAHA!'

I tell him I'm not trying to be funny.

'I am!'

'How old are you?'

'How old am I? Depends what newspaper you read, man.'

'No, how old are you?'

'Yeah, and my answer, for the third time, is: it depends what newspaper you read, man. Yeah, man.'

He won't look me in the eye. Why won't he tell me how old he is? 'Because I have. Come on, man. You're makin' issues at this precise moment.'

I've heard blue-rinsed old ladies being less evasive. 'I'm 27, man. I'm like Cliff Richard. Put that down. HAHAHA!'

He stares at his feet. I tell him I have no problem with him, and that knowing someone's age, even approximately, helps you get a better picture of that person.

No response. How old was he when he got into hip-hop? 'Hmm ... ' What year was it? 'Probably...'79. And I came out DJ-ing around '82.'

When he was nine? 'I don't know, man. I'll have to work it out. Next question.'

'Why won't you tell me how old you are?'

'It's not an issue, man. Paul, do I know how old you are?' Paul coughs.

'Come on, man. Let's move on.'

Does he think it's a strange question? 'No...come on, man, I'm in showbusiness, man. Not showbusiness, but...the music, um...showbusiness. Showbusiness, man. Come on, man. You can understand that.' I tell him I could understand it if he was 75. 'I ain't 75, brother.'

It's hopeless. I ask more questions but he just keeps taking offence.

'So, hip-hop's become your life?' 'Yeah? And? What's your life, man?'

When I tell him we're done, he exhales, long and hard, before bemoaning at some length those who 'be hatin' on me.' Eventually, we – me, him, and Paul – leave.

Outside, a baffled man in Hare Krishna garb stares at the bright red van. I shake Westwood's hand, looking at a pleasant but hugely over-sensitive guy in early middle age. He looks at me as if I'm the devil. Then he heads toward the van. The last time I see him, he and the Krishna devotee are knocking fists.

'Yo, man, yo. Wha' appenin', man? Yo, man…whassup?'

Source: *The Guardian*, 1 November 2000

Biography

Tim Westwood is regarded as the most influential figure in hip hop in Europe and as a pioneer of the UK scene.

Westwood began as a DJ on pirate radio, LWR, and then as one of the co-owners of Kiss FM during the station's pirate years. After presenting the Rap Show on Capital FM for seven years, he joined Radio 1 in December 1994. Westwood has also hosted his own television show on ITV's Night Network and has presented and co-produced several music documentaries.

Westwood is also very active as a club DJ throughout the country and organises his own Radio 1 Rap Show events. Last year, Westwood held a regular Saturday night event at the Temple Nightclub in North London. Every week the night attracted over 3,500 people and featured Hip Hop stars such as Funkmaster Flex, Busta Rhymes, Jay Z, Lil Kim, Mase, EPMD, K-Ci and Jojo, Gang Starr and the Jungle Brothers. Westwood also hosts the Main Stage at the Notting Hill Carnival, an event which attracts over a million people. Westwood organises the top UK and US acts to perform at this free open-air event.

Westwood is committed to supporting UK talent on the Radio 1 Rap Show and promotes unsigned talent through open mic competitions and showcases.

Westwood has won the Sony Award for Best Specialist Music Programme in 1990, 1991 and 1994 and he has been voted the Number One Rap DJ by the readers of Hip Hop connection for the past ten years. In addition, he won the Best Radio Show at the Muzik Magazine Awards 1999.

Radio 1 Rap Show

The Radio 1 Rap Show broadcasts nationally on Radio 1 97–99FM on Fridays 11pm–2am and Saturdays 9pm–12am to over one million listeners every week. It is also available on the Astra Satellite in Europe.

The Radio 1 Rap Show is the only national rap show in the UK. It is known for breaking records into the mainstream, playing new music first and establishing new talent.

Once a month Westwood broadcasts live from New York with Funkmaster Flex for the 'New York Rap Exchange' and with Marley Marl for 'New York Live'. Once a month there is Mixmaster where local DJs have an opportunity to show their skills. Every Friday, UK artists guest in the studio and there is a NYC Update with Max Glazer. On Saturday, Westwood features hot guest DJs such as Cipher Sounds from Funkmaster Flex's Big Dawg Pitbulls. Recent guests include Method Man and Redman, Jay Z, Puff Daddy, Busta Rhymes and Eminem. The Radio 1 Rap Show is hot – so check it out.

Source: BBC Radio 1 website

Part Eight

TV Drama

The overarching focus for any project under this subheading should be research into the significance of TV drama. The headings below outline the general areas which would be appropriate to study for this topic.

The placement of TV drama in the schedules

A research topic within this area could begin with the study of TV schedules. TV listings magazines are the perfect resource to begin an analysis of the percentage share which TV dramas are given to programming within particular channels. How many TV dramas are offered might help you assess the aims of the channel and reflect the target market at which the channel is aiming. Remember that you do not have to restrict your analysis to terrestrial TV channels or to British ones.

Consideration of channels which show only TV dramas, whether these be new or repeats, would present interesting questions concerning audience profiles and also the attitude of the channel's parent company to TV drama.

What kinds of TV drama are placed at which times within the TV schedule would also provide an effective topic for study. Are there particular sub-genres of TV drama which dominate schedules? If this is the case, do you think that scheduling is determined by audience demand, by TV stations attempting to secure existing and create new audiences, or a combination of both these factors?

Sub-genres of TV drama and their target audiences

One way of beginning a study of TV drama sub-genres would be to use TV listings magazines (as mentioned above) to note down all of the examples of TV dramas that appear in schedules today and then try to describe their sub-genres. Your list will probably include at least those identified below, especially if you consider digital and satellite stations as well:

- soap operas
- costume dramas
- medical dramas
- crime dramas.

Your project might focus on any sub-genres that emerge as the most common within schedules and then evaluate what it is about these sub-genres which appeals to both the institutions behind the shows and the audiences who view them. This might include analysis of the particular conventions of the sub-genre and how the presentation of these relates to audience expectations.

The Sopranos

Eastenders

Drama documentaries

Drama documentaries, or examples of 'faction' as they are sometimes known, are a specific sub-genre of TV drama and therefore have their own set of conventions. The general focus of your project should be the significance of these conventions to producers and audiences. In terms of the specific questions you might effectively ask yourself about drama documentaries, there are a number of possible areas. You could select a group of drama documentaries that all use the same events as the basis for the programme and then comment on any differences within the presentation of the events across the different programmes. You could then extend your analysis to question why these differences might have occurred. Does the reason concern target audience, the political backdrop that existed when the particular programme was made, the time the programme was broadcast or any other reason?

You might look more generally about the aim of the drama documentary and its relationship with its audience. With this kind of project, you would need to analyse specific examples of drama documentary in order to deduce the strategies used to present events, but then this textual analysis should be extended to a consideration of the varying functions of the sub-genre. Do audiences view drama documentaries to be informed, educated, to have their own preconceptions confirmed or just to be entertained? If you consider there to be an ideological or campaigning thrust behind any particular

You will need to choose a national cinema, consider which film genres are evident (and most dominant) within it, and then discuss the attitudes of film producers and film audiences to those genres.

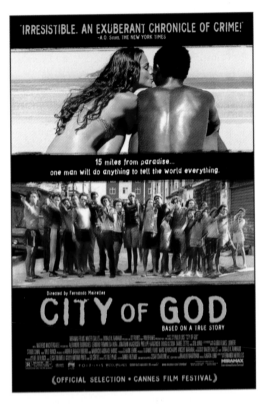

Poster for Brazilian film *City of God*.

If your research indicates that other national cinemas do have culturally specific genres, but also include those recognisable to British and American audiences, then your task will be to discern whether or not these 'recognisable' genres include similar sets of conventions or have adapted those conventions for the specific national audience. If the thriller genre exists in Japanese cinema, for example, are the set of conventions we expect evident and are they presented in the same way?

Cinematic hybrids

This sub-topic could be translated in two different ways. One possible direction for your project could be the study of whether the same kinds of hybrid genres that we experience in the UK exist in a different national cinema, whether there are any similarities in the conventions that have been combined and whether these hybrids have comparable popularity within another country. Action-adventure films are a significant feature within British cinema schedules, for example. Does this particular merging of genres exist outside of the USA and the UK? Are the same conventions combined in a similar way in a different national cinema? Is the hybrid genre given the same kind of exposure within cinema schedules? Is it popular with a similar profile of audiences?

Influence of world cinema on US and UK cinema

This sub-topic provides the inverse of the type of study that has been proposed for cinematic hybrids. Here you would have the opportunity of considering the influence of any other national cinema on that which exists in the USA and the UK. It would be of more interest, and more effective, to broaden your study, for example, by researching the influence of one particular national cinema on recent Hollywood or British film products. Have elements of this particular cinema been 'imported' because of audience demand, financial impetus, critical acclaim for that other cinema or any other reason?

Cultural independence

If your interest is more within the realm of how a particular country's national cinema is distinguishable from any other, then this sub-topic would be of interest to you. You could begin by looking at the contextual issues connected with the film texts produced within your chosen country. How important is a film industry to the country on which you are focusing? What kind of financial support does the film industry receive from the government of the country? Do the films produced have a market purely within that country?

Poster for French film *Amélie*.

The next area which would be worthy of study is the way in which the films produced within your chosen cinema represent the culture of that country. If a nation is to have a cinema that is deliberately independent from other cinemas, then a representation of the cultural difference of that country from others is usually a feature within the films produced. The question is really, to what extent does the cinema you are studying contribute towards a representation of the culture from which it came?

World cinema and politics

As you are probably very well aware, the relationship between cinema and politics is long and complicated. As a global medium, cinema has the potential to reach millions of individuals and thus to transmit particular messages to an incredibly wide audience. If you choose this sub-genre, you could look at particular points within a country's cinema history in which cinema has been used for explicitly political ends. This use might take the form of government propaganda or an expression of discontent with the dominant politics of the time. If the films you have chosen to study are challenging in tone, then you will need to investigate how those in control of the country treated the producers of those films. As a final debate within any study under this sub-topic, it would be very useful for you to consider what you think of the potential of cinema to affect politics.

Poster for German film *Goodbye Lenin!*

Poster for Chinese film *House of Flying Daggers.*

CASE STUDY

Japanese fantasy cinema

One possible avenue for your research under the heading of World Cinema could be the relationship of genre to audience within a particular national cinema. You would need to begin by specifying a genre of film on which to focus, so that your project did not become too broad and unmanageable. You should consider which conventions seemed to exist within this particular genre and how these are presented within a group of films. Your study would then need to extend into discussion of what audiences within your chosen country expect from the genre you have identified. Below is an example of a review that could be used within this type of study. It discusses an example of fantasy cinema from Japan.

Gods and Monsters

Lead review: *Spirited Away*

Andrew Osmond salutes *Spirited Away*, a Japanese animation film that mixes fairytale surrealism with a belief in empowerment through labour

Spirited Away (*Sen To Chihiro No Kamikakushi*), a Japanese animated fantasy about a little girl's adventures in a realm of gods and monsters, invites comparisons to the Alice books,

The Wizard of Oz and even Harry Potter. First and foremost, though, this remarkable film is embedded in the personal universe of its auteur-director Hayao Miyazaki, whose standing in Japan is comparable to Steven Spielberg's or, indeed, J.K. Rowling's in the west. From its opening in 2001, *Spirited Away* has become the biggest Japanese release in history. It is also the most successful 'foreign' film ever made, with the bulk of its revenue earned in its native country. The film shared the Golden Bear at last year's Berlin festival, followed by an Oscar for best animated feature. It is released in Britain both dubbed and subtitled, the dub produced by Disney and directed by Kirk Wise, who co-directed *Beauty and the Beast* and *Atlantis The Lost Empire*.

It's the baggage *Spirited Away* carries as a Miyazaki film that may bewilder British audiences. The director's previous film, the medieval fantasy *Princess Mononoke* (1997), is available on UK video, but to steal a phrase often applied to Woody Allen, both it and *Spirited Away* depart from Miyazaki's early, funny pictures. Not that *Spirited Away* is humourless; it has some splendid gags but it's deeply recursive, uniting themes and images from across the director's past work. To take the most obvious example, the soot-sprites that toil in the boiler room of the spider-man Kamaji here appear in a different role in Miyazaki's *My Neighbour Totoro* (1988), while many other elements form part of what might be called Miyazaki-land: his fascination with flight, ecology, elaborate buildings, strong girls, weary gods, overbuilt machinery, empowering labour, even the pigs' heroine Chihiro's gluttonous parents turn into. *Spirited Away* is not a sequel or spin-off, yet it's part of a one-man brand some western critics gloss as that exoticising standby, inscrutable orientalism.

Then again, the film's opening demonstrates the cross-cultural universality of fairy tales. A family wanders, or is lured, into a magic place where the parents eat tempting food and turn into pigs. Miyazaki cites Japanese folk tales as his influence here, but one could equally invoke Hansel and Gretel or Circe in Homer's *Odyssey* (a work referenced by Miyazaki in the past). The first minutes slide from normality to unease to menace as Chihiro's unwitting parents poke round what they think is a theme-park recreation of old Japan. The crescendo climaxes as the sun sets, the lanterns glow, and Chihiro finds her parents grotesquely transformed. She's not just scared, she's revolted, grossed-out; her body wriggles with nausea before she breaks and runs. The scene evokes the darker moments of classic Disney but with more edge than Walt's balletically styled terrors. Then with barely a pause the mood switches as the heroic boy Haku takes charge, pulling the hapless girl on a dizzy dash to a bathhouse patronised by gods and spirits (where most of the film is set). The delicacy of the score by Joe Hisaishi (a regular musician for live-action director Kitano Takeshi) gives way to bolder strokes a la John Williams, announcing a transition to high adventure.

From here on the audience is at Chihiro's eye-level, to sink or swim in a fantasy world somewhere between Wonderland and Harry Potter's Hogwarts, less soap-bubble surreal than the first, more quirkily digressive than the second. Here a spider-man works beside walking frogs and soot-balls with eyes, but there are also boilers, elevators, even an amphibious train. The bathhouse is furnished in lavish mosaic detail, from the painted partitions to the patterns on the cushions. No doubt this reflects the director's expressed desire to do justice to Japan's design heritage – the bathhouse blends architecture from various periods – but then Miyazaki has always been a craftsman of imagined space, creating eminently explorable, 'solid' drawn worlds that owe little to *Spirited Away*'s fairly sparse CG effects. Miyazaki's world-building has been compared to that of some videogame adventures, which also depend on first-person exploration, but analogies are legion, from the baroque-gothic labyrinths of Mervyn Peake's *Gormenghast* to the play-worlds of Rupert the Bear.

Initially Chihiro stumbles through her world, hurtling down steep stairs and being magically yanked across hallways. Her switch to active protagonist is signalled in the second half, when she hitches up her worker's uniform, runs along a treacherous metal pipe that nearly drops her to her doom, then climbs the bathhouse to the top. What causes this change? Miyazaki's answer is hard work, but of a different order from the jovial capitalism of Disney's dwarves.

One of the director's most popular earlier films, *Kiki's Delivery Service* (1989), was about a teen witch making flying deliveries while coping with adolescence. *Spirited Away* has a similarly offbeat work regime with Chihiro tending Japanese gods and learning responsibility and purpose. This has less to do with stereotypes of the industrious Japanese than with Miyazaki's own leftist leanings and belief in empowerment through labour. What makes it more than dreary moralism are the witty riffs on the theme. Chihiro's first trial is to help a soot-sprite carry unnaturally heavy lumps of coal; she succeeds, only for all its co-workers to drop their burdens before her en masse.

Later the bathhouse manager Yubaba (a huge-headed matriarch seemingly modelled on the Duchess in Tenniel's Alice illustrations) tries to steal Chihiro's name and identity. However, instead of depicting the girl's new job as dehumanised drudgery, Miyazaki turns it into a heroic, Herculean struggle. As Chihiro strives to clean a stinking gloop-god, stumbling, banging her head, trudging through faecal slime, there's a palpable sense of the once weak girl building an identity through toil, redefining the labour as her own. Eventually the bathhouse inmates rally to help her in a multi-species display of worker unity, but it's she who stands alone at the end as the revealed deity intones a transcendent "Well done". Meanwhile Yubaba's doppelganger Zeniba lives in a thatched farmhouse pursuing handicrafts, while Yubaba's giant baby, now a mouse, becomes a comic proponent of unalienated labour.

At the farmhouse Zeniba gives the characters an Alice-style tea party, which fits with the film's recurring images of eating, cleansing and purging. These range from the sublime (a storm that leaves the bathhouse surrounded by sea) to the outrageous (the monstrous No-face burying Yubaba in a diarrhoea-like avalanche of vomit). A passing mention of Japan's 'bubble' economy, with its associations of national indulgence, foreshadows the gluttony of No-face and Chihiro's parents, not to mention the great baby ensconced among painted mountains and palaces, refusing to go out for fear of "bad germs". Thematically, this marshalling of motifs and images is sound; more contentious is the film's narrative structure, which introduces new characters and strands half way through while leaving Chihiro's parents almost forgotten in the mix. It's an eccentricity that may not have been fully intended by Miyazaki, who reportedly altered his story outline in mid-production. Yet it makes aesthetic sense: why shouldn't Chihiro's adventures wrong foot the audience? The unpredictability can be wearing but also bracing, an antidote to the pat rollercoaster climaxes of such animations as *Monsters, Inc.*

Disney's dub (featuring Lilo voice-actress Daveigh Chase as Chihiro) is a creditable effort, though it lacks the spontaneity of original animation soundtracks and some of the 'extra' voices are weak. Western audiences may chafe at the sub-Disney frame rate (much of the animation is done on 'threes', or eight distinct frames a second) and the cartoon acting can't match that of the best US studios. That said, Chihiro's fearful, clinging behaviour is well observed, while her character design with a thin gawky body and pipe-cleaner legs is inspired.

In any case, cartoon acting was never the sine qua non of Miyazaki's films, which are built instead on heightened situations and sublime fantasy landscapes. Even if CG cartoons come to dominate Japan as they do much of the world, there's a corner of the animation field that will be forever Miyazaki.

Source: BFI website, *Sight and Sound* review

Summary

The aim of this section has been to introduce you to the main research topics outlined within your Critical Research Study unit and to describe some of the possible sub-topics you could investigate. Each section has aimed to give guidance on both content and project structure. Remember that the examiner will want to read a comprehensive, well-structured and original answer. You should bring into play all of the analytical skills and Media Studies knowledge that you have gained so far in your A Level course. Feel confident that your own informed and substantiated opinion will be rewarded.

SECTION 3
MEDIA ISSUES AND DEBATES

Introduction

This part of your Media Studies A2 Level requires you to show that you can bring together all the various concepts and skills that you have developed and apply them to a range of topic areas which encourage you to think about issues.

Issues is a commonly used word – there are always 'issues to consider', people have 'issues' they need to resolve. We rarely stop to think what the word means when used in this way. Media Issues are the concerns that people argue about, the discussions we have as a society about the role of the media, and the relationship between individual people, media organisations, producers and governments. The debates are the discussions themselves. In recent times, for example, the status of computer games as entertainment and/or educational tools has emerged as an issue, and people with different views (those who believe computer games are cognitively stimulating, rich resources for developing strategic skills and others who believe young people's consumption of games is denying them other opportunities to develop literacy or social skills) have debated the issue. Your task with this part of your Media Studies course is to understand the debates and come to a decision in each case about where you stand in response to the issue. Some examples of these issues are:

- Should violent films be censored?
- Should we have to pay a licence fee if we only want to watch subscription channels?
- Why are 90 per cent of the films shown at our local multiplexes American?
- Should journalists be able to intrude on people's privacy in the public interest?
- Is reality TV exploitative?

These questions have one thing in common: there are no right answers, but instead a whole range of facts, opinions and different areas of debate. Your job is to understand the subject matter, the factual, historical and political context, so that you can draw your own conclusions in an intelligent way. You need to show personal engagement – that you care and have a view, but only after you have explained each point of view.

The interesting thing about Media Issues is that they involve you as a citizen. It is not just a case of gaining knowledge. Instead, it is about discussing how the media represent you, take profit from you, serve you, provide for you, include you and exclude you.

Some of the topics involve understanding the government's (changing) role in regulating the media. Contemporary British Broadcasting involves not only analysing current TV and radio programmes, but also knowing about some legislation that impacts on both television and radio producers and us as the audience. At the same time that technology has changed, so too has the playing field for the BBC and its competitors. We are in the midst of great historical change and this topic puts you at the centre of it, deciding which point of view you support. Should Public Service Broadcasting be protected in the national interest, or has BSkyB increased the quality and choice of TV in Britain?

The process of learning about the British press gives you insight into the rules and regulations that journalists work to, so that you can understand the debates about press intrusion, libel and disregard for the truth from an informed angle.

Film censorship is also a rich topic for discussion. Who has the right to judge what we can and cannot see, and what is offensive? You probably have your own view on this, and now you can weigh it up against the opinions of others.

Other topics ask you to consider issues of quality, representation and labelling. For example:

- How does music television reflect the music industry's response to its audience turning into 'the ipod generation'?
- Does our national cinema represent Britain as it is in the twenty-first century, or as the Americans like to think it is?
- Does the magazine industry profit from perpetuating damaging gender **stereotypes**, or just tell it like it is?
- Why are so many of the films we see using the same genre formulas over and over again, or, if we look more closely, are they?

Some topics ask you to consider the role the media plays in **gatekeeping** our understanding of local, national and global events. If you study the local press, you will be asked to think about your own local community and the news service the press provide for you. At the other end of the spectrum, a study of broadcast news and current affairs cannot avoid a high degree of immediate relevance. The war in Iraq, the subsequent Hutton Inquiry and the London bombings represent a hugely significant chain of events for the future of international relations that we only understand through the media images provided for us, and which are now subject to increasing state intervention and scrutiny.

Since Media Studies was introduced in schools, colleges and universities, there has been much debate about its academic status. The thousands of students who have opted for it have provided evidence of its relevance to their lives. Far from being a 'Mickey Mouse' subject, Media Studies now places you at the heart of vital democratic questions about how news constructs our understanding of our culture. This part of the course offers opportunities for you to think about the relationship between the mass media and your own citizenship.

This section contains starting points for each of the nine topics in the OCR Specification. For it to be most effective you should work through the activities and use the content as a springboard for your own work, finding your own examples to integrate into your exam responses. Within each area there are hints for links with other units and at the end of each topic there is a practice exam question, similar in scope and demand to the real thing you will encounter on the big day!

Part One

Music Programmes on Television

Unit links

In other A2 units, you could:

- *Film* or *animate* and edit a music video.
- *Produce* a TV music programme.
- *Design* a website for a music programme.
- *Research* music TV as a form of advertising.

Introduction

The key concepts (ones you will be familiar with from your studies so far, and which link across all the different units) for this topic are:

- *Genre*: Is the music programme a television genre? If so, are live music shows, programmes that feature exclusively pop videos and music documentary broadcasts all sub-genres? How has the genre changed over time in terms of conventions and audience expectations? To what extent did MTV revolutionise the genre? Can we understand music programmes as separate entities to the music itself, or are they simply promotional vehicles? If the latter is the case, then what difference to the genre has downloading made in recent years? Or are music programmes clearly multimodal (in which case it makes little sense to apply genre as a categorising device)?

- *Representation*: How do music shows, and the videos they broadcast, represent people and ideas, most significantly within a broader question about how youth is represented to itself? Do music programmes offer youth subcultures a degree of autonomy and self-expression, or has the corporate parent culture used music programming as a cynical tool for profit? Are there representations in music programming that might cause you concern?

- *Audience and popular culture*: To what extent does audience behaviour, in terms of subcultural expression, consumption and creative contribution (through new technologies in particular) shape the development of music programming? How do different music programmes target different audiences? Does MTV exist as a homogeneous entity or does it attract different audiences for its range of scheduled material? More broadly, how do audiences use music programmes? While *Top of the Pops* was a hugely successful weekly show in the traditional context of the schedule and collective viewing, are music programmes today a pioneering example of 'on-demand' access to media?

What's on offer today?

We currently enjoy a variety of music programmes. On terrestrial channels, one week's viewing might include highlights programmes of concert performances (from 4Music most usually), *Top of the Pops* and its nostalgic offspring *TOTP2*, *Later with Jools Holland*, *Never Mind the Buzzcocks*, *Pop Idol*, an 'In Profile' documentary of a band and considerable amounts of Saturday morning kids' shows that are devoted to music. That said, there is much greater choice available on digital television, with whole channels devoted to music, such as MTV (which offers nearly ten formats), VH-1, TMF, The Hits, The Box, Kiss, Kerrang, Smash Hits, Q and Magic, to name just a few of the range available at the time of writing.

The future of *Top of the Pops*, currently still a survivor despite being shifted to Sunday evening, is uncertain to say the least, and this is due in the main to its reliance on the UK singles chart, which is becoming increasingly marginalised in the era of ringtones and downloads.

The most successful response of the traditional TV schedule to the on-demand era has been the reality TV music show, shaped, like *Big Brother*, by interactivity and suspense, and made entertaining in the vicarious pleasure offered to the viewer when the wannabee is scrutinised by the industry judge. The same debates arise here as with *Big Brother* – is this just cheap TV yielding maximum returns through the multi-platform set-up, the revenue from phone calls and SMS votes and the premium on advertising space? Or can we see in such shows a new, democratic access to the networks for ordinary people?

ACTIVITIES

In a group, conduct audience research with music fans in your area. Produce data which allows you to draw some conclusions about:

- what music TV people are watching
- how people are using music TV, compared to other TV formats
- the role music TV plays in determining what people consume (purchased CDs, downloads, concert tickets)
- the extent to which the audience for music TV is broken down into smaller groups, or niche audience groups.

The history of music TV

In the days before music video (which arrived during the 1970s and was firmly established as indispensable by the start of the next decade), programmes like *Top of the Pops*, *The Old Grey Whistle Test* and, previously, *Ready Steady Go!*, relied on a combination of live performance, interviews with musicians, chart news and input from the studio audience. *Top of the Pops* offered two unique elements: the performers mimed to their own recorded music and, when performers were not available for such simulation, the viewers were treated to a group of scantily clad female dancers with the single in question as the soundtrack.

As music video became a convention, *Top of the Pops* combined live acts with videos, and programmes like *The Chart Show* emerged, reliant purely on videos. A more 'adult' format, primarily offering live music, was provided by *The Tube* (a precursor of *TFI Friday*). In the 1980s, MTV arrived in the UK and, some suggest, the rest is history.

The MTV generation

MTV appeared in the early 1980s and became a part of the UK audience's TV landscape when Satellite TV became the norm in our homes. Now, of course, a variety of music TV channels come as standard in the basic 'bundles' we subscribe to. Owned by Viacom, MTV has been pioneering in forming partnerships with big business, such as Motorola recently. The reason this has been possible is that MTV, more than any other television channel in history, is synonymous with youth culture (as the subheading above suggests).

Corporations believe that association with MTV is to be seen as part of global, postmodern, US-driven teenage life, and this market is clearly huge as people of this age spend millions on entertainment and technology, as opposed to furniture and insurance. MTV has also been keen to pioneer genre-transforming programming, and much of the standard offer on music programmes today (message bars, interactive features, voting for videos and 'mashing') were first seen on MTV. Two key debates for your studies are:

1. Has MTV changed the nature of music, or is it simply a platform for the music?
2. Has MTV been responsible for a narrowing of youth music consumption (or, more broadly, of **hegemony**, where potentially radical cultural activity like popular music is incorporated into the mainstream, repackaged for corporate profits and made 'safe' as a result)?

Manufactured pop?

It might be considered a surprise that, in the wake of wall-to-wall video channels and the rise of MP3, the music industry turned to terrestrial, scheduled TV for a new cash cow, but that is what happened when Simon Fuller and others created a new version of manufactured pop bands. Whereas the Stock, Aitken and Waterman era and the grooming of bands like Take That and Boyzone had been obviously made to order as opposed to live and organic, the new twist was to make the manufacture visible to millions by televising the auditions and, cleverer still, allowing the audience to play a role in making the band.

The debate for you to grapple with is this: is it a reduction of music to nothing more than commerce producing music with little spirit or creative authenticity (in which case television ratings are the driving force as much as CD sales), or is this simply a transparent playing out of what pop music is anyway – a negotiation between musicians, corporate executives, PR and audience response?

As a Media Studies student (as opposed to someone analysing music itself), you need to analyse the pleasures offered by *PopStars* and its genre associates. These include the construction of a collective viewing experience (the 'water cooler moment', as the saying goes), which offers people a conversational topic over a period of time. In this sense there is a demystification of the music industry taking place, and thus possibly the feeling of involvement in the process on the viewer's part. This is interesting because it might mean we feel less exploited as a result. Additionally, *PopStars* and *Pop Idol* provide an active audience experience. Whether the music as a cultural form of expression is actually very important to this is another question, but nevertheless an important one. Placed alongside a text like *Later with Jools Holland*, we might well ask whether *PopStars* is really a music programme at all.

ACTIVITIES

Produce a pitch for a new music programme with a reality TV element. This must be original, but similar enough to successful shows to engage the audience. However, you must focus on a genre of pop music previously neglected by this format.

Once you are ready, work in a group with three or four others and vote for the best idea from your group. Then 'jigsaw' with other groups and vote again, until the whole class or a larger group of students has voted for the single best idea.

Finally, the whole group should split the development of the idea for the show into a range of tasks, for example, the presenters, the show's graphics, voting conventions, interactive features, attracting advertisers, further audience research, the studio design, and take the pitch to a more polished level.

A live music television deconstruction of pop music?

Music video

Music programming (with the exception of programmes focused only on live performance and reality pop shows) tends to be highly reliant on music video. It is therefore worth spending some time analysing this form of media text as a subsection of this topic, especially if you are making a music video for the practical part of your course.

A key theorist in this area is Andrew Goodwin. He suggested that the pop video essentially builds on visual associations provided by the music, rather than starting from scratch. An interesting exercise, therefore, is to listen to a piece of music for the first time and develop some ideas for the video, then to watch the video and check the degree of similarity (in this way you might disprove the theory).

Videos are a form of advertising of course, and this is interesting in terms of analysis because it means they require simple narrative in order to be successful (adverts must be memorable but avoid complexity for this reason). So if a video is an advert, can it be a piece of art? Well, some would include advertising in their description of what art can be, but others would disagree. The former are usually in the postmodern camp, where the boundaries between art, commerce and culture are blurred. Another debate for you to consider!

A key convention of music video is the editing, cross-cutting between representing narrative and a band or artist performance. This makes the form very interesting in terms of **realism**. The audience is required to suspend their disbelief and engage with a fictional representation of the music, while being reminded of the 'reality' of the song and its performance. More postmodernism.

Some videos are set up to transcend the limitations of the song form and become an additional product, as opposed to a mere vehicle for the music. At the time you read this, there will be current examples you can draw on, but a few classic contributors to this kind of text are Madonna, Michael Jackson, Eminem and Johny Cash.

Multimodality

You might decide that it is inaccurate to describe music programmes as a genre at all, because they are made up of such a range of media elements (recorded music, music performance, music video, documentary). If so, you are thinking of music programmes as multimodal, which means they combine a wide variety of forms of communication (dance, spoken language, visual language, editing, rhythm, various elements of music). Kress and Van Leeuwen (1996) offer a theoretical approach for multimodal analysis. Looking at texts this way, we need to:

1. Identify the medium (or media) chosen for production.
2. Identify the modes of communication chosen for the design of the text.
3. Identify the various ways in which the text is distributed.
4. Identify the kinds of discourse being communicated (the dominant representations of people and the world).

Music programmes are multimodal because of their reliance on combinations. It is helpful to use a theory like this if we think that the kinds of media texts we are dealing with are more complex and involve more combinations (mainly due to technology and new audience behaviour) than the traditional concepts of Media Studies can deal with. Once again, it is an issue for you to work with.

Exam practice question

Is music TV anything more than a continuous stream of advertising?

Part Two ■■■

Broadcast News and Current Affairs

Unit links

In other A2 units, you could:

- *Produce* a TV or radio news broadcast.
- *Research* the relationship between current affairs, politics and news media.

Introduction

This section deals specifically with television and radio news, as broadcast in the UK, and includes the relatively recent emergence of rolling 24-hour news provision. However, you can benefit from studying news as a whole, including the press and the internet, as an awareness of how these other media provide news will yield useful comparative understanding.

This topic relates to the key conceptual framework of Media Studies as follows:

- *Genre*: News itself is a genre, of which broadcast news is a sub-genre, and television and radio are further sub-genres. However, there is not only TV news or radio news, but local, national, international and global news, and then the different styles of news within even those categories. You will need to look into how different broadcast news programmes offer different types of news with varying conventions.

- *Narrative*: Although news is not fiction, it still involves a high degree of storytelling. Investigating how one story is treated and constructed differently for different purposes is essential to this topic. News has characters, conflict, disequilibrium and various stages of resolution, and so theories of narrative will be just as relevant to the analysis of news broadcasts as they are for soap opera or action films.

- *Representation*: How people are represented in news tells us much about our culture and society. As news and entertainment merge, the portrayal of individuals, groups and issues becomes an increasingly contested area of debate. There will be interesting differences between local and national representations.

- *Audience*: The way news stories are selected, constructed and presented varies, depending on the broadcasters' assumptions about the audience they are informing. News is seen by some as an essential public service, at the heart of state-supported media, while for others there are new, innovative ways of delivering news to audiences.

- *Ideology*: News values inform the process by which events are reported. These values relate to the dominant ideas of the culture in which they circulate. News changes over time and its presentation varies from culture to culture. Issues of freedom, control, bias and public interest lie behind the study of news. Recently, the Hutton Inquiry into the BBC's reporting of the government's use of Ministry of Defence intelligence foregrounded major issues around democracy, the status of the BBC as a self-regulated news provider and the public's faith in the impartiality and transparency of the reporting of current affairs.

ACTIVITIES

In a group, consider what difference it would make if interviewees could also speak directly to the camera. Why is it that the newsreader and reporters speak to us directly, while the subjects of items speak to the side of us? This should raise issues of control, authority and trust.

CASE STUDY

The Hutton Inquiry

It is impossible to scrutinise broadcast news and current affairs in the UK now without paying significant attention to the Hutton Inquiry. The BBC is owned by us but funded through government. It applies for charter renewal and in return for its side of the bargain (impartiality and range), the government justifies to us its protection from commercial competition. The BBC receives 85 per cent of the licence fee carve-up. The other 15 per cent is split between the other terrestrial channels, and in turn they have public service obligations. Public service broadcasting means programming that caters for entertainment, education and information in equal measure, as opposed to just offering programmes that get the highest ratings. The future of public service broadcasting is threatened both culturally (by the success of subscription and download TV) and by the changing relations between state, regulator and broadcaster. All of the terrestrial presences are facing uncertain times.

In March 2005, the BBC's charter was renewed until 2016, providing that the Board of Governors is replaced by an independent board of trustees. This governmental intervention arises directly from the Hutton Inquiry and the feeling of cabinet that the governors were confused in their dual role of regulator and management.

Hutton investigated and reported on the battle between Greg Dyke's BBC and Alastair Campbell's New Labour, and this provides a case study through which we can look into this debate over contemporary public service broadcasting. A BBC radio journalist, on Radio 4's *Today* programme, alleged that the government had 'sexed up' the potential threat represented by Iraq's weapons of mass destruction (which we now realise were non-existent). There was immediate attack from the government, and controversy over Hutton's appointment as mediator (the BBC believed that his track record made a whitewash inevitable). The debate hinges on the claim by Richard Sambrook, Director of BBC News, that 'Number Ten tried to intimidate the BBC in its reporting of events leading up to the war and during the course of the war itself.'

If this is true, then it is very serious because it leads us to doubt that we live in the kind of democratic society where we are given objective information (as opposed to state-controlled societies in which information is provided by government).

News values

Before we deal with TV and radio news specifically, it is helpful to consider some models and theories that have become conventional in discussions about how news is selected and constructed. These theoretical offerings all provide useful ways of understanding a very simple concept. This is that we only get to see or hear about things people choose to tell us, and that we only ever hear versions of events as seen by journalists. In other words, the news is not fact; it is not a transparent 'window on the world'. Instead, it is a collection of stories chosen for their 'newsworthiness' according to a set of values, related to ideas the journalists have about their audience. An obvious example in print news is the difference between the reporting of stories in *The Sun* and *The Guardian*. In broadcast news, the comparison tends to be less extreme.

Galtung and Ruge's famous (but overused) description in 1965 offers us the characteristics of news values.

> 'Journalists tend to think that stories are newsworthy when they offer recency, currency, continuity and simplicity. Alongside these are the benefits of stories that are close to home, feature celebrities or elite and powerful people, relate to human interest and, more often than not, are negative. We get to know about events that can be made into stories relating to where we live, involving people who are famous, offering us things with which to relate or empathise, and involving bad news which tends to be more interesting than good news.'

For a detailed reference to news values, see page 13 in Section 1: Advanced Practical Production.

Analysis of the 'values' of two news events

Galtung and Ruge arrived at these values of news by analysing news stories over a period of time. It is useful to look at two news events that feature all the values listed here first.

The terrible attacks on the World Trade Center in New York and the Pentagon in Washington on 11

September, 2001 and their aftermath dominated the British news for a long time and led to extended news coverage replacing scheduled TV and radio programmes. Just under four years later, perhaps as a result of Britain's role in subsequent wars in Afghanistan and Iraq, suicide bombers targeted London, and the news focus was similarly sustained. The values offered by the events themselves and those that followed readily relate to specific news values.

Recency, currency and continuity

The enormity of these terrible events and their implications for national and world security, financial markets and our fears of war and reprisal ensured that the story would be long running. And while the actual attacks would become further in the past each day, responses to the attacks, the attempts of rescuers and the investigations into the events and their perpetrators were guaranteed to offer long-term, day-to-day interest across the globe. Indeed 'post 9/11' has become a stock phrase to describe the supposedly different times we live in.

Simplicity

With 9/11, there are complex undercurrents underlying the events in terms of the political and historical details. However, the atrocities of such terrorism could not be simpler in terms of villains and victims. Unlike many political stories where news offers a simplified version in order to intrigue and involve the audience, this story offers total unambiguity in the form of universal horror, outrage, shock and anxiety. The London bombs were equally easy to simplify in the immediate aftermath (the public in danger, eyewitness accounts, calls to 'carry on as normal'), but as events unfolded, a series of less straightforward elements emerged – the shooting of an innocent man wrongly suspected of terrorism, the debate over whether the (unsupported) war in Iraq was a direct cause, security failures and the Government's desire to introduce legislation and increase surveillance of Islamic activists. The broadcast media's response, post-Hutton, to Home Office activities is an interesting case study.

Closeness to home

The British news broadcasters, in the aftermath of 9/11, were able to focus on British victims, the political alliance of Britain and the USA, the possible deployment of British troops and the increase in security at British airports. Furthermore, Britain's own experiences of terrorism offered comparison and context. Local bulletins focused on victims from specific areas and regions of Britain. The London bombs were followed by police activity in Yorkshire and the West Midlands and security alerts across the nation. So while London is only home to a minority of the population, its status as the nation's capital accentuated the sense of imminent danger for the whole audience.

Negativity and human interest

In both cases, the events were clearly terrible and nobody could fail to be horrified by the number of casualties and the scenes of chaos. The most resonant human interest aspects were offered by eyewitness accounts and the stories of people searching for their lost relatives. One curiosity of the London bombings was the inconsistency of eyewitness accounts and the possibility that some witnesses, in a state of shock, were responsible for giving misleading anecdotal information.

Celebrity and powerful people

World leaders were involved at every stage of the 9/11 narrative, and the aftermath centred on the reaction of President Bush and the threat of war. The USA is the world's most powerful nation and much of the devastation arose from the shock that such a dominant country could be attacked in such a way.

The London bombs placed Tony Blair, Charles Clarke (the Home Secretary at the time) and Ian Blair, the Chief Constable of the Metropolitan Police, centre stage. The possibility of a cover-up in the wake of the mistaken shooting at Stockwell added a flavour of conspiracy and demonisation of authority figures.

Television news in Britain

History

Radio dominated news broadcasting until the 1950s, when the BBC started producing its own visual news material. The 1953 coronation of Elizabeth II was probably the first event to be covered in the way we expect today, with the nation watching a major event in the comfort of the living room. Soon after, the BBC was rivalled by ITN's *News at Ten*, first broadcast in May 1955. ITN's style was slightly less formal than the BBC's, and to this day the BBC has been more reluctant to consider news as a form of entertainment. Since the 1950s, the two institutions have consistently offered slightly different news styles.

Conventions

News is increasingly gathered, produced and transmitted with the benefits of digital technology. Our appetite for instant information has accelerated the haste with which news is communicated across local, national and global boundaries. There is an increase in anchor footage recorded by members of the public and some of the traditional practices of the broadcast journalist are ever changing. However, while the means of gathering and transmitting footage might be evolving at a rapid pace, the style of presentation, in the main, has remained very traditional. Broadcasters are apparently reluctant to challenge the conventions of the formal bulletin for risk of being accused of dumbing down or offending their audience.

As with all moving-image analysis, deconstruction of camera angle, movement and position is important, not only in the studio but also when considering the construction of footage or location/outside broadcast material. Depending on the events being covered, you will see different choices of shot type, varieties of editing and decisions about camera position that can manipulate the way we understand news events.

Pictures are selected for the bulletin when they complement the narrative and conform to the news value of simplicity. Semiotically speaking, pictures must instantly provide the viewer with a clear range of **signifiers**. Narration or voice-over is only used alongside when it can meaningfully add to these self-explanatory images.

News relies on experts or eyewitnesses being interviewed. The conventions for this are clear – the interviewee is profiled in three-quarter style, looking slightly to one side of the camera, where the questioner's shoulder might be seen. If you set up this type of interview yourself, you will see how forced and unnatural it actually is, emphasising the power of conventions that have become commonplace or 'natural'.

When there is a break in continuity, news broadcasters use cutaways, such as the questioner nodding or images that relate to what is being discussed. They are used to link sequences, break up the tedium of talking heads or anchor the subject matter. For example, most news items on the NHS feature shots of ambulances, waiting rooms, patients and the outsides of hospitals.

It is important to remember that seemingly trivial factors like the use of cutaways, 'noddy' shots or edits of interviews can cause conflict between broadcasters and the subjects of news items, since these techniques mediate our understanding of events.

The most classic of all TV news conventions is the 'piece to camera', where a reporter stands in front of a news location (sometimes the scene of dramatic events, like military conflict or a disaster, sometimes a building where political talks have taken place) and speaks directly into the camera, summarising the story or concluding the item (having the final say).

Agendas

Those who select, construct and present the news we receive have enormous power to control the flow of information in our democracy (one of the reasons why Media Studies is so important for citizenship). The combination of the news values a particular news broadcaster holds, the conventions they use for the delivery of their stories, and the political or ideological positions they maintain are described as the broadcaster's news agenda.

Rolling news offered continuous coverage of the July 05 bombs.

Over the course of a week, record for analysis examples of British news bulletins (try to cover a range of broadcasters) and some peak-time output from CNN, Sky News and BBC News 24 (all three of these go out to an international audience).

Compare the national news provision with the international material, using these three perspectives:

1. Conventions
2. News values
3. News agendas (identify what you think are the priorities and intentions of the broadcasters in each case).

The changing nature of TV news

Digital television affords us the opportunity to consume 24-hour news from the BBC, ITV, CNN, Sky and others. The extent to which this facility proposes a threat to the conventional, edited narrative of the half-hour news bulletin is open to debate. You might conduct some audience research, taking a demographic cross-section sample of the television audience in your locality, in order to gather the following data:

- Who is using rolling news?

- How are they using it (is their use of it event driven, or time driven – do they turn to 24-hour news when major events happen, or do they watch it at the same time regularly)?

- Does rolling news replace or complement scheduled broadcast news for these viewers?

Comparison – *Outfoxed*

Although the focus of this topic area is news broadcast in the UK, the digital subscription era has shifted the boundaries and made news increasingly international. That said, some argue that so-called global news tends not to disguise its corporate and cultural agendas. Comparing BBC News 24 with Fox News (from the USA) is an interesting exercise in this respect. *Outfoxed* is a documentary film that investigates the news practices of Fox News, owned by News Corporation (Rupert Murdoch's media empire). According to this text (which of course is taking a particular stance), Fox News is a direct outpouring of the political views of its owner, through direct control of journalists' work and a clear, undisguised policy of influence running through the organisation, despite the network using the slogans 'Fair and Balanced' and 'We Report, You Decide' to promote itself.

Radio news in Britain

As we have seen, it was not until the royal coronation in 1953 that television began to emerge as the 'natural' outlet for news information (alongside newspapers). However, television has not reduced the power of radio news. This is due largely to its portability (whether that means commuters receiving live updates on the way to work, or people tuning in to the BBC World Service on tiny radios all over the world). In the absence of the raw images we have come to expect, radio news has to have its own conventions that compensate and offer alternative benefits.

Nowadays, digital technology allows for ever smaller recording equipment and ISDN lines offer the journalist instant transmission to the studio. Although this new wave of technology has made lives easier in terms of carrying equipment and communicating quickly, the radio journalist still has to observe the same conventions of sound, ethics and presentation. Sue MacGregor of Radio 4, when asked about the differences digital radio would make, remarked, 'The pressure is on for quantity, not quality. We may even be the last generation to know and appreciate the excellence of good radio; to realise that the best of good radio produces unforgettable pictures in the head.'

Local radio is an interesting area to explore in order to understand both radio news conventions and to approach issues of access, democracy and equality. Together with the local paper, these broadcasters offer information to small local areas that television cannot. Carrying out a small case study on radio news provision in your local area will raise some useful issues about the function of news as a public service.

Note: Public Service Broadcasting as a concept was mentioned in the introduction to this section (page 115) and features in detail in the next topic, Contemporary British Broadcasting (page 130). A glance at that area will also help you with this topic.

ACTIVITIES

Arrange an interview with a local radio news journalist and find out about their working practices and how the format of the radio programme they work for determines the way they gather news. Focus in particular on the unique qualities of radio news as opposed to newspaper or television journalism.

Digital radio

The radio stations only available on digital radio are currently dominated by music and sport, but the technology does offer a wider range of news provision. One example is the BBC's Asian Network News which broadcasts digitally, and another is LBC News, from London. Like their visual counterparts, these stations offer a more fluid news narrative with a much slower rhythm, and they tend to be dominated by speculation rather than packaged synopsis. However, as more stations like Asian Network emerge, we may see a broader set of news agendas, and Media Studies students will be able to investigate the degree to which we will be able to select our broadcast news by cultural and political preference (as we do for newspapers).

> Exam practice question
>
> Broadcast news offers a constructed, mediated version of current affairs, while claiming to provide objective, transparent reports. Using examples, explain whether the level of mediation is equal for all broadcast news.

Part Three ■■■

Contemporary British Broadcasting

Unit links

In other A2 units, you could:

- *Produce* a documentary, magazine feature, newspaper supplement or website covering audience responses to new broadcasting technologies and delivery methods (e.g. downloaded hard-drive TV).

- *Design* promotional materials for a new subscription TV channel or piece of hardware (e.g. a rival to SkyPlus).

- *Research* the impact of new technologies in sports coverage and the response of armchair viewers to new arrivals like pay-per-view.

- *Research* audience use of community radio in your locality, providing both quantitative and qualitative data.

Introduction

Essentially this topic requires you to understand factual detail, historical developments and political issues, and there is a body of knowledge that you must have at your disposal. However, in order to engage personally with the issues and debates that surround the current broadcasting scene in Britain and to understand its future possibilities, you will need to develop your own point of view on the topic, ideally through some personal audience research. To this end, this section will introduce you to:

- The Peacock Report, the Broadcasting Act and Deregulation (the facts).
- Issues and debates surrounding deregulation, technology and audience response.
- The future of broadcasting in digital Britain.
- The significance of BBC Charter renewal.
- Possibilities for audience research.
- This section will focus on television, but will take into account that broadcasting includes radio and there is interesting work to be done on that medium too.

ACTIVITIES

For this topic you will need to research certain political, historical and sociological terms and ideas. You should produce for your own use a 'dictionary' consisting of definitions and examples of the following:

- privatisation
- the licence fee
- the public sector
- the private sector
- state regulation.

A brief history

In 1986 the Peacock Report was published and paved the way for the Broadcasting Act of 1990, which changed the institutional context of TV and the ways in which we consume it.

Margaret Thatcher's Conservative Government wanted to increase competition in broadcasting and to decrease the control the state held over TV. As part of Thatcher's wholesale privatisation, it was decided that it was preferable for companies to bid for transmission rights (called franchises) and for the government to stop seeing television as part of the public sector (like education or the NHS).

Public Service Broadcasting and the licence fee

For over 80 years, British broadcasting has operated under the state-imposed ethos of Public Service Broadcasting. This means that, although commercial and subscription channels are on the increase, there still has to be material which serves the public by educating, entertaining and informing us. These three criteria were put in place by Lord Reith, who was in charge of the BBC in the 1920s. Today, the BBC is still 100 per cent PSB-driven.

The difference between the BBC and BSkyB is clear – the BBC exists to provide the nation with programmes that fit the three categories mentioned above in equal measure. We, the public, own the BBC, paying for it to exist through the licence fee. Therefore, we have a legitimate right to be represented in its programming. There must, quite literally, be something for everyone on offer. BSkyB, however, exists as a profit-making organisation, funded by the considerable capital of Rupert Murdoch and by advertising and sponsorship. The reason that the BBC does not carry advertising is not just because it does not need to create revenue in this way. It is also because it was felt that commercial interests, such as those of advertisers, would compromise the BBC's ethos in the race for bigger ratings.

The key point is that Reith, and many since, believed in the fundamental principle that what is popular does not appeal to everyone and that minority audience groups deserve a share of transmission time. Hence, Public Service Broadcasting can be seen as a democratic right.

Commercial TV has to reflect the interests of those who own and fund it and so it needs to make money. In this case what serves the public might be secondary to what attracts audiences. Therefore, competition does not necessarily lead to an increase in quality. In fact, Reith and the subsequent directors of the BBC have believed the opposite – that it is precisely the lack of competition and the BBC's status as a neutral, public utility that has allowed for its quality programming.

Those who believe in PSB think that choice is created through the avoidance of commercial imperatives. Those who subscribe (literally) to the principles of the free market and paid-for TV think that more channels with more specialist output (e.g. Sky Sports or the Sci-Fi channel) create more choice.

DISCUSSION

What difference would it make if the BBC took advertising?

Why do we have to pay a licence fee to fund the BBC if we want to watch mostly Sky Sports, for instance?

The answers to these questions may not spring to mind as readily as you expect.

The 1990 Broadcasting Act

To summarise, this Government White Paper put forward the following changes:

- Government intervention in broadcasting content to be reduced, providing that taste, decency and 'quality' are maintained.
- Subscription television to increase, with new methods of transmission encouraged.
- Advertising and sponsorship of programming to be allowed in new ways and advertising rates to be kept in check by increased competition.
- Competition between broadcasters to be encouraged (moving away from the BBC/ITV duopoly).
- The introduction of a fifth terrestrial channel and more satellite services.

What this meant in real terms was good news for Rupert Murdoch's BSkyB and a wake-up call for the BBC and ITV.

Deregulation

There are two kinds of regulation that were attacked by the government at the beginning of the 1990s: editorial regulation (over content – the PSB ethos) and economic regulation (control over how many channels should exist, who owns them and what other institutions they own – in other words, regulation that protects the BBC's existence from commercial competition).

We saw earlier how Margaret Thatcher's Government was anxious to privatise the airwaves in order to increase free-market ideology in broadcasting. In this way, Thatcher viewed broadcasting as a service no different from any other; different providers of the service should compete for audiences. The key debate rests on the question of whether competition increases quality or minimises risk-taking.

Channel 5 was launched as a new commercial channel in 1997. There were many early transmission problems (many viewers could not receive the signal), but the channel promised to push back boundaries and offer new, innovative kinds of television. Many sceptics saw Channel 5's ideas of innovation as indicative of the inevitable dumbing down brought about by the 1990 Act.

After the revolution of the Broadcasting Act, it was necessary for the government to consider the future development of the BBC. What place was there for a public service institution funded by the taxpayer through the licence fee in the face of the free-market, satellite and subscription services? The government proposed that the BBC should continue to exist as a public service, with the licence fee maintained, but that the organisation should become 'more efficient'. What this meant in reality was that the BBC would have to develop cable and satellite methods of transmission alongside their terrestrial provision. The outcome of such a proviso has been the introduction of BBC News 24, BBC Choice, BBC Knowledge and BBC Online. These might seem fairly innocuous projects in the current climate, but they have been very controversial. Critics have questioned the value of these as licence fee-funded channels. Again, where you stand on this depends on how you feel about PSB, populism and notions of 'quality'.

Interactive TV

The possibilities brought about by the advent of digital broadcasting, combined with the freedom of the market following the 1990 Act, are already in effect with pay-per-view, interactive TV, hard-drive stored TV and internet TV growing in popularity.

SkyPlus, for example, has a large hard drive to store huge amounts of TV digitally without the use of tape or disc, and perhaps the most attractive feature of SkyPlus is its ability to pause live TV. Other variants (such as TiVo) even suggest programmes you might like by 'learning' from your viewing habits over a period of time. The catch is that this memory facility is not just used for your convenience. Shortly after installing TiVo, viewers start to receive information about products and services that are targeted at the groups to which TiVo thinks they belong. It is now possible to pay for films to be downloaded via your phone line and viewers can now decide exactly when they want *Little Britain* to be transmitted to them.

These innovations do not just mean that the technology is different. They may revolutionise our viewing habits to the extent that we will look back in affectionate amusement to the days when we all used to sit down and watch the television at the same time – a context for broadcasting that has been commonplace since the coronation!

Narrowcasting and the death of the schedule?

In the contemporary broadcasting scene digital providers encourage us to fragment as an audience and move away from the collective viewing experience (although not for event TV like *Big Brother* or live sport). Critics of this current scene claim that high formatting has led to an era of 'narrowcasting' in which producers, in ever increasing anxiety about competition from more and more channels fighting for smaller audiences, play safer than ever before.

If this is true, then a proliferation of quantity has led to a decrease in quality, or at least choice. However, the programmers would argue vehemently against this notion and suggest that the incredible amount of programmes to choose from means that a viewer interested in art, for example, is far more likely to find television content of interest on any one evening than they were in the days of prescribed public service scheduling.

Digital television (and interactive services made possible by it) is an arena for dispute and debate. Some would have us believe that scheduling as we know it is doomed, as we will all shortly be watching programmes downloaded and played back at our convenience. If this is the case, and programme guide information on our televisions becomes ever more sophisticated at leading us to our preferences, then the notion of channel will erode, so we do not really know the origin of what we are watching, never mind when it was 'broadcast'. Others take a more sceptical view and say that the 'water cooler moment' will always remain, as human beings will always enjoy the pleasure of the 'big moment', such as the *Big Brother* eviction night or the climax of a major soap opera storyline.

A further area for debate is the forthcoming 'switch off' of the analogue signal by the government at some point later towards the end of this decade. Cynics argue that this is an ill-judged plan that is only being carried through because the powers that be are committed to it. This argument is based on evidence that many older people and those with less money have no intention of transferring to digital voluntarily, which begs the question – who pays for the future?

What about PSB?

A good way to understand the issues and debates about current broadcasting and its future arises from looking at how the BBC has reacted to the challenges described earlier. Financially, the BBC is still sustained principally by the licence fee. This is justified by the view that, free from commercial imperatives, the Corporation can guarantee the preservation of quality and programming diversity (rather than relying on successful formulas or dumbing down to attract the mass audience). It is also argued that the BBC sets the standard for others to follow and, as a result, commercial broadcasting offers higher quality than would be the case without the BBC as it is currently funded (this is referred to as a 'virtuous circle').

However, the BBC is divided internally between two kinds of activities – those funded by the licence fee and its commercial activities. The latter tend to be internationally driven.

Since the 1990 Act, the BBC has changed. Under the leadership of Sir John Birt it has restructured to become more efficient (in the economic sense) and now broadcasts a range of programmes produced by independent companies (these can only be non-news programmes). The BBC has also embraced the internet, creating successful sites for news and education within BBC Online. Importantly, the BBC has worked in partnership with private sector companies on its new media initiatives. Whereas BBC Online exists as a public service website, beeb.com is a commercial venture that controversially showcases material funded by the licence fee.

The BBC has invested heavily in its online activities and, alongside the News 24 channel, this represents considerable investment in activities either peripheral to or outside of its traditional remit. The decision to commit a 'strategic investment of public service assets online' would, according to many commentators, substantially diminish the original Reithian principles of Public Service Broadcasting.

The BBC has ventured into new areas editorially, financially and technologically since the 1990 Act, to the extent that Birt declared the institution a 'major media global player' in 1999. The impulse to explore new areas has arisen due to outside pressure exerted on the BBC since Thatcher's attacks on the fundamental validity of the licence fee structure. In 1999 the Davies Committee published 'The Future Funding of the BBC'. This suggested that the BBC's request for increased revenue from government for its online projects was unrealistic and that it should be operating with roughly one-third of the suggested budget.

The situation will have changed since this section was written. You will need to keep up to date with the operations of the BBC and commercial/digital broadcasters. Although the internet is not broadcasting in the traditional context, the BBC's embracing of the medium will yield some interesting ideas related to the concept of PSB.

The internet is said to have destabilised the boundary between the BBC and commercial media. In this sense, the internet has broken down and made meaningless the traditional boundaries between different media and also between the Corporation's commercial and publicly funded activities. Furthermore, the web has confused the link between the licence fee and the national audience.

In March 2005, the BBC's charter (granted by government) was renewed until 2016, with the condition that the Corporation should avoid narrowcast programmes for high ratings. This compulsion was in response to arguments from other broadcasters that the BBC was 'having it both ways', by justifying the licence fee on the back of its public service ethos while outbidding other channels for US imports. The Green Paper on the future of the BBC cannot be separated from technological developments. Its rationale for the modernisation of the state's broadcaster is entirely grounded in a sense of the Reithian values (that television should inform, educate and entertain in equal, prescribed measure) no longer holding firm in the digital world.

On your course you will have studied the cultural implications of digital technology, and as a major broadcaster the BBC is experiencing a swings-and-roundabouts relationship with such innovation. On the one hand, technology has been the main threat to the BBC's existence, providing as it has the possibility for subscription channels and downloaded TV. On the other hand, the BBC's website is hugely successful and it has embraced both digital TV and radio itself. But ultimately, if audience expectations are the driving force, as opposed to the original public service obligation to inform, educate and entertain, might we choose a diet of American television, as we have largely done with film?

ACTIVITIES

Audience research – how do we use broadcasting today?

The best way to gain an insight into how all these developments affect people's lives is to carry out two kinds of research with people you know or with members of your local community. These will be quantitative and qualitative types of research. **Quantitative research** is concerned with gathering data or figures to demonstrate trends or changes in order to measure audience behaviour. **Qualitative research** is to get a sense of what people think by researching their attitudes and feelings about the future of television.

Here are four activities to get you started:

Decide on a community or sector of the population that you can work with easily – you may decide on a small local area or an age group in the area, a gender or college students. Work with your teacher to construct a suitable focus group. Then conduct the following research activities with the same group:

1. A survey to find out how many of the group subscribe to either Sky, Telewest, Cable TV providers or NTL, and how many of these people object strongly to paying the licence fee in addition.

2. Consumption tracking to acquire the following data. Of those above that do subscribe to digital, satellite or cable providers, find out the percentage of their average weekly viewing that is broadcast by:

   • The BBC (terrestrial only)
   • Commercial terrestrial channels
   • The BBC's digital broadcasting
   • Digital broadcasting from ITV
   • Subscription channels

3. A survey to find out the percentage of digital viewing that is scheduled and the percentage which is downloaded and viewed at another time.

4. Interviews/attitude tests to find out how much people know about the reasons for the licence fee and how the money is used (this should be with a cross-section of the original sample, not just subscribers).

5. Interviews to find out how people feel about the BBC's online and international/global activities, some of the funding for which is generated through the licence fee.

The first two activities are quantitative, the latter two qualitative. Hence, 3 and 4 will need some organising and serious thought about research methodology (covered in the section on Critical Research on page 60).

You must remember not to lead your respondents into the answers, and bear in mind that no research can be 100 per cent objective – you will inevitably interpret the answers through your own critical perspective.

Part Four ■■■

Contemporary British Cinema

Unit links

In other units, you could:

- *Produce* a trailer or sequence for a new British film.

- *Design* a DTP promotional campaign (film posters, stills, video sleeve, magazine cover, reviews and features, soundtrack cover, and so on) for a new British film.

- *Research* women in the British film industry or the representation of women in British films, or women as an audience in Britain (or perhaps a tighter focus, like Asian women and Bollywood in Britain).

- *Research* an area of world cinema in comparison to the UK film industry.

Introduction

The key areas of knowledge and understanding for this topic are:

- The current state of the British film industry.

- The relationship between British film, European cinema and Hollywood.

- The representation of contemporary (and changing) Britain in films.

Careful selection of material is required for this topic: you cannot cover every kind of film made in the UK in the last few years, so you will have to work out what is significant. To get the most from this work, you must not merely describe the industry and the films it makes, but consider issues and debates in relation to contemporary British film.

This topic covers the major areas of enquiry and offers a framework within which you can study selected films. It is useful to recognise that the majority of films most of us see at the cinema or on video or DVD are from Hollywood. However, there are a notable number of films that portray British life and, because our society is diverse and multicultural, Bollywood cinema and other national cinemas draw large audiences in many of our major cities. You may consider whether Hollywood films manage to be 'universal', or whether it is important that a nation has a cinema which reflects its specific social issues and its people more 'locally'. Another question might be to ask what 'Britishness' is and how cinema reflects such diversity in the twenty-first century.

ACTIVITIES

Britain is not just England.

Whether you are describing film ownership, cinema chains, directors and stars or representation of people in the films themselves, you must remember at all times to specify whether you mean the whole of Britain or just England.

Before generalisation takes over, research cinema from Scotland, Ireland and Wales and produce a brief sketch of each of those three nations' film industries at the time of study.

Context: a period in time

Thinking in terms of periods in British cinema history helps us to understand the workings of historians more than the role of cinema in society. For example, if this topic covered the 1960s, we would immediately think of kitchen-sink drama, realism, Swinging London, Bond and *Carry On*, and a whole host of ways in which Britain represented itself anew. However, this would be to see that decade through the filtering effect of a particular retrospective spin.

The advantage of studying contemporary British cinema is that you are immersed in such cinema as you study it. Hence, any labels used or grand claims made for the impact of specific films or groups of films and their authenticity of representation (or not) will be of your own making and negotiation. As you study films like *East is East, Billy Elliot, In this World, Love Actually, 28 Days Later, Bend it Like Beckham, Vera Drake, Dead Man's Shoes, Harry Potter* and *Ae Fond Kiss*, you need to reflect critically on the very different ways in which these films portray the Britain you live in or look back to earlier times.

Multicultural Britain

Themes

It is important that you think thematically about the contemporary as a time period – let us define this roughly as since 2000. It is neither possible nor desirable for you to cover the output of British film-makers or the manoeuvres of the British film industry chronologically from the turn of this century. You need to address the way British films have depicted changes to society in diverse ways, consider the major funding and institutional contexts and look at the film audience in Britain to reflect on demographic factors. An interesting strategy is to project yourself forward in time to 2050 and think about how the 2000s will be written about by film historians and theorists in retrospect. What were the main movements? Who were the key industry players? What changed, and for whom?

Before any study of British film can begin, we have to return to the timeless question of what is a British film? The industry is increasingly fragmented, many films are co-funded across national boundaries and many British directors are working abroad. Equally, there is the issue of whether we can any longer (or ever could with accuracy) group films together under the British banner. Films like *Wimbledon* and *Bend it Like Beckham* have little in common either institutionally or representationally with *Sweet Sixteen* or *Ratcatcher*.

The idea of representing Britain cannot be understood in isolation from an understanding of context and purpose – who is being represented by whom and to whom? Hugh Grant's awkward upper-class charm in *Love Actually* may appeal to an American audience who would struggle to understand Martin Compston's dilemmas in *Sweet Sixteen*.

The Films Act (1985) provided these criteria for defining a British film: the film will have either a UK or EU production context (the 'maker test'); at least 70 per cent of the production cost must be spent in the UK (the 'production cost test'); 70 per cent of the labour costs must be paid to residents of the UK or EU (the 'labour cost test'); and no more than 10 per cent of the content can be from an existing film. Additionally, the British Council say a British film must satisfy at least three of the following criteria:

- a British producer
- a British production team
- a British director
- a mostly British cast
- subject matter focused on British life or experience
- a review in *Sight and Sound* magazine that defines the film in terms of British identity.

It is useful to begin with an attempt at categorisation by institution, funding, director, audience and genre, in order to get a broad view of the texts in question and how they relate to the exam questions further down the line. Research into the areas described below can act as starting points.

Twenty-first century Britain: politics and culture

There have been many changes to British society that will have formed the backdrop to your own childhood – new technology, the post-Thatcher and New Labour eras, globalisation, the war in Iraq and subsequent terrorism, changes to popular culture consumption (or the privatisation of culture) and arguments about dumbing down.

Think about Britain as an advanced multicultural society, linked to questions about national identity in the face of globalisation, American dominance of culture and its exhibition, and arguments over Europe. In sociological terms, the New Labour era can also be understood as a post-industry era, with the dominance of the service economy and claims of a leisure society. There is a new economic phrase to describe this – *Wimbledonisation* – we do not produce anything significant (Tim Henman only) but we host the event. Economically, we act as a host nation to overseas industry and multinational corporations (the McDonald's effect). This makes a difference to people's lives in areas of Britain historically reliant on employment in manufacturing.

Contemporary ownership and institution

In terms of production, most film companies in Britain are either small scale, working on a film-by-film basis or subsidiaries of larger companies. British broadcasters moved into film in significant ways in the 1990s, with Channel 4, Granada and the BBC all involved. The majority of distributors sharing the market in Britain are still American. In exhibition, those who yearn for diversity have been dismayed by the fact that the increase in the number of screens with the rise of the multiplex has done little to increase the range of films shown. Equally, the visible increase in cinemas and screens has failed to help film producers in Britain get their films shown.

The 1990s was a period in which the internet emerged, along with other technological developments, and changed the face of all media production and consumption, not least in cinema. Film-related websites, DVD, IMAX and pay-per-view movies were all introduced.

Alongside the technological fervour, Britain had a new government, with a minister devoted to film. In 1998, Chris Smith, the Minister for Culture, Media and Sport, commissioned a review called 'A Bigger Picture', which investigated national film policy and made recommendations for the future. The outcome of this was that film distribution (essentially marketing) was recognised as the most significant area for attention, not production.

The Arts Council and the National Lottery handed out nearly £100 million to film producers who had successfully applied.

However, in the second half of the next decade, it still remains the case that there are no large companies producing films in Britain, and thus one disaster release can bankrupt our studios. The medium-sized companies that operate in Britain tend to be parts of bigger international corporations. These companies mainly concentrate on one film at a time. This means that there may be almost as many production companies as there are films produced in Britain (one or two films each, essentially) at any one time.

Funding for British films can be generated through access to the Film Council's resources, which are divided into Development Funds (for screenplays); a Premiere Fund (usually for bigger budget films or films from established directors); a New Cinema Fund (to support diverse projects from new origins); and the Regional Investment Fund for England (which carves up funds for the nine Regional Screen Agencies). However, it is important to recognise that there has been a major shift in intent. The current Film Council is focused on supporting projects that will return a profit from British audiences primarily.

Traditionally, countries have chosen between two types of film industry: a studio system like Hollywood – a 'factory' system with huge capital, exporting its products worldwide and from where all the major players operate; or a state-funded system where the government provides money for films that will reflect domestic life, in order to preserve national identity and resist the pull towards a 'universal' American culture. In Britain, neither system operates and our film-makers have neither the corporate system of Hollywood or government money to support them. This is the reason why so many 'British films' are only British in terms of their film-makers, artists or part-finance, and why for decades many of our most talented directors and stars have gone to Hollywood.

An additional problem is created within the areas of distribution and exhibition. Because our cinema screens are mostly owned by large American corporations, who tend to play it safe when booking films for exhibition, British film-makers have trouble getting their films shown in Britain.

These days, only around 20 per cent of British films are released on over 30 screens, about 15 per cent get a limited release and the remainder are never screened! We also struggle to see foreign, non-American films, which tend to be shown at independent or art-house cinemas only. This is where most of our own famous 'realist' directors, like Mike Leigh and Ken Loach, have their films shown as well.

Many British films have been more successful abroad than at home, then becoming popular in Britain once reputation is established through award-winning and critical acclaim elsewhere.

When looking at the contemporary British film industry, you will realise how difficult it is to find a 'purely' British film institutionally, and to distinguish between those that are funded and created through British creativity and money, those that are co-funded with European or international partner companies but feature 'British content', and those which are really foreign films with some British investment. It is useful to look at films from these institutional backgrounds and to bear in mind these factors when dealing with representational issues.

Consider the example of a film you are unlikely to have seen or heard of, *The Man Who Killed Don Quixote*. The National Lottery provided £2.3 million for this film by Terry Gilliam, through the Film Council, a government organisation. This was an example of state-sponsored domestic film-making. However, this lavishly expensive film was set in Spain and featured largely foreign talent. Moreover, the rest of the money for the film came from Pathé Pictures (France), Le Studio Canal Plus (France) and KC Medien (Germany). Here we have a truly international co-production, so how do we define it?

ACTIVITIES

Arrange an interview with representatives of your nearest independent cinema and your nearest multiplex on the subject of the current state of British cinema.

ACTIVITIES

Interview a relative or family friend who was a regular cinema goer in either the 1940s, 1950s, 1960s or 1970s. The further back the better! Ask them to recall their experiences, not just of the films, but of the social experience, who they went with, where they went, what the cinema was like, how they chose the films. Let them speak uninterrupted for as long as possible and record their memories if you can.

Compare their experiences to your own.

The fall and rise of cinema in Britain

Cinema-going (as opposed to watching films at home) has survived some major setbacks over the last 60 years. Cinemas have survived the advent of television, the VCR, digital subscription services, DVD and pay-per-view. Part of the reason for American dominance is that, in order to fend off these 'home comforts' and tempt people back to the cinemas, exhibitors had to create new kinds of spectacle and lure us to a 'cinematic experience'. Bigger screens (and more of them), comfortable seats, lavish foyers, surround sound and special FX help this cause. Arguably, British films that are traditionally more narrative-driven are less tempting to a new audience who are seeking spectacle. New IMAX developments could be seen to take cinema back to its origins, when the audience cowered at the sight of an approaching train on the screen and marvelled at images moving for the first time. Stories were secondary to spectacle when cinema began, and it might be argued that the 'multiplex age' has a lot in common with the dawn of film in this sense.

The British film industry is enjoying a boom period, but it is important to think about exactly what this means. You will probably find that at the time of reading this, most of the top box-office hits in Britain are American. It is likely that even successful British films will be partially financed by American companies, and that the cinemas where tickets are sold will be mostly American owned.

In 2004, the British public went to the cinema more often than at any point since 1972. Crucially, 25 per cent of what they paid to see was, on the surface at least, British output. According to the Film Council, films like *Harry Potter and the Prisoner of Azkaban* and *Bridget Jones: The Edge of Reason* were only beaten at the box office by *Shrek 2*.

However, if we return to the question of how we define British films, the degree to which this success represents an upward trend is a more complex issue. Both *Harry Potter* and *Bridget Jones* were US-funded. In the case of *Harry Potter*, most of the money made from the British audience's choices goes to Warner Bros. But it could be argued that the cast and crew were all British, so in terms of career development the benefits go to British personnel, and the cultural content of the film is British. But using the BFI's criteria, which foreground economic criteria, it would be difficult to herald a renaissance for the UK film industry on the evidence of the Hogwarts franchise. The most successful 'purely' British films of recent years have been *Shaun of the Dead* and *Touching the Void*, while *Love Actually* and *Calendar Girls* were the most successful UK/US co-funded movies. What is significant here is that neither of the 'pure' films offer a **social realist** depiction of working-class British life, so be careful not to make assumptions that US-funded films tend to be escapist and UK-funded films introspective. This is simply no longer a valid argument.

It is important that you find out about those films that you do not normally get to see. We only know about a minority of the films that are produced. Some do not even get to cinema screens and those that do are ones purchased by distributors who are confident of a profit (there are exceptions to this, but this is the norm). While the British film industry is enjoying a boom period at the time of writing,

ACTIVITIES

Select three films released in the last two years.

Criteria a)

- One film must be purely British, in the sense that both the money and talent come from Britain.
- One film must be co-funded with both British and foreign investment.
- One film must have mostly foreign investment, with a small British input in either money or creativity.

Criteria b)

In one of the films chosen, the subject matter shall be related to contemporary British life or an aspect of it. Preferably this should be a film which represents either a 'minority' group, one of the other home nations (Scotland, Wales or Ireland) or portrays a representative cross-section of our society.

In another of the films, Britain should be represented in a way that is highly specific to a non-minority specific group (e.g. white working-class males or the aristocracy). In one of your films it should be clear that a traditional, stereotypical portrayal of Britain is being employed to appeal to an international audience.

Compare the three films in terms of their production contexts, levels of success, representational elements and social themes. What view of Britain does each present and in what ways is this linked to the film's funding and creative personnel? Research the background to the films in order to trace publicity and critical reception in each case.

You will then be able to draw conclusions from this close analysis that will help you to discuss wider issues in an exam context. Moving from the specific to the general in this way is the most fruitful strategy for covering such a broad area.

Time constraints

You will not have time to cover all three films in great depth and so you should have a hierarchy of detail. One film should be analysed in depth, one used for meaningful comparison, but in less detail, and the third should be for reference only.

this does not mean that there is a growth in choice or diversity. If you look at what is on offer at multiplexes in your local area, you will probably find that they offer a very similar range of titles.

You will need to find out about local independent or art-house cinemas and examine their film listings. Consider why these films are not exhibited at the major chains.

British film and changes to national identity

You need to approach this topic in a triangular fashion, combining awareness of the UK film industry, films as texts (particular directors' approaches) and films as representative devices. This third area now demands our attention. Some critics argue that, compared to other national cinemas, British film has suffered from a burden of representation, and since we share a language with the USA, directors have tended to choose between portraying Britain in a way which will attract an international audience and subsequent riches, or to focus more on social issues for the domestic audience, who, perhaps ironically, have tended to prefer the other model anyway!

What you must avoid is lumping together diverse films into misleading categories. Many American-funded films are rich, complex, subtle narratives, while British-funded films are equally likely to be formulaic and predictable. A sensible approach is to take a particular aspect of representation, which is clearly contemporary, and analyse the range of representation on offer, in terms of who is being portrayed, how, with what intent and, most importantly, with what range of responses. Looking at the representation of asylum seekers, in comparison with the recent success of films dealing with issues faced by British Asians, is useful. Whereas *East is East* looks back with some nostalgia at 1970s Britain in the era of Enoch Powell, *Bend it Like Beckham* offers a glossier, upbeat investigation of the challenges facing an Asian female in Britain. But both might be guilty of stereotyping, or at least filmic shorthand. *Beckham*, after all, has the US audience very much in its sights, as soccer is a game played more by women than men in the States.

Taking the main characters and deconstructing them as types, we can see how each text sets up a range of different **discourses** that are placed in conflict, and in each case one view of the world comes out on top, the assumption being that the audience will share this. Ken Loach's *Ae Fond Kiss* adds another example to this emerging genre. In all cases, no matter how sensitively the director prepares the discourse, conflict in the form of the religious parent tends to be set up as the 'problem discourse', or at least this is the preferred reading for the western(ised) audience. You will make up your own mind, of course.

East is East – filmic shorthand or social realism?

Films like *In this World*, *Last Resort* and *Dirty Pretty Things* are different in that they represent the experiences of people seeking British nationality. Michael Winterbottom adopts a semi-documentary approach for *In this World*, after going to a refugee camp in Afghanistan and asking two of the residents to be filmed on a journey to London. The issue of asylum was brought into sharp focus during the 2005 election, and the Muslim community in Britain has been under intense scrutiny since the London bombings. So these films cannot be interpreted outside of these very difficult social questions about contemporary Britishness. Your job is to explore the variety of possible responses to each text and to come to some conclusions about how film is documenting the changes in Britain.

> Exam practice question
>
> 'It is increasingly difficult to define a British film'. With particular reference to the way that films are funded and the representation of changing Britain in recent cinema, discuss this point of view.

Part Five

The Concept of Genre in Films

Unit links

In other A2 units, you could:

- *Produce* a film trailer or sequence in a particular genre.
- *Create* a new magazine aimed at fans of one film genre.
- *Research* the relationship between film genre and gender.
- *Research* film genres from different world cinemas.

Introduction

This topic requires you to understand how genre works as a concept and a theory. You will already be familiar with genre from your AS work, but because this is one of the Issues and Debates areas, you now need to evaluate how useful genre is as an analytical tool.

Essentially this area of investigation is about formula and pleasure. However, genres do not comprise an unchanging set of rules, rather they are templates from which directors and studios may deviate.

Many established film genres have been parodied by directors, who take the classic conventions and revisit them and exaggerate the conventions to humorous effect. Directors are able to give the genre a twist (new kinds of Westerns have sprung up in recent years that return to the wild west and examine it from different points of view, and horror films have arrived that play with the history of the genre).

Ultimately it can be argued that we are now in a postmodern era of film-making, where films do not just offer representations of the world, but take a *filmic* reality as their starting point.

Most importantly, you need to challenge the idea of genre and adopt a sceptical approach. This means thinking seriously about whether it is the films themselves that are formulaic and predictable in the pleasures they offer and the conventions they adhere to, or whether it is actually our way of thinking about films in genre terms that is formulaic.

ACTIVITIES

Working in pairs, decide on two genres that you want to consider. One should be a genre that has enduring appeal and the other should be a newer genre or a sub-genre. An example would be to consider the Western and the serial killer horror film, or the Hollywood musical and the 'Masala movie' from Bollywood.

From your existing knowledge of these kinds of films, list the classic conventions they might include that relate to:

- narrative (subject matter, storyline conventions)

- representation (who are these films usually about and who is represented in a positive or negative light?)
- iconographic codes (*mise-en-scène*, settings, lighting, visual style)
- technical codes (use of camera and editing, FX, etc.)
- sound (kinds of music, sound FX, dialogue)
- ideology (what kinds of messages do these films tend to offer?).

Imagine you are writing a genre guide that offers an explanation of the pleasures of each film genre. Write a three-sentence statement for each of your genres. These can then be copied for everyone as a quick reference guide to film genre pleasures.

Looking at the guide as a whole, can you find any pleasures that may be said to be universal, that all the classic film genres offer?

Finally, consider the reasons why some genres have lasted so long and whether the fact that they have tells us anything about our society.

Genre theory

As you will know from your other work in Media Studies, the word 'genre' does not only relate to film, nor does it just belong to the subject of Media Studies, nor indeed to the study of texts in general (there are also literary genres and musical genres). Genre comes from the Latin *genus* and means kind or type – it was first used to classify biological phenomena. Since the nineteenth century it has been used mostly to define texts.

One important difference between film and TV genres and those of literature is that in written fiction, genre labels were used by theorists and critics to compartmentalise literary output long after poems, plays and novels were in existence. In moving-image production, however, genres were in the minds of producers and directors as well as audiences, critics and academics from the start.

Genre relates to the three 'phases' of the film industry in different ways. To the producer, the genre acts as a template for the film; to the distributor/promoter it provides assumptions about who the audience is and how to market the film to that audience; and to the viewer (at the point of exhibition) genre acts as a label that identifies a liked or disliked formula and thus acts as gatekeeper and filters our tastes. Genre regulates our consumption, but it also provides rules of engagement for the spectator in terms of the anticipation of pleasure.

In this way, as genres become 'classic', they exert great influence over all the areas of cinema. Production can be quicker and more confident; screenwriters follow tried and tested formulas and create characters that fit standard 'types', appropriate to the genre in question. Actors can be filtered into genres, their raw material (acting ability) transformed into star quality at the point when their mannerisms, physical attributes, ways of speaking and acting fit a particular style. Directors, cinematographers, sound people and costume designers all have a ready shorthand to work with. Films can be produced as products on an assembly line. As viewers, we become generic spectators.

The generic audience knows what to expect from a horror film or a comedy and judges it according to prior experience of the genre – in this sense we do not consume films as individual entities, but in a fundamentally **intertextual** way. Films make sense in relation to other films, not reality (film can be described as a postmodern medium in this way).

Genres have rules (conventions) that should already be clear to you from your textual analysis work for AS Level. Genre can be understood as a contract between producers and consumers, the assumed pleasure of the latter determining the creative output of the former in a cyclical manner.

However, genre texts do not work by simply copying other texts in the genre, but by adding their own contribution that strays more or less from the norm, depending on the director's intentions. Sometimes directors deliberately frustrate the audience by leading them down blind genre alleys. This frustration is not negative as usually it leads to a more interesting experience for the viewer, but for it to work, it depends entirely on whether the generic template is firmly entrenched in the audience.

ACTIVITIES

Find a film that is ambiguous in generic terms.

Use promotional materials, academic responses and critical reviews to research different viewpoints on the film.

You may find that the same film takes on a variety of different genre elements, depending on what audience the poster, review, feature, website or article is for.

Fandom

For genres like science fiction and horror in particular, there are groups of fans associated with each sub-genre that develop a deep interest in certain kinds of films within the genre (for example, Japanese Manga animations) or a particular series of films, such as the *Star Wars* films. When the latter happens you might come to the conclusion that a series of films becomes a sub-genre in itself.

Some interesting sociological and media research has been carried out into fans and their interests in certain kinds of films. This research has looked at the ways in which people identify with certain kinds of films and the psychological reasons for this. It has looked at fans in terms of subcultures – groups of people who adopt whole lifestyle traits around film types. This is more common for popular music than film, but particular kinds of science fiction attract people who collect all kinds of memorabilia and clothing or videos and DVDs and attend conventions and social events. An hour on the internet searching for sites related to *Star Wars*, *Star Trek*, *Planet of the Apes* and *Blade Runner* will introduce you to this world.

ACTIVITIES

Interview the editor of a fanzine/magazine or the creator of a fans' website (you could carry out an electronic interview) about the pleasures offered by a particular film genre.

CASE STUDY

Science fiction

The science fiction genre can be traced back to the beginnings of cinema itself. The Lumière Brothers, who are credited with the invention of moving images, created an early film sequence in which a pig was fed into a machine and sausages were produced at the other end. This machine was not real, but it was considered scientifically possible.

In 1902, Georges Méliès made a surreal film about a trip to the moon and in 1910 the first adaptation of the novel *Frankenstein* was made. So, in the first 15 years of cinema history the three central narrative themes – scientific/technological discovery, space travel and other worlds/life forms and creation/existence – were already in place.

Here are some important questions to ask about any genre that has survived for such a long period of time:

- What are the common themes that underpin the narratives of individual films?
- How do these themes relate to our society's concerns and preoccupations?

Science fiction is a genre that has centred on three central themes since it began as a literary genre:

- What are the limits of science (how far can or ought we to go in the desire for progress)?
- What is the relationship between science, nature and religion?
- What do we consider to be the future for the human race?

These themes have been explored through a number of story types, involving space exploration, alien invasion and terrors of technology or dystopian visions of the future. Many of the narratives relate to what is known as the 'Frankenstein myth'. In Mary Shelley's novel, Dr Frankenstein creates a man he cannot control, with disastrous consequences. Films like *Blade Runner* (1982), *Terminator* (1984), *Jurassic Park* (1993) and *The Matrix* (1999) all deal with the same theme – humans using science and/or technology to 'play God' with nature.

At the heart of the genre, which may seem to be completely fantastical and escapist on the surface, lie a number of serious political, philosophical, existential and metaphysical questions. In some ways science fiction relates to the important questions about humanity, namely, why are we here and where are we heading?

ACTIVITIES

Research the history of the science fiction film genre, making notes on the following:

- science fiction conventions
- hybrids such as the sci fi/horror alien
- common themes
- pleasures.

Keep a list of examples of key films under each heading.

Choose another classic film genre and consider the issues that are addressed within it, for example, the representation of women in horror films. You will be able to do this for horror, romantic comedy, action films, musicals and Westerns.

Build a genre file: in a small group, each choose another genre and, having done some basic research, present a short genre history for one another.

CASE STUDY

Bollywood

Bollywood itself is not a film genre, but an industry rivalling Hollywood in terms of worldwide appeal. It produces an average of 800 films a year with global appeal. The term 'Bollywood' describes popular Indian cinema from Bombay. In Britain today, several cities and towns have a Bollywood cinema showing Indian films. Bollywood cinema is an interesting case for this section because it has been argued that its treatment of genre is very different to films made in the West.

If you do an internet search for Bollywood you will immediately see the massive scale of this kind of cinema. Bollywood films often revolve around spectacular song and dance routines which carry the narrative; central ideological themes that relate to cultural issues and conflicts such as East and West, tradition and modernism and family and individual desire.

For our purposes, the most interesting comparison between Hollywood and Bollywood is the

fact that while the former employs a range of classic stock genres, Bollywood cinema offers the 'Masala movie'. This is where any one film offers something for everyone, a blend of different generic elements, including the themes of love and romance, thriller, crime, family drama, social realism and musical. Thus, strict adherence to a single genre does not occur in Indian cinema. This is more complex than merely a genre hybrid. The reasons for this vary from the legacy of mythological epics to the idea that cinema-going in India and Bollywood cinemas in Britain is more of a whole family experience. Audiences expect to see favourite elements of individual films, rather than favourite types of films. Whatever the reason for this different approach, it provides an interesting perspective on the norm that we have come to expect from Hollywood genre films.

Bollywood – mixed genres is the norm.

So how useful is genre?

We have looked at how genres stay popular, researched some classic genres, looked into sub-genres and fandom and compared Hollywood genre films with Masala movies that operate in a different way. Lastly, but crucially, we need to problematise the concept of genre. This means that we need to consider whether it is a useful way to think about films or whether it is simplistic and reductive. A good way to start is to think about pop music.

ACTIVITIES

Get as many of your class together as you can and draw up a list of pop music genres. When you cannot think of any more, decide which are actually genres, and which are styles that cut across a whole range of genres (e.g. is dance music really a genre?).

Next, break down each genre into sub-genres, and then each sub-genre into further sub-genres, and so on, until you can go no smaller.

Finally, each person should list their top five CDs of all time and then identify which genre they are in.

Was this an easy task? Did everyone agree? Usually the answer is no. This is because if you have a keen interest in something, it is harder to use a blunt tool like genre to define it since you are more aware of the nuances and individual features of each item.

So why should we think of film in terms of genre? Why is it that television programmes are usually described in terms of format rather than genre? Could it be that every film has individual features that defy any one simple act of labelling? If so, why does genre exist and whose interests does it serve? Perhaps it serves our lazy nature – efficient packaging saves time when making choices. Certainly it serves marketing people and their ideas about audience appeal and targeting strategies. Some say that it serves an overly commercial view of cinema. In other words, we are denied access to a rich variety of unique films which never get made because the studio executives prefer funding safe bets – films which can be packaged and sold because they adhere to tried and tested formulas.

We also need to consider the use of genre as a derogatory term, as a form of cultural snobbery. Literature, ballet and opera are rarely explicitly categorised in this way. Critics of popular culture tend to argue that popular (especially Hollywood films) lack originality and are 'easy' to watch, due to their repetition of conventions. This argument ignores the highly complex parody and intertextual referencing at work in a great many 'genre movies', of course.

Adopting a sceptical approach to genre works by simply starting the other way around, that is, with the film, not the genre. Rather than saying that there is a romantic comedy genre and films within it look like this, you ask the following questions:

- Is it possible to categorise films in different ways, and if it is possible, why is it useful – how does it help us?
- If we can come up with categories, how are these best defined – are they related to themes and issues, narrative and characters, or content, the visual style or 'look' (i.e. *mise-en-scène*)?

Most importantly, you need to examine the ownership of genre definitions. Think about who labels films and why; whether the label is fixed (i.e. we all agree) or open to debate; and whether it has changed over time or remained the same as a label.

Consider how elusive a genre is. Do texts from within it cross over into other genres? Are there sub-genres within the genre, and is it possible to come to a clear, final categorisation of any film within this group?

Might we say that contemporary films can be analysed in relation to genres, but they are not produced by them? And if Media Studies students are to be encouraged to analyse and to some extent expose the use of stereotyping, should we not be careful not to use genre as a shorthand set of generalisations?

Do we come to the ultimate conclusion that all films are Masala movies? Does every film tend to contain elements from several genres in a hierarchical fashion, which means that one genre becomes dominant and this is the one we use for our simplistic desire to label?

Your own examples of such films will lead you into some interesting findings about the way that genre can serve the interests of the industry and lead the audience down blind alleys. In this sense, genre is a profoundly restrictive tool.

> **Exam practice question**
>
> How useful is genre as a way of understanding films?

Part Six ■■■

Censorship and Film

Unit links

In other units, you could:

- *Produce* a documentary on film censorship and public views, a newspaper/magazine supplement feature, a radio discussion programme or either a pro- or anti-censorship website.
- *Research* women's responses to films that contain violent and sexual imagery to see whether responses to 'shocking' texts are gendered.
- *Research* the effects model in relation to a research project on children and media.

Introduction

When you think of film censorship, the examples that spring to mind tend to be of violent or sexual content that has led to outrage and claims that the fabric of society has broken down. However, there are a great many films that may not have been banned, but either by a process of self-regulation on the part of the director or studio, or through some cuts on the part of the censor or (and far more commonly) through classification, are either released in a form different to the original, or are only released for some of us to see.

Even the record-breaking success of *Harry Potter and the Philosopher's Stone* (2001), though not censored, raised concerns. In this case it was teachers who warned that a dangerous interest in the occult could be a possible outcome of the film's huge influence over children. As is often the case, it was only the film release that raised any concern (the same was true of *A Clockwork Orange* and *Crash*, both apparently perfectly acceptable in novel form).

Harry Potter – teachers called for censorship

The question that needs to be considered at the beginning of this topic and throughout is, simply, who decides?

All the Media Issues and Debates topics demand an opinion and personal engagement to the degree where you have your own informed view to argue in an intelligent and balanced manner. For instance, what is the cultural value of soap opera? Has deregulation provided more choice for consumers? Is the press free from bias? Is Hollywood domination imposing cultural imperialism on the British film industry?

The difference with the topic of film censorship is that you probably have your own opinion already, before you learn about the academic perspectives.

The key issues for this topic are:

- History of film censorship.
- Different motives for censorship.
- Arguments for and against censorship.
- Debates concerning effects theories.

You will need to relate these issues to contemporary examples. This section will point you towards some famous examples, but at the time of reading there will be new, 'present-tense' films that are either being censored, banned or causing certain sections of the public to call for their withdrawal from circulation.

The British Board of Film Censors/Classification

When judging whether film content is acceptable (and acceptable to what age groups) or whether it needs to be cut or censored, there are a number of areas of concern that must be addressed by the British Board of Film Classification (BBFC). While the BBFC is apparently neutral and independent, the fact that it is made up of industry representatives makes it self-regulatory, although there are suggestions that, despite this claim, it is accountable to government. The areas of concern are:

- sexual violence
- emphasis on the process of violence and sadism
- glamorisation of weapons that are both particularly dangerous and not already well known in Britain
- ill-treatment of animals or child actors
- details of imitable, dangerous or criminal techniques
- blasphemous images or dialogue.

The BBFC is not the only body that can influence what we get to see in cinemas and on television or DVD. The Home Office can make decisions in extreme cases, and ultimately the power to decide what we see is held by local councils. They almost always comply with BBFC recommendations, but they do not have to by law. The two famous exceptions from the last ten years are the decision by Westminster Council to deny the public access to *Crash* and the decision by Camden Council to allow the public to see *The Texas Chainsaw Massacre*.

In 1912, the BBFC came into being in order to ensure that the Cinematagraph Act of 1909 was enforced. This meant that cinemas were licensed by local authorities and that films were classed as either suitable for everyone or just for adults. In the 1920s, a middle ground was introduced, involving films that children could see under the supervision of parents, and in the 1930s horror films were classified separately as 'H'. Shortly afterwards the 'X' rating was introduced for any film seen as entirely unsuitable for under 16s. In the 1970s, the age for 'X' went up to 18, and 'AA' was introduced for age 14-plus only. In the 1980s, the framework became U, PG, 12, 15 and 18 and was also applicable to video retail and rental.

In 1982, the board changed its title from British Board of Film Censors to British Board of Film Classification to acknowledge the fact that, in the vast majority of cases, their role was not to prevent the exhibition of films, but to control their audience.

ACTIVITIES

Produce a short statement explaining what changes occur in a person's life at each of the key ages defined by film classifiers (i.e. 12, 15, 18). How do these changes make them able to respond safely to different kinds of films? Given that many A Level students are under 18 you may find this difficult, but put yourself in the mindset of the censor if you can.

The history of censorship

Before the 1909 Act, censorship was voluntary in the sense that film-makers wanted their new medium to be established as a respectable art form. The Act led to the establishment of the BBFC and then films were either cut or banned fairly frequently when they were deemed unsuitable for the public. This notion of unsuitability has always been fiercely contested. Who can say what is suitable? Who has the right to judge? Censorship has tended to operate around the following key kinds of examples:

- *Sexual content* – in 1919 *Damaged Goods* (the story of a soldier with a sexually transmitted disease) was not given a certificate.

- *Violence* – in more recent years both *Reservoir Dogs* (1992) and *Natural Born Killers* (1992) have fallen foul of the censor at the video release stage.

- *Taste* – a much harder category to define, many films have been controversially censored for this reason. In 1959, *Night and Fog*, a film containing real footage of corpses found in Nazi concentration camps, was cut before release.

- *Politics* – an even more controversial area, censors have refused to classify films for release if it was felt that their political content could lead to public unrest. *Battleship Potemkin* (1926), a famous Russian film with a socialist/communist slant, was banned in Britain because the BBFC were concerned about a possible revolution.

- *Blasphemy* – the Monty Python film *The Life of Brian* (1979) was banned in some areas of Britain (local councils reserved the right to make local decisions) because of its comic treatment of the story of Jesus.

- **Moral panic** – this term describes the hysterical reaction that mainstream society sometimes has to groups of people who challenge conventions and behave in ways that threaten the status quo. Films that offer an insight into such subcultures are often banned or edited lest they serve to encourage people to participate. For example, *The Wild One* (1954), starring Marlon Brando, is a film about Hell's Angels that was banned in Britain because it was seen to set a bad example to the young.

The BBFC today

The BBFC's relationship with the State is usually described as a 'gentleman's understanding', which means that Parliament observes from a distance and the BBFC regulates itself in accordance with the ideology of the government in each period. The BBFC website publishes its guidelines and the organisation arranges public consultation on a regular basis, through roadshows across the regions. The website also gives details of the (rare) cuts made to films. Currently the board is predominately a classifier rather than a censor, and it is important to recognise the distinction between these two practices.

The only legislation the BBFC adhere, to is the Obscene Publications Act, which is used to censor films which are likely (although of course this is a matter of opinion) to 'deprave or corrupt' viewers. This is usually interpreted in terms of the likelihood of viewers acting criminally as a result of film viewing. As you would expect, the Act, and all censoring and classifying, tends to be evoked as a practice of 'othering'. In other words, it is always 'other people' who we imagine being depraved!

Since the New Labour Government came to power in 1997, the BBFC has been seen to be mellower in its response to films. In September 2000 the Board published new guidelines, relaxing the 18 category, but becoming tougher at the younger levels. Most significantly, but least publicised, the 'new BBFC' regime liberalised the R18 category, which essentially means that some forms of hard-core pornography are now legal in Britain.

The notion of harm and, subsequently, the importance of protection remain at the heart of this debate. A famous recent example of this was the cutting of a few seconds from *Fight Club* (1999). The cut was criticised by many as merely 'tinkering' and unlikely to have made a tremendous amount of difference. BBFC News justified this: 'There were two scenes in *Fight Club* in which the violence was excessively sustained. In both scenes there was an indulgence in the excitement of beating a defenceless man's face into a pulp. The Board required that cuts be made.'

The BBFC intend to move towards a less mandatory, more advisory system and thus place more trust in the public. To this end, the BBFC have experimented with a 'PG-12' rating which allows the parent to decide whether a film suitable for 12-year-olds might be suitable for their 10–11-year-olds. This revolves around a trust of the public to decide for themselves and a form of self-regulation as opposed to imposition from the censor.

Since 2001, monitoring of the BBFC has been conducted by the Department of Culture, Media and Sport. This is seen as an interim measure, as the government's long-term intention is to bring all broadcast media, film and video/DVD into Ofcom's remit (the new regulatory body for broadcast media and communications, who have a Media Education remit also, interestingly). This might have serious implications for the BBFC both economically (if Ofcom classify DVD releases, this would take money from the BBFC) and culturally (perhaps these two bodies will disagree on classification decisions?).

Fear and loathing

Examining the discourses of censorship and outrage is a useful way to understand and discuss its functions. The following are all quotes from either censors or other groups who have chosen to publicly express their shock at the content of films, ranging from the 1920s to recent years.

The Exorcist (1973): 'the most shocking, sick-making and soul-destroying work ever to emerge from filmland' – *Daily Mail*.

Battleship Potemkin (1926): 'damaging references to controversial politics' – the BBFC.

The Wild One (1954): 'the police were shown as weak characters and the teenagers did not get the punishment they deserve' – the BBFC.

Straw Dogs (1971): this film features a controversial rape scene – 'if anyone tries to re-enact this, God help Britain.' – *Sunday Times*.

Crash (1996): this film is about sexual auto-eroticism – 'a movie beyond the bounds of depravity' – *Evening Standard*.

ACTIVITIES

Just one example is given above of each of the most common kinds of censorship.

Research some other examples and find at least three more of each type (some you will already know about). Try to get an old example from the early days of censorship, an example from the 1960s or 1970s, and a current or recent example.

For each film, answer the all-important question: Who was being protected, and from what?

DISCUSSION

Why is it that many texts that start their life as novels only provoke calls for censorship when they are made into films?

Arguments *for* film censorship

Those that believe in some form of film censorship hold the view that censorship protects the moral values that are prevalent in society, thus censorship reflects our values. The counter-argument is that censorship imposes the values of certain people, who do not necessarily represent the rest of us, and it assumes that we are not capable of mature, safe responses to 'immoral' material.

You will probably have found from your discussions with other students that most people's views on censorship depend on the context. There is a kind of continuum – at one end there is the view that media, including cinema, influence people and teach behaviour, like a hypodermic needle injecting 'effects' into passive viewers. At the other end, there is the anti-censorship view, which feels that we are able to understand texts as works of fiction or art. If an individual commits an act of violence in response to a media experience, then the psychological condition of the perpetrator is the problem, not the film. In between are those of us who think that classification is needed and those who believe that some kinds of films might be 'harmful', but that others are not.

One famous advocate of censorship was Mary Whitehouse. For many years she lobbied for the banning of films and television programmes, on the grounds that media images of sex and violence are in part responsible for the decline of moral standards in society.

Whitehouse claimed that it is indisputable that young people are vulnerable to harmful screen images. She used accounts from psychologists and researchers to apparently prove the link between violent acts and exposure to violent images. In particular, Whitehouse decried films where violence is depicted without a moral context, or where violence is not punished. In this sense, those concerned about the effects of film images differentiate between the contexts for such images (i.e. the rationale for, or the justification for the violence).

Whitehouse believed that the burning issue is one of protection, arguing that it is a matter of getting film-makers to accept a sense of their own responsibility for the health and welfare of the whole of society, especially for the welfare of children. She may be a rather extreme example of the pro-censorship lobby (and here we have dealt only with violence, remember there are at least six other criteria which have been used to scrutinise film content), but her views do resonate, in part at least, with those who believe that:

- Films are potentially influential.
- Viewers of films receive messages which, in some cases, they need to be protected from.
- There are certain people who are capable of judging what others should be able to see.

DISCUSSION

Examine the statements above. What do they have in common? What do they all assume about the viewers and the effects of films on them?

ACTIVITIES

Using the internet, investigate an organisation that campaigns for censorship. Summarise its views and offer opposing points of view.

Arguments *against* film censorship

There is a difference between an argument that disagrees with all three statements above (i.e. a view that suggests films are not influential) and an argument that asserts that films can influence, but that citizens should not all be treated as though they cannot interpret filmic images safely. What is really at stake is the assumed link between viewing and behaviour. This is referred to as the media effects debate

The media effects debate

This debate rests on whether or not people agree with the 'effects model'. This way of understanding the relationship between film and viewer is grounded in behaviourist psychology, which examines taught behaviour and stimulus-response. In this framework, viewers of violent images take part in various tests. These determine the extent that people's likelihood to respond to certain situations violently is increased, as a result of exposure to violent images.

However, this approach has been refuted by those who think that this way of examining media and violence is 'topsy-turvy'. That is, looking first at film violence and then at the social problem of violence as an effect is less useful than looking at the social problem first and researching the violent behaviour and the experiences and psychological profiles of violent people. David Gauntlett, a much published critic of the effects model, suggested that this approach is like implying that the solution to the number of road traffic accidents in Britain would be to lock away one famously bad driver from Cornwall! In other words, the effects model tries to approach things the wrong way.

The many academics who have opposed the effects model have all argued against its central thesis – that we receive media messages passively, that violent films have a causal effect in the same way that cigarettes harm the lungs. While effects experiments and hypotheses have offered different spins on this notion, they have all tended to assume this passivity.

Another outspoken critic of the effects model and the justification for censorship that it offers is Mark Kermode. It is useful to look at two arguments he has put forward against censoring films. The first is his account of his own interest in horror movies. Kermode argues that, to the true horror fan, the pleasure of the genre lies in the ironic, excessive send-up nature of graphic scenes. Hence, the horror fan is a sophisticated reader of filmic references. Horror can offer a post-modern approach to film (where horror films all relate to each other in what is essentially an intertextual game). This means that nobody is more aware that horror films are not real than the viewers who the censors are trying to 'protect'. To take this argument to its logical conclusion (and it is up to you to decide whether you agree), the only people truly qualified to judge how harmful a horror film might be are people who have seen other horror films and have viewed them with the sophisticated engagement that only a fan is capable of. Kermode claims that the reason for the difference of opinion between censors and genre fans is not because horror fans have become hardened or insensitive to violence through years of exposure to sadistic material. Rather, the experienced horror fan understands the material through knowledge of a history of genre texts and this actually makes any sense of arousal, sadistic or otherwise, unlikely.

ACTIVITIES

This section has introduced you to some of the arguments for and against censorship and/or classification. However, the most useful way to move towards a personal, informed response is to test these perspectives on a case of your own. While you are working on this topic, there is sure to be a film released which is either banned or provokes calls for censorship. Investigate the reasons for the reactions to the film, noting the following:

- provocative content
- type of censorship/type of censorship called for
- arguments in defence of the film
- arguments against the film
- notion of protection (who and from what)
- your views.

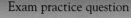

Exam practice question

Describe, through examples, how film censorship relates to notions of 'protection'. Explain your views on the issues.

PART SEVEN

The Magazine Industry

Unit links

In other A2 units you could:

- *Design* a new magazine aimed at an established target audience or a website for the magazine, or a webzine.

- *Produce* a documentary on the impact of the new 'lad mags' or on the responses of young females to women's magazines.

- *Research* advertising in magazines.

Introduction

This area of your course (unlike AS work you may have done on lifestyle magazines) requires you to understand the workings of the *industry* as well as to demonstrate skills of textual analysis. The trick is to combine the two, but the main focus is on the ways in which audiences are 'delivered' to advertisers by the industry.

Magazines in general

Magazines in Britain are mainly published by a few dominant companies. Publishing, like all media industries, is a phenomenon of convergence, **cross-media ownership** and oligopoly (a small cluster of bodies controlling a large market).

Being purely descriptive, we can say that magazines have colour covers, are generally glossy, and publish weekly, fortnightly, monthly, quarterly or biannually. There are fiction and non-fiction varieties and they appeal to mass audiences or niche audiences. Most magazines have a specific target audience, often a particular age and gender group attached to a hobby, interest or lifestyle choice. In fact, if we believe that media audience groups present an accurate view of the demographics of our society, we could identify the kinds of people living at any one time by the magazines on offer. Of course, by this stage in a Media Studies course you should be sceptical about such 'transparent' ideas about media representation!

To be analytical, rather than just descriptive about magazines, you need to understand the following:

- What are the conventions of magazines and can these can be organised into genres/sub-genres? How is this related to target audience?

- Who owns magazines and publishes them?

- What is the relationship between editorial content and advertising in magazines?

ACTIVITIES

Organise a focus group to discuss the relative success of a magazine that is a newcomer to the magazine market.

ACTIVITIES

Look at the range of magazines on offer (a trip to a large newsagent with a pen and paper may be the quickest way to do this) and list items under genre and sub-genre.

Can you think of any group of people for whom there is a gap in the market? If so, identify the gap in editorial terms (what would the magazine offer in terms of articles, information and features) and then consider the kinds of products and services that might be advertised usefully in the magazine.

In a group, research one magazine publisher (other than Emap). Using the internet, find out all the titles they produce and the readership figures for each. Then select one title and contact the magazine, asking for the advertiser's information. This will, in many cases, offer not just financial information, but also a kind of narrative about the perceived typical reader, their personality and consumption habits. From this information, draft ideas for a new magazine to compete for this imagined reader's attention.

CASE STUDY

Men's Health

Men's Health, published by Rodale, features articles about working out, exercise in general, health tips, sports and action activities, work-related problems and solutions, relationship and sex issues and style and cosmetics.

It has the tone of a 'friend' and tries to emphasise a problem-sharing ethos among its readers, even to the point of men writing in with tips and solutions to common problems and anxieties. Its unique selling point is simple – this is an area in which men have never before been comfortable, but by mixing this advice with style and images of attractive, muscular, successful men in designer clothes, the magazine achieves the same blend of problem solving and anxiety creation as its female counterparts.

Men's Health has to be very careful to get the balance right. An example is the cover, which always features a topless man with an aspirational physique. The editors always use black and white for the cover image and there are three reasons for this. First, black and white fits the identity and branding of the magazine, which is black, white and red throughout. Second, men's bodies look more angular and powerful when printed in black and white because muscle tone is better emphasised than in colour. Third, and perhaps most important, black and white creates a safe distance for the reader who needs to feel comfortable when buying the magazine. The editors believe that heterosexual men feel less anxious about buying a magazine with a semi-naked male on the front if the image is in black and white.

An analytical reading of *Men's Health* shows that the overriding theme of the title is control and the quick-fix solution to common anxieties. Throughout the text, the theme of control over work, stress, style, relationships, diet and sex arises. Every edition offers a highly short-term (yet near impossible) solution to an image problem, such as a six-week six-pack workout or a fortnight weight-loss programme.

Funding

In the early days of magazines, the cover price raised enough money for a profit. But as more magazines emerged, competition meant fewer sales for individual titles. When the tax on advertising was removed in the 1850s, the cover prices were lowered so that the revenue from sales did not even cover the costs of production. The reason was simple – the majority of revenue could be accrued from advertisers.

Advertisers use figures from the **ABC** (Audit Bureau of Circulation) and the **NRS** (National Readership Survey) to gauge which magazines to use. In addition, the publisher's materials (most magazines produce a pack for advertisers) break down the figures into groups of people and make bold claims for the importance of the title in the lives of their readers. It is essential to send off for one of these for a magazine you are studying or to download it from the magazine or publisher website – they are invaluable in encapsulating the identity the title wants to have, especially when it relates to a gender and age group.

The British magazine industry is worth over £7 billion. The market has three subsections – the trade press, magazines aimed at specific customers produced by business and the huge range of titles aimed at the general public. Advertisers spend more than £2 billion each year on magazine placement, and media analysts generally agree that, compared to other media industries, the magazine sector is robust, despite the perceived threat of new digital technologies to such 'traditional' media.

The thousands of magazines that are available have different functions. Some are related to specific business areas, trades or work practices. Others are related to hobbies or interests. Some are, broadly speaking, consumer-focused and some are entertainment-based, although the latter usually relate closely to particular kinds of consumption, such as music, film or football.

As well as targeting age and gender groups, or occupation/interests, magazines also appeal to particular socio-economic groups. However, this is rather a blunt instrument when it comes to categorising people and the next section comes with that disclaimer!

Publisher profile: Emap

Emap started life as a local newspaper company in 1947 and is now a major player in the magazine industry, producing over 150 consumer titles globally. Emap Consumer Media comprises the majority of the Group's consumer magazine portfolio in the UK, publishing nearly 70 titles ranging from *heat* and *FHM* to *Closer, Empire, Max Power, Angling Times* and

Today's Golfer. It is currently the second most successful publisher in the UK magazine industry.

Emap Consumer Media's titles are grouped into the following areas:

Special interest titles (Emap Active)

Bird Watching
Country Walking
Coach & Bus Week
Digital Photo
Garden Answers
Garden News
Model Rail
Practical Fishkeeping
Practical Photography
Rail
Steam Railway
Trail
Your Horse
Natural World
Nintendo
Angling Times
Golf Weekly
Golf World
Improve Your Coarse Fishing
Match
Match Angling Plus
Sea Angler
Today's Golfer
Trout & Salmon
Trout Fisherman

Automotive titles (Emap Automotive)

Car
Parker's Car Price Guide
Parker's Used and New Car Chooser
Land Rover Owner International
Max Power
Revs
Practical Classics
Classic Cars
Classic Bike
Motor Cycle News
MCN Sport
Performance Bikes
Bike

RiDE
What Bike?
Automotive Management
Fleet News

Young women's titles (Emap élan)

New Woman
Top Santé
Bliss
more!

Entertainment and style titles (Emap East)

Arena
Arena Homme Plus
Pop
Empire
FHM
Period Living & Traditional Homes
ZOO Weekly

Celebrity and women's weekly titles (Emap Entertainment)

heat
Closer

Music magazines (Emap Performance)

Smash Hits
Kerrang!
Mojo
Q
Mixmag
Sneak

When analysing any one magazine using the key concepts from Media Studies, there is a danger of making assumptions about editorial policy if you are not aware of its institutional context. For example, *ZOO Weekly* is unlike other titles in the Emap entertainment and style titles portfolio, but very similar to *Nuts*, produced by a rival publisher. So as well as delivering audiences to advertisers, publishers are also attentive to market trends and competitors' new titles.

Socio-economic categories

The socio-economic groups are labelled A, B, C1, C2, D and E. They refer to people's occupations, economic status, education and background. While we all know that labelling people into 'types' in this way is fairly inaccurate because it misses people's individual tastes and interests, advertisers have used this system for years and it therefore has some validity.

As well as this blunt way of categorising people, magazine publishers and editors, and the advertisers they rely on, also use segmentation to cluster us into one of seven groups: succeeders, aspirers, carers, achievers, radicals, traditionalists and underachievers. They also define us in terms of our opinions and values, whether we are traditionalist, materialist, hedonist, post-materialist or postmodernist. For example, a magazine might be launched to attract young female hedonist B and C1 aspirers! Or middle-aged male traditionalist achievers in A and B.

Labelling a magazine's audience

The notions of audience outlined above depend on substantial research to test consumption, lifestyle habits, tastes and responses to issues. The media in general often seem preoccupied with trends, scrutinising what we think, eat, buy and worry about, then categorising us with new labels such as 'ladette', 'spice girl', 'new man', 'new lad' and 'middle youth'. This does not only involve the young. Other labels coined in recent years have included 'the oldie'. Advertisers, in particular, are aware of the fact that, because we now live longer and remain healthier and more mobile into our senior years, there is a whole new sector of society emerging, which can be described as the 'young-minded older person'.

It is argued that some magazines collectively form an encyclopaedia of insecurities about health, lifestyle, looks, body image, success, material wealth and relationships. Therefore, a well-balanced person has no need of these magazines. The fact is that hardly any of us look like the men and women we see in *Men's Health* and *Elle*. The variety of shapes and colours that people come in are not represented by these titles. The rise of male grooming products reflects a new market of narcissistic men to whom advertisers can promote their cosmetic products, playing on the kinds of anxieties that have traditionally been women's property.

CASE STUDY

Word and *Mojo*

These two monthly music magazines are targeting a mature (30+), primarily male audience. *Word* (currently priced at £4.20) is published by Development Hell and is edited by Mark Ellen, an established music journalist, contrasting with *Mojo* (priced at £3.95), which is part of Emap's wide portfolio (see the case study on Emap above). Each magazine is reliant (in almost every issue, but not all) on a free CD. Whereas *Word* offers a sampler of between twelve and fourteen tracks from new albums, *Mojo* provides a themed CD (for example, music chosen by the band featured on the cover, or a set of cover versions of songs by the featured artist).

Both of these are a form of 'below the line' advertising for the artists in question. Advertising that is directly paid for from the promotional budget of a record company (for example, a

---

video, TV ads, half-page magazine ads for a new CD) is described as 'above the line'. 'Mutual benefit' promotional items, such as CDs with magazines, are described as 'below the line' because they are a less direct, more discrete form of advertising. The net result is the same – readers of *Mojo* and *Word* in September 2005 will buy more new Baxter Dury CDs and download more legal copies of Bob Dylan's 'No Direction Home' as a result of the symbiosis of new release, magazine feature and free listen made possible by this below-the-line activity.

The music press and the music industry have, for these kinds of reasons, enjoyed an interesting relationship for decades. The one is reliant on the other, yet the more 'interesting' artists have always strived to appear less media-friendly and enigmatic than the manufactured bands, and, equally, the music press have traditionally been less interested in the 'packaged' variety.

Unlike the computer game magazine described below, there is much objective criticism of product in Word and *Mojo*. However, the 'free CD' does throw this objectivity under the spotlight to some extent.

Front cover of *Mojo*

The music press

To explore the relationship between audience pleasure, industry and advertising, it is interesting to consider the function of 'free' CDs that are now a standard convention of music magazines like *Mojo*, *Word*, *Q* and *Kerrang!*, and a frequent feature also of *NME*.

Conduct some audience research with the readers of these titles in order to produce some useful data from which you can draw conclusions about the following:

- Whether readers are subscribers, frequent buyers of one title, or whether they choose the magazine that offers the best CD, according to their tastes.
- The extent to which consumers purchase or download music as a result of sampling new material from the free CDs.
- The relationship between the CD and the magazine. Are there readers who do not actually read much of the magazine, and, conversely, are there consumers who are not overly interested in the CD? This third area is qualitative research, whereas the previous two are quantitative.

Content analysis of *Play* magazine

Play describes itself as 'the UK's best unofficial PlayStation magazine' and as such concedes its lack of endorsement by Sony. This lack of official sanction might be perceived as a selling point, as it allows for potential criticism of Sony products. A monthly title, it sells at £3.99, and, to take an example the October 2005 issue includes two additional items. The first is a CD containing cheats for *Medal of Honour: European Assault*, *Tekken 5* and *Batman Begins*, a range of codes for seven other games and some downloadable game saves. In terms of audience pleasure, the option to cheat at computer games is an area of some sociological research you may have come across in other parts of your course. Certainly magazines such as *Play* rely on players' interest in such an alternative to completing a game 'honestly'. The other freebie is a preview magazine for the new PSP portable console and all its launch games.

The October 2005 magazine consists of 132 glossy pages, of which 26 pages are advertisements. In addition to this, the entire editorial content of *Play* is promotional, in the sense that it is essentially a preview magazine for new games. Even the 13 pages of news are devoted entirely to the new PS3 and PSP consoles. The one area that exhibits an edge of criticism is a feature on action games related to Marvel Comics.

The cover feature for this month is a comparative review of two wrestling games: *Smack Down* versus *Raw*. The article is designed to reflect the conventions of a wrestling bout, with the two players set up as the fighters. Alongside a detailed analysis of the strengths and weaknesses of each game, the reader is offered a 'play by play commentary'.

The advertising paid for in the pages of this edition promotes computer games for the PS2 on seven pages. Other gaming magazines are advertised on four pages, six pages are devoted to adverts for hardware (in-car game-playing systems), and the remaining nine are for downloadable games, ring tones and a great deal of pornography for mobile phones. This last detail is crucial for pinpointing not only a range of gender assumptions made by advertisers (with the help of editorial prompts), but also attitudinal stereotyping.

Constructing ideas of gender

If a focus of this topic is audience and gender and the debate we are considering is the extent to which men's and women's magazines construct ideas about gender rather than just reflect them, then (like all of the topics on the Issues and Debates paper), this is an area where strong feelings and disagreements should be common among your peers.

Some of you may be of the mind that 'men are from Mars, women are from Venus' and that magazines simply appeal to our different gendered ideas and tastes. Others may think that without the media's perpetuation of old-fashioned sexist ideas about women, females would have a stronger stake in society. Much of the discussion is concerned with the nature–nurture debate.

The nature–nurture debate

The process of gendering begins from the day a person is born. A child will be dressed in certain clothes, put in a nursery with certain wallpaper and given certain toys that relate to its gender. But gender is different to biological sex. We are born into a biological sex, but the gender roles we are asked to take as men or women are cultural.

Some people argue that the reason men like cars and women like flowers is not cultural but natural. It is just the way it is, a natural instinct to form certain interests which relate to women's maternal and domestic programming. Others argue that culture dictates everything and the reason that men and women often have different gender-specific ideas and tastes is because of the way we are socialised.

Women's magazines: a feminist reading

There has been something of a backlash against feminism in recent years. Many people (including many women) have argued that we are living in a post-feminist world where the battles for equality have been won and we can all relax about gender and move away from so-called 'political correctness'. However, it is important to remember that the essential feminist debate is concerned with equality for women so they can operate on a level playing field with men and we can do away with sexism just as we want to do away with racism, for instance.

Women are still under-represented in Parliament, in managerial posts in business and in much of industry and the professions, and there is still inequality in pay and status. Worse, many women feel threatened by a media culture which constantly places great emphasis on the way that women look. The rise of eating disorders reflects this. Thus, when we are looking at women's and men's magazines, what we are asking is, what kinds of images are men and women given of themselves and do these different images challenge, reflect neutrally or actually construct inequality in society?

Contemporary women's magazines have moved on a great deal from their historical origins, offering visions of femininity that involve independence and confidence as well as beauty and domestic concerns. However, a feminist analysis of magazines like *More*, *Red* and *New Woman* will still find that women are encouraged to look good in order to attract men. On the other hand, it could be argued that the new crop of men's magazines, such as *Men's Health*, do exactly the same for men. However, the feminist response would be that two wrongs do not make a right; both these genres are still perpetuating an obsession with appearance that discriminates against women, for instance, in the work place.

Men's magazines: a new market

Since the mid-1990s, a crop of very successful magazines aimed at young men has emerged, spearheaded by the controversial *Loaded*. Followed by a range of imitators and variants on the theme, *Loaded* was celebrated by some as a refreshing, post-politically correct opportunity for men to rediscover their masculinity. *Loaded* was condemned by others as a dumbed-down 'year zero' in bad taste and analysed by yet others as an ironic postmodern text through which men can enjoy being 'new lads' without really being sexist.

More recently, IPC and Emap launched *Nuts* and *Zoo* simultaneously in 2004. *Nuts* was ultimately more successful, and it is easy to describe the title as a kind of 'post-feminist year zero', in which women are only ever depicted as objects and men's interests are reduced to soft porn, sports, gadgets and various forms of fighting.

ACTIVITIES

In groups of three or four, choose two other magazines aimed at men (ones where gender is the focus of the magazine) and two aimed at women. Taking one title each, produce content analysis notes, using the following as prompts:

- price
- frequency
- cover
- design and layout
- editorial approach
- advertising
- promotional techniques
- content.

This activity works best in a mixed-gender group, with each person analysing a magazine that appeals to the other gender. It is essential that you get together to discuss your findings and to make sure that your assumptions about the other gender's interests and ideas can be challenged.

Having studied some 'gender magazines' in more detail, try to come up with an original idea for a new magazine aimed at one gender and age group. Produce a rough treatment, covering the following areas:

- justification/gap in the market
- audience
- title

- content
- incentive to advertisers.

Share your ideas with other members of your class and vote for:

- the most original/challenging/refreshing
- the most predictable
- the most offensive.

Now decide which magazine would be the most successful.

The postmodern audience?

Clearly there is an argument that magazines like *Nuts* profit from reinforcing some pretty damaging stereotypes and encourage the male reader to see females in a very reductive way. But theorists who favour a more postmodern approach to media audiences, such as David Gauntlett, describe the 'pick and mix' reader, who can enjoy a magazine such as *Nuts* (or *Cosmopolitan*, for that matter) without taking the content literally. In other words, they are more discerning, selective and 'playful' with the kinds of identities presented for them by the magazines than the simple effects model of interpretation suggests.

However, Alex Kendall's research into the reading habits of young people in the West Midlands in 2002 showed that male readers tend to be less critical than their female counterparts. The female readers were more able to negotiate and therefore reject some of the gender codes presented in their magazines, whereas males demonstrated less selective acceptance of meanings. Perhaps this is because the women's magazine format is more mature, and thus the titles involve more self-parody than the likes of *Nuts*, *Stuff* and *FHM*.

Summary

This topic foregrounds the workings of the magazine industry – publishers, their profiles (the range of magazines they have in their portfolios) and their relationships with other media industries. For example, alongside the unofficial PlayStation magazine described in this section, there are other titles owned by publishers who are subsidiary companies of the same multinational corporations that operate in the games market and in software and hardware. So at the institutional level, this part of your studies takes you to the heart of cross-media ownership. In addition, audience research is essential – you need to get out there and find out who is reading what, in what ways and with what effects (if any). The third point of this triangular approach is conceptual – magazines set up, from their cover images to the adverts they house, a coherent world (or ideology) for the ideal reader. While we need to take the idea that media audiences swallow such ideas without reflection with a very large pinch of salt, we do need to analyse how magazines represent the world to the reader, the reader to the world, and the reader to him or herself.

Exam practice question

Magazines exist to deliver audiences to advertisers. Discuss.

Part Eight

Local Newspapers
Unit links

In other units you could:

- *Produce* a new local newspaper.
- *Design* a website for a local newspaper.
- *Research* the relationship between local politics and the local press.

Introduction

These days we are often told we are living in a global village, where boundaries of time, space and culture are broken down by multinational corporations, brands and images which transcend national identities. The apparent trend shows that people shop at out-of-town supermarkets (rather than the local grocer), eat McDonald's when abroad rather than the local cuisine, and wear clothes that everyone else across the globe either wears or wants to wear. Children in Britain and across the world grow up supporting Chelsea, rather than their local football team.

As a Media Studies student, you will be interested in how much of this globalisation is related to media imagery and advertising. It has been argued that the McDonald's yellow 'M' and the Nike 'swoosh' have become images as instantly powerful as the Christian cross in our consumer-media society. You will also be concerned with the relationship between globalisation and community. Local media, such as local papers and local radio, still play a hugely important role in maintaining community, and their survival and enduring importance demonstrate a forgotten resistance to global trends.

By far the best way to get to grips with the conventions of local newspapers, the different types of papers, their audiences and what they provide, and the relationship between local papers and their national counterparts, is to work on a case study in your local area.

Here you are given an overview of the local press in Britain at the time of writing, a summary of the key issues relating to local news provision and an example of a case study, focusing on the local news provision available to the residents of Halesowen in the West Midlands. To get the most out of this topic area, use the case study as a template for your own research and analysis of where you live.

ACTIVITIES

Visit the offices of your local paper and find out about daily working practices and how the news is gathered. Then interview the editor, a reporter, photographer or someone from the advertising department and record their views on the role the publication plays in your community.

Functions of local press

In terms of the amount of specific local information that any one medium can provide, the local press is by far the leading provider. Regional TV offers frequent bulletins and a half-hourly dedicated broadcast each day, although the regions are usually quite large. Local radio provides valuable time for discussion, but not the quantity that the local paper can offer. In this sense then, the local paper provides a public service. Most local areas have a paper that can be financed by advertising from the community.

Within the journalism profession it is assumed that the local paper serves as a nursery from which talented reporters graduate to the larger regional or metropolitan titles and then to the nationals. However, the local press has its own distinct role: being the first to uncover stories where they happen, enjoying large and loyal readerships and attracting large amounts of classified advertising. Even the internet and interactive TV do not seem to pose a significant threat to the cheap, regular 'local rag'.

Nevertheless, as with any media market, threats to established titles frequently arise. Free sheets depend entirely on advertising and achieve high levels of saturation in an area, up to 100 per cent in some cases. In 1970 free papers only accumulated 1 per cent of the regional press's advertising revenue, but 20 years on this had grown to 35 per cent. Recently, the launch of the free Metro titles, distributed in the mornings on public transport, has been another attempt to undermine the appeal of the paid-for paper in the local community.

Editors of the paid-for titles argued that the quality of journalism and the community ethos was undermined by free titles. However, readers voted with their wallets and the existence of free sheets has inevitably heralded a partial decline of the paid-for paper. As both types of paper proved able to survive alongside each other, publishers began to realise that the relationship could be complementary. Now, the same company will often own both titles in one area.

Institutions and ownership

Over 50 per cent of local newspapers are owned by the 'big five' companies (another media example of an oligopoly). These companies are:

- Trinity International
- Northcliffe
- Newsquest
- United Provincial
- Johnston Press.

ACTIVITIES

Find out who owns your local papers, both free and paid for. Is it the same company? Is it a subsidiary of one of the five companies above? If so, which other titles does that company own?

CASE STUDY

Halesowen

You can use this model case study as a template for a case study on local newspapers in your area.

Halesowen is a small town in the area of the West Midlands referred to as the Black Country. It is situated 11 km from Birmingham, 5 km from Dudley and on the border of Worcestershire. Residents of Halesowen do not consider themselves to be from Birmingham. Because of this, Halesowen offers an interesting example of the relationship between local and regional news.

Local papers on offer in Halesowen include:

- *Black Country Evening Mail* (local version of the Birmingham Evening Mail) – daily.
- *Black Country Bugle* (a paper consisting of local history features) – weekly.
- *Sandwell Express and Star* (Sandwell version of a paper that covers the Black Country) – weekly.
- *Halesowen News* – weekly.
- *Birmingham Evening Mail* (in many shops one can choose to buy the Birmingham or the Black Country edition) – daily.
- *Birmingham Post* (the only broadsheet of the bunch, a much larger paper with several separate sections) – daily.

The best starting place for information about newspapers, ownership and circulation, as well as for contact numbers for the various publications, is the current edition of *The Guardian Media Guide*, produced by the newspaper annually. It is highly likely that the Media Department at your school or college will have at least one copy and it may be in the library.

Ownership

The *Evening Mail* is owned by the Mirror Group, and with a circulation of almost 200,000, is one of the top five regional dailies. Also in the top five is the *Express and Star*, owned by the Midland News Association (which also owns *Halesowen News* and the *Halesowen Chronicle*), with an almost identical circulation to the *Evening Mail* (the circulation figures include all local editions).

Midland Independent Newspapers owns both the *Birmingham Post* and the *Sunday Mercury*. Other papers covering the same or nearby geographical area are the *Dudley Chronicle*, *Dudley News, Sandwell Chronicle, Stourbridge Chronicle, Wolverhampton Chronicle* and the *Kidderminster Chronicle* (all owned by the Midland News Association).

There is a vast range of individual daily papers available to people in this region, but many of them are local versions of a larger regional title (for example, the *Evening Mail*, the *Express*

and Star). The Midland News Association dominates the Black Country provision, with the Mirror Group and Midland Independent Newspapers competing for the Birmingham titles.

Content analysis of the papers

Comparing newspapers on one particular day can be a useful way of examining and comparing their content. Below is an analysis of a number of newspapers available in Halesowen on a particular day.

Specifications

Both versions of the *Evening Mail* are tabloids, and both consisted of 56 pages in one section. The centre spread and the front and back covers were colour, with the remainder red, black and white. The content for both was divided into approximately 34 pages of news, features and public announcements or information, and 22 pages of advertising, including both display adverts and classifieds.

The *Birmingham Post* offered a main section of 13 broadsheet pages, a business and sport section (again, broadsheet) of 14 pages, and a style tabloid of 32 pages. Taking the three parts as a whole, editorial content made up 33 pages and the remainder was either advertising or, more commonly, features that contained promotional content or **advertorials**.

The *Express and Star* consisted of one 40-page section sized between a tabloid and a broadsheet, 25 pages of which were editorial.

The *Black Country Bugle*, again a larger tabloid, offered 36 pages. This was harder to break down because each page contained a mixture of smaller ads and articles, but roughly 19 pages were editorial.

In all cases at least one-third of the publication's content was advertising or promotion and this rose to half for some titles.

Front cover designs

The *Express and Star* had one image taking up 90 per cent of the page and another small picture used as an inset. There was one main story accompanied by a larger headline, surrounded by seven smaller stories and some news in brief in a left-hand column. The only colour on the front page was a blue text box for a smaller story and a red poppy symbol alongside the masthead.

The *Birmingham Post*, the only broadsheet, featured a large rectangular box, using two colours to promote a car competition on the cover. The most dominant text on the page related not to a story but to the value of the car to be won. Four stories were featured on the front page, with one clearly dominant, taking up one-third of the cover, and the other three descending in size, with the smallest accounting for only 19 cm². The front page also used a logo for a campaign related to one of the stories.

The *Black Country Bugle* cover featured just two stories, a left-hand column listing the content within and one photo taking up one-sixth of the cover. Adverts accounted for over one-third of the page. Just below the title was a strapline – 'the voice of the Black Country'.

The two versions of the *Evening Mail* were interesting to compare. The Birmingham edition featured the most visually striking, tabloid-style cover of all, with a large emotive headline, an equally striking strapline and 11 photographs situated with clock graphics indicating the progression of time. However, the Black Country edition featured the same story and images, but the size was reduced so that a more local story could be situated alongside it. The number of images and graphics was reduced from 11 to 5 to allow for this.

Below the masthead in each paper was a blue banner featuring two content links. The first, a sports story, was different for each paper (focusing on the local team in each case) and the second, a promotional item, was the same for both versions.

Editorial material and news values

Space does not allow for anything more than a cursory glance at the main stories and the editorials of each publication here. A fuller case study would employ content analysis techniques to explore the full range of stories, the organisation of the paper (its narrative) and the ratio of each category of content. By doing so, comparative conclusions about the news agenda of each paper could be drawn. Nevertheless, by using the front pages and editorials alone, we can make the following points about the papers chosen for analysis.

The *Evening Mail* versions clearly indicate the differences in local focus. The Birmingham edition shouts 'You Idiots', referring to local people parking their cars in illegal places in the city centre, days after a bomb had exploded in a busy area. The use of clock graphics next to photos of people's cars indicates where the cars were parked and at what time. This method is clearly intended to accuse irresponsible members of the community and it has an inbuilt public/police information role.

The editorial ('The Mail Says') moved away from this to deal with the success of an organ-donation scheme in nearby Walsall (calling for the rest of the country to follow its example) and there is a smaller statement urging shops not to open on Christmas Day in order to preserve the tradition of one day free from commerce.

The Black Country edition reduced the size of the 'You Idiots' leader to devote equal space to a story about a glassworks factory closure in Stourbridge and the subsequent loss of 200 jobs, an all-too-common staple of local paper content. The editorial was the same as the Birmingham edition, as it always is.

The *Express and Star* also led with the glassworks factory story, alongside another main story featuring a local woman who had escaped with her children from a house fire. The cover photo is almost a classical stereotype of the local press, with the woman featured in her burnt-out home with one of her cats, rescued by firemen. Other smaller stories on the front page (unusually self-contained in the main, rather than leading to other pages) included the ex-Beatle George Harrison's cancer fight, a story about the murder of an ex-local politician and two more 'bad news' stories, about a gun raid in a local shop and a local criminal being imprisoned. Finally, two stories were headlined almost with a tone of **parody**, with 'Tortoises taken from pet shop' and 'Cold spell on the way'.

The editorial 'Comment' on page 10 featured three statements in descending order of column space and importance. The main issue was the return of Concorde to the air, followed by the success of British beaches in passing EU regulations (and a call for Mediterranean beaches to follow suit) and a jokey sentence or two about Oxford United FC blaming bad results on a Gipsy curse. Unusually, none of the editorial related to local stories, people or events. It is important to analyse the ways in which local and regional newspapers react to stories of national and international significance.

The *Birmingham Post* led with an ongoing story of the bomb in Birmingham, this time updating the story with images from the police footage released that day, anchored by the headline 'Moment Hundreds Escaped Blast Death', offering positive elements to a negative story. To raise the emotive style and the impact on the local reader, a pull-out quote from the Assistant Chief Constable was used, saying, 'It is not unreasonable to think that virtually all of those people could have been casualties'. Many of the readers will have been in the area at the time of the blast.

Alongside this was a more positive story to offer balance, mocking Ken Livingstone's attempt to sabotage Birmingham's bid for the national stadium with his claim that water voles would cause problems for the project. This story clearly sets out to take a comical angle on what could be a serious aspect of the planning, in order to back the local project. The story is anchored by a 'Bring it to Birmingham campaign' logo. This is a common technique of the local paper – adopting a local issue or project in order to raise its community profile.

The *Post*'s editorial, which is untitled, went with the Walsall organ donation story ('Walsall shows it is easy to save a life') and also a statement drawing attention to an increase in sales figures for locally manufactured cars.

Finally, the *Bugle* led with a photograph taken 90 years ago of local (Blackheath) Sunday school children winning a competition. The story informs the readers that the banner the children won is now on show in the local Black Country Museum. Here the paper serves as a promotional tool for the local tourist industry, all-important in an area hard-hit by the collapse of industry.

ACTIVITIES

Look back at Section 3, Part 2: Broadcast News and Current Affairs (page 122). Using the list of news values identified, find examples of them in the case study content listed above. In particular, focus on local human interest and local negativity, as opposed to more national-based stories.

When you carry out your own detailed case study, you are advised to focus in more depth on two publications, looking at content, news values and news agendas, layout and advertising, as well as institutional details to do with ownership and circulation. The information on the Black Country papers is only intended to get you started.

Your focus should be on:

- the ownership, circulation and funding context of local papers in your area
- the news values and news agenda of specific papers
- the representation of your community in the paper.

To consider how fairly all groups are represented, you may need to do some demographic work on the range of people living in your area.

You might be able to find a time when a local story is also a national story. It would also be fruitful to compare local press coverage of specific items on local television and radio in order to test the claim that the local paper offers something more immediate and in-depth than local broadcast news.

The threat of technology?

There is clearly a set of threats to the highly traditional and perhaps old-fashioned local paper, such as the decline of newsagent delivery of news (in the face of competition from sales at supermarkets, garages, and so on) and the availability of news on the internet, on mobile phones and on 24-hour digital radio and television. That said, evidence suggests that the specific services and pleasures offered by the local newspaper, in particular its role in maintaining community identity (perhaps in times of increasing social alienation), make its chances of survival very good. Another factor worth considering is that national news is often formed by cherry-picking from local news, while broadcast news is usually derived from newspaper stories. So rather than these other forms posing a threat to the status of the more organically produced local news story, they are in fact dependent on it.

In addition, there is the simple fact that online news cannot offer the local detail and variety of services (job ads, property pages, classifieds, local sport analysis, and so on) that the daily paper provides. Equally, local papers have their own websites that can enrich their services, in particular archive search opportunities (local newspapers are a tremendous library resource for historians and genealogists, as well as the general public).

On the other hand, local papers in big cities have clearly been threatened by free listings facilities on the internet, such as Gumtree and, to some extent, Ebay. Time will tell whether the Google News smartsearch resource will have an impact, and you need to keep an eye on the ever increasing use of blogging as an alternative news source, which is ideal for local specificity.

Perhaps a more significant threat at the moment emerges from the free *Metro* newspaper, which is available on public transport. The *Evening Standard,* in particular, has suffered from this rival, as to date, traditional audience behaviour has been to read the *Evening Standard* on the way home on public transport. While the local paper and *Metro* are not similar in what they provide, it has been suggested that, over time, the newspaper audience are being 'groomed' to expect newspapers to be free, and for this reason local papers will be forced to put down their cover price, which in turn will create an economic threat to their existence.

Exam practice question

Will we still read local papers in ten years' time?

Freedom, Regulation and Control in the British Press

Unit links

In other units you could:

- *Design* a website campaigning for a free press in Britain.
- *Produce* a documentary on recent cases that led to differing views about the press and regulation.
- *Research* the freedom of the British press to cover politics without constraint.

Introduction

The vast majority of people consume the outpourings of the press, whether *Telegraph* or *Sun* readers, and as a Media Studies student your job is always to consider texts as constructions.

For much of the time the public display ambivalent attitudes towards the press, but events regularly occur that engender debates concerning how free the press should be and how they should be controlled and regulated. Events in recent years that have brought press practices to public attention have included the death of Princess Diana, the political bias of *The Sun* newspaper and its shift of allegiance from Tory to New Labour and the printing in *The Mirror* of fake pictures of British soldiers abusing Iraqi prisoners. These incidents bring up three different aspects of this topic:

1. Princess Diana – raises the issue of our obsession with celebrity and the intrusion of the press into public figures' privacy. Newspaper journalists and photographers usually defend this on the grounds that it is in the public interest, but others call for greater regulation. Because Diana died abroad, the actions of the paparazzi could not come under the scrutiny of British law in any case.

2. *The Sun*'s political slant brings up issues about the ownership of papers and concerns about the relationship between a successful newspaper entrepreneur and the political parties. These concerns strike at the heart of our notions of democracy and the freedom of the press to be neutral and truthful.

3. The fake pictures published in *The Mirror* bring to attention questions of self-regulation in the context of editorial ideology. Although the editor resigned his post in the aftermath, there was no available legislation to prevent the printing of the pictures.

The aftermath of the death of Princess Diana is a good place to start with this debate. Her brother, Earl Spencer, famously declared that the owners and editors of every newspaper that had paid for pictures of the Princess, infringing her rights to privacy, had 'blood on their hands'. This was an exceptionally emotional and hard-hitting condemnation of our press. The British nationals have always enjoyed a double-edged status internationally. On the one hand, we have a free press that can operate without government interference, reporting events in the public interest. On the other, we have some of the most infamous tabloid papers in the world, notorious for their stretching of the truth and their obsession with celebrity, royalty and the so-called 'build them up and knock them down' philosophy. Diana's death mobilised debate about tighter control of press intrusion.

Earl Spencer's harsh words also caused the British public to question their own contribution to the paparazzi's hounding of Diana (who died in a car crash while fleeing from photographers in Paris). After all, those photographers would not be paid to go to such lengths if there were not a readership at home hungry for the latest candid pictures of the royals and celebrities.

ACTIVITIES

What do you consider to be the essential differences between newspaper stories that are 'of interest to the public' and 'in the public interest'?

Press ownership

Newspapers in Britain, like other media industries, are today characterised by an oligopoly (a small cluster of powerful companies controlling a large market). The largest company is Rupert Murdoch's News International, enjoying a 35 per cent share of circulation through *The Sun*, *The Times*, the *Sunday Times* and the *News of the World*. The only daily newspaper which is not owned either by a tycoon or a multinational corporation is *The Guardian*, controlled by The Scott Trust.

Murdoch's influence on the newspaper industry has been huge since the 1980s. He introduced the kind of tabloid journalism style we are now so used to when he took over *The Sun*. He then moved his operations to Wapping, and with the support of Margaret Thatcher, the prime minister at the time, took on the previously strong print unions. Then, the Conservative Government wanted to reduce union power and introduce deregulation so that entrepreneurs such as Murdoch would have more freedom to run media organisations like his newspapers and BSkyB (see Contemporary British Broadcasting, page 130, for more background on this). Whether you see 'the Murdoch effect' as increasing choice and offering the kind of infotainment that the British public really want, or a dumbing down of our national news provision, depends on your point of view. There is a saying that 'the British people get the press they deserve'.

Another view, often expressed, is that newspaper owners exercise 'power without responsibility'. This phrase is really at the heart of this topic, for the British press enjoy a great deal more freedom than their broadcasting counterparts. Broadcasters are not allowed to express political bias, whereas newspapers are merely controlled and regulated within the scope of their own self-regulation and statutory controls.

Some argue that the legislation in place is outdated, as it was established in the pre-tabloid era, and that since the Murdoch effect, tabloid practices have outgrown the self-regulatory context. Equally, it has been suggested that it is impossible to scrutinise the regulation of the press without considering the issue of how ownership is regulated. In other words, if ownership restrictions were tighter and there was a more diverse control of editorial policy, self-regulation would work more effectively.

The Press Complaints Commission

The Press Complaints Commission replaced The Press Council in the early 1990s. This body introduced a code of practice for journalists and photographers: a press complaints tribunal system and legislation relating to intrusion of privacy through hidden cameras, telephoto lenses and bugging devices. Editors and owners agreed to the code of practice since it is essentially a form of self-regulation and they preferred this to direct censorship laws. However, as we have seen, the death of Princess Diana brought the issue of tighter controls into the public domain. As a result, a revised code was introduced, covering issues of:

- accuracy
- the right to reply for individuals that are written about
- the need to distinguish clearly between comment and fact (i.e. not to mislead)
- privacy and harassment
- misrepresentation
- chequebook journalism
- intrusion into grief or shock
- identifying relatives and friends of convicted individuals
- the reporting of issues relating to children
- dealing with victims of sexual assault
- confidential sources
- the definition of the public interest.

ACTIVITIES

In a group of four, each take three issues from the above list and research more information on what exactly the code of practice states for each of the areas. Then share your findings, so that each group member has a complete overview of the code.

Press freedom

Despite the introduction of a more rigorous code of practice, we still have a free press in Britain, which means that there is no censorship of news, government interference or controlled licences that can be removed. Anybody can publish a newspaper in Britain as long as they remain within the law. Nobody has the right to exclude the press from enquiries that are seen to serve the public interest.

In practice, this does not mean that our newspapers are free from bias; clearly the opposite is the case, with different papers showing allegiance to political parties and offering distinct opinions and specific views in most major current affairs. However, what we do have is a variety of publications representing an array of political ideological positions. These positions are so well known that you may have heard people using stereotypes, such as 'liberal *Guardian* readers', '*Sun* reader' or '*Daily Mail* mentality'. In the case of *The Sun* it has been said that Tony Blair's greatest coup was *The Sun* switching sides, when it turned its back on John Major's government after years of right-wing propaganda.

A thorny issue to consider is whether tighter controls on the press would be 'double-edged' in the sense that the possible benefits on restricting some tabloid practices would be outweighed by the restrictions that would be placed on so-called 'serious' journalists working for the broadsheets.

Although the press may be free from official state censorship, unlike film, broadcasting or advertising, there are forms of legislation that force impositions on this freedom. The press refer to these as elements of 'the creeping censor'. These include the Official Secrets Act and the Libel and Defamation Laws.

The Official Secrets Act

Passed in 1911 and revised in 1989, this Act means that civil servants, soldiers, the police and various other people who officially work for the Crown cannot speak on matters that are related to various forms of government activity. Editors of newspapers can be served with 'D-notices', which prevent information being published on matters of national security, but these are normally issued as a story is in progress rather than after publication.

The Freedom of Information Act

Established in 2005, this piece of legislation gives the press (just like every member of the public) access to government information. This development, it is argued, makes the restrictions on the press ever lighter.

Libel and defamation laws

This much-used legislation gives members of the public the right to sue newspapers which print stories that damage their character and/or their livelihood. While newspapers are regularly threatened with libel action, very few of these threats become court cases because of the expense involved. However, this is a crucial form of 'creeping' or 'covert' censorship since the possible threat of libel action often makes editors withdraw stories. In this sense it is a form of self-regulation. Furthermore, people can take out injunctions by appealing to court and, if granted, this prevents a story being published until the court has considered evidence. On Sunday 11 November 2001, the *Sunday People* published a story about a footballer in a sex scandal without the names of those involved because the player had successfully applied for an injunction of this kind. This was a historical event because no similar judgement had previously been given. The press were outraged, arguing that many of the most important pieces of investigative journalism in history would never have made it to the pages had judges behaved in this way, and that the public interest was being undermined.

Other restrictions on reporting

Contempt of Court is a broad restriction on any reporting that might impede the workings of the court. For example, the publication of a photograph of an accused person who has not yet been identified in court, or providing comment on factual information which is before the court or criticising a judge while the case is being heard.

There are various other acts of law that journalists have to know inside out, such as the Sexual Offences Act and the Race Relations Act. The bible for journalists has always been *McNae's Essential Law for Journalists*, 18th edition, edited by Welsh, Greenwood and Banks (Oxford University Press, 2005). This guidebook is highly recommended as a source of research.

ACTIVITIES

Interview a journalist or, ideally, an editor from your local paper about the restrictions they have to be aware of in their daily working practice.

Exam practice question

'The price we pay for a free press is invasion of privacy by tabloid journalists. We cannot have one without the other.'

To what extent do you agree with this statement?

SECTION 4
WRITING SKILLS

Introduction

As you have discovered during your AS studies, a Media Studies course requires you to complete a number of different written tasks. Within your A2 studies you will also be asked to write essays, Production Logs and research projects. This section aims to help you create thorough, systematic and comprehensive written pieces. It will offer you guidance on using terminology appropriately, organising contents clearly and effectively and constructing critical debates. Some of the skills in this section are generic to all your writing tasks and others are specific to particular parts of the OCR A2 course.

Written work

During your Advanced Practical Production project you will need to be able to create two types of written work. One is assessed and one non-assessed, but they are both of equal importance to the overall success of the project. The first piece of written work will be a Production Log, in which you keep notes on the process of your project. The second piece is the Critical Evaluation, which will be submitted as part of your assessment.

2733: Advanced Practical Production

The Practical Production Log

In order to be able to submit a comprehensive Critical Evaluation, it is essential to keep a record of your project while creating the practical work. Your Log will provide your teacher with a guide for assessing how you have planned the project. It will also provide a template for you when referring to research, planning and process in your Critical Evaluation. The Log can be organised in a number of ways, but should include particular information. Try to ensure that you update your Log throughout the planning stages of the project. You could keep a separate folder for these notes, with divided sections for each of the areas below.

Initial ideas

In your first lesson of planning your project, you should brainstorm possible ideas. You will only develop one of these, but your initial responses to the task are an important indicator that all the process stages of your project are being gone through systematically. Try to elaborate and expand on these initial thoughts because you may need to go back to one of these ideas if your chosen one becomes unworkable. For each idea, make a note of the potential impact that your product would have on its target consumer and what its context would be in terms of existing media products. You could present initial ideas in the form of a diagram or as a series of bullet points.

Group organisation

How is your group going to be organised? Is each member going to take on specific roles in the planning process or is the group going to tackle all parts collaboratively? You will need to keep careful notes on exactly what you did within the project and the roles of others.

Changes and developments

Within any media text production process, ideas will develop and change after the initial ideas have been noted. Changes are developmental and provide the person assessing your project with a clear indication of positive and focused process. If you have embarked on the production of a particular product and then continually scrap one idea for another, your project will appear disorganised. However, if you show modification and informed alteration to your product, this will indicate that you are continually researching and checking its many elements and its impact on the target audience.

Practical planning: storyboards/shooting schedules/drafts/mock-ups

The contents of this section will be defined by the particular type of media product you have chosen to create for your Advanced Practical Production. If you are producing a television programme, a video or a film, you will need to produce storyboards, shooting schedules, equipment lists and location reports and descriptions. If you are creating a piece of print-based media, then page mock-ups, sample photographs and article drafts would provide evidence for this section. Practical planning for an ICT/New Media product could be in the form of a paper draft for a new website (including linked pages). For a radio programme, recorded pilot shows, drawings for programme logos and detailed scripts (that include dialogue, any sound effects and technical direction) would provide good practical planning evidence.

Context research

Contextual research requires you to investigate other products that are similar to the one you are planning to produce and to analyse your potential target consumer's profile and preferences. When you have collected texts and products that are similar to your own, you will need to comment on their context of consumption and their position within the marketplace. You will need to ask yourself:

- How many possible consumption contexts do your researched products (and by extension your own product) have?
- What does this mean in terms of the potential target consumer?
- Are there specific conventions that you have identified in your researched products?
- How have you used these conventions within the production of your own product?
- Is the product you have chosen to create original within the marketplace or is it placed within a tradition of such products?

All the notes you produce regarding the context of your product will provide essential reference material when you come to write your Critical Evaluation.

Audience feedback

Your assessed written work requires you to comment on how an audience has responded to your product and it is extremely useful to ask for audience feedback in the planning stages of your work. Once you have defined your potential audience, you could begin by forming a focus group of target consumers with whom you discuss initial ideas and practical planning work. Make a note of what your focus group says about your ideas (both the positives and the negatives). You might alter certain features of the product in the light of the feedback you receive or you may have your ideas confirmed as successful. Within an industry context of production, audience expectations and feedback would be taken into account and your project and Critical Evaluation will also benefit from audience comment.

The Critical Evaluation

The Critical Evaluation is the written part of your Advanced Practical Production task and enables you to describe the process of your production and evaluate its success. You will have 3000 words in which to apply the key media concepts you have learnt throughout your A2 course (Media Forms and Conventions, Media Institutions, Media Audiences and Media Representations) to the product you have produced. The most systematic way to organise your Critical Evaluation is to divide it into four sections: an introduction that does not count within the word limit, and three other sections of roughly 1000 words.

Introduction

The introduction should explain the differences between the brief that was undertaken for your AS Practical Production project and the one you have completed for A2 Advanced Practical Production. Your medium will be different for the A2 project and you need to make clear in your introduction what the differences are within the briefs for the two pieces of work. Do remember, however, that you are able to work with moving image in both AS and A2. Film and television are counted as different media despite both being submitted on video.

Part one

In your Evaluation you should analyse the design process from its inception through planning to realisation. You should include reference to your research notes, clear indication about your chosen genre and your chosen approach. You may include selected deconstructions of similar texts that have influenced you. You should also include reference to your planning processes and highlight the creative decisions you have made. You should take care in this section to identify your particular role and responsibilities if you were working in a group, and to relate the production work closely to the genre and style, institution and audience that you are targeting.

Part two

The second part of your project asks you to step back and analyse your project as a finished product. This is where you will need to use your knowledge of key conceptual areas to comment on what you have created:

- How does your product use conventions?
- Have you followed conventions literally or subverted them in some way?

- How does the form of your product work to generate meaning for your target audience? For example, does it include some form of narrative and, if it does, what impact does this have on the target consumer?

- How does representation operate within your finished product? You can apply real media theories to your product when analysing in this section.

- Are there intertextual elements to your product and how do these impact on the target audience?

- Does the presence of intertextual elements place your product within a postmodern debate?

Part three

This section justifies your production in the wider context of Media Institutions and Audiences by analysing the ways in which your product compares with other products of the same genre. You should include a detailed evaluation of the response of your target audience and also include evidence that you have tested your text and evaluated the feedback received. Use the research information that you gathered for your Log to discuss your product in relation to examples of real products. You could also include the focus group or audience feedback that you received during your planning to evaluate the effectiveness of your product in relation to real media examples. Where do you think your product would be placed in the media marketplace? What would its potential context(s) of consumption be? Do not forget that this section should also include the conclusion to your project and should offer summarised comment on the effectiveness of your product.

Finally

Remember that you have only 3000 words to include all this information and analysis, so you should use supportive appendices and references effectively, but sparingly. Your text must be credible within a realisable context and you must be able to demonstrate competent and secure handling of the challenges and opportunities arising from this level of understanding and appreciation.

2734 Critical Research Study

The Critical Research Study needs to be detailed and organised in a way which allows you to access relevant information easily. The Critical Research Study section goes into more detail concerning structure, content and methodology, but below is one possible way of organising your notes.

Generating the research title

Once you have chosen your topic, you should then brainstorm areas that may be of interest to research. Make sure that you choose an area that you will be able to explore fully, one in which you will be interested and around which you can build an interesting thesis. It might be useful to create a more specific research area under one of the following general headings:

- Issues of representation, the relationship between product and audience.

- The individual producer's relationship with the industry in which they are working.

- Historical changes within the chosen area.

- The role of the medium in which an individual producer is working.

- Conflicts or controversial issues within the topic area.

Finding references and materials

There are three main sources that you can access when searching for references and materials: the internet, print publications and visual materials. The internet can be used to find reviews, critical writing, popular criticism, surveys and institutional information. Make a note of the websites that you use and the authors behind the materials so that you can give correct references in the exam. Print publications may be books of media criticism, media-related magazines, biographies of particular individuals, newspapers or guides relating to specific texts. Note the author's name, the publication's title and the date of publication. Visual materials may include not only texts related to individual or institutional producers, but also TV programmes that discuss an issue concerning your chosen area.

Keeping organised notes and using reference materials effectively

You will need to organise your notes and materials in such a way that allows information to be easily accessible to you. You should use sectioned folders to store your findings, but you will also need to break these down into particular areas. Below are some headings that might help you to organise your Critical Research Study.

Primary research

Interviews, questionnaires, questions on message boards and your own textual analysis.

Secondary research

Secondary textual analysis

Notes on academic and popular criticism that have been written on texts related to your chosen area.

Biographical information

Information concerning particular individuals who are significant within your chosen area.

Contextual information

Information on the social, political and ideological context relevant to your area. You may have looked at, for example, the impact of political shifts on your chosen topic area, the role and perception of producers or texts in a particular period, or controversial issues which may be relevant to institutions or textual production.

Institutional detail

Your notes will include details of the companies and organisations which are significant within your research area. You may have information concerning their attitudes to and intentions behind the media texts produced, their role within new developments (either technical or ideological) or their attitudes to certain groups of people who work within them.

Audience-related research

You should have information concerning the audience for the texts related to your particular area in terms of their profile, expectations, consumption modes and contexts. This section should include any academic research that you think is relevant concerning audience reception, as well as details of audience research that you have carried out.

Finding and applying critical frameworks

Remember that this unit has been designed to enable you to use the materials you have created during your research to develop an independent critical response. Whatever ideas and frameworks you use from established critical work should be incorporated into your own arguments. You should remember, however, that established theorists can be challenged and your study should include discussion of the relevancy and pros and cons of using certain critical frameworks.

Creating your own critical response

Your own ideas and responses should always be fully substantiated, using examples from your primary research, and systematically argued. Your ideas may challenge much of the existing criticism you have read and this can provide a thought-provoking study if your argument is backed up by specific examples. Remember to refer directly to your area of research when you are creating your own response and not to formulate ideas that are irrelevant to your title.

The four-page booklet

We have already looked at how to organise your notes effectively. When you come to the exam you will need to select the notes which are specifically required for Questions 1 and 2. Always present your notes clearly, writing in full sentences and offering well-substantiated points. The examiner will want to see that you have:

- identified reasons for your topic of study
- thoroughly and appropriately researched your topic
- made relevant use of existing criticism
- considered the profile, expectations and text reception of your identified audience
- understood the nature and impact of institutional questions
- analysed the historical and social context as factors which influence your topic area
- used your research to form conclusions about your chosen topic.

You will need to make sure, therefore, that your research notes include information that will be able to satisfy all the requirements listed above.

2735 Media Issues and Debates

Exam essay writing skills

There are many factors to consider when you are sitting an exam: question choice, your approach to the question and, the element that is often forgotten when you are under pressure, the structure and style of your writing. Below are some guidance points for you to remember when you are approaching any exam essay question.

Planning

It is extremely useful to make a plan before you commence writing. This can be a list of bullet points that indicate to you the areas to be covered in the exam. It is also worth making a brief note of any references or examples you are going to include in your essay. You should aim to spend up to five minutes making your plan.

Overall structure

The most obvious point to remember is that your essay needs a clear introduction and conclusion. Your introduction should address the essay question specifically and describe the particular approach to the question that you are offering. Your conclusion should offer a summation of your argument and not introduce new points.

What lies in between the introduction and conclusion should be a systematic and relevant development of your ideas. One paragraph should feed into the next. The examiner will not want to read a disjointed piece of writing. Avoid repetitious points and make sure that whatever you do write is fully substantiated by references to textual detail or theory.

Clear organisation is essential if you want your argument to have clarity. The organisation of the piece is up to you, but certain systems of organisation are particularly effective:

- If you are closely analysing a text it is much more useful to structure your paragraphs by 'area' (for example, genre, *mise-en-scène*, editing, sound) than to work through the text chronologically.
- If you are comparing texts then the same kinds of headings can be used.
- With a question concerning genre conventions a systematic 'journey' through each of the relevant conventions and how they have been used is most effective.
- If you have chosen a question that asks you to discuss an issue, then paragraphs that explore the key areas of the debate and include within them the different arguments offer a more systematic and comprehensive approach.
- If you are creating an essay which offers a personal thesis (idea), you do not need to give the alternative arguments, but you do need to set out your ideas logically and avoid too many personalised statements, such as 'I think … ' or 'My opinion is … ' The examiner will be able to recognise original approaches and will be happy, provided your statements are fully substantiated.

For all these possible essay styles, it is essential that you refer back to the title of your essay and connect your content and movement of argument to the original task. Try not to move off onto tangents within the topic area that may be interesting but have little connection to the essay title.

Paragraphs

The first thing to remember concerning paragraphs is that you must use them! Clarity of argument is always lost when you adopt a 'stream of consciousness' style of writing. Try to make sure that each of your paragraphs follows the structure below:

- Open with a topic sentence – a statement that identifies the point you are trying to make.
- Follow this with a clear (textual) example.
- Next you should elaborate on your original topic sentence.
- To close the paragraph, try to refer to the viewer/audience's response to the issue you have raised.

Language

In an exam you are expected to produce a piece of writing which has suitable academic form, tone and content. You should avoid the following.

Slang or imprecise terms

You are creating an academic piece of writing and slang terms that you may use in your everyday descriptions are not appropriate. By the same token, your essay will lose fluency and weight if the terms you use are either imprecise or wrongly attributed. You should use specific media terms where appropriate. The examiner will not want you to clutter your essay with too much terminology, but you should use it where applicable. Use words such as narrative, genre, *mise-en-scène* and **iconography**. They will give clear indication that you know exactly what you are talking about. You should, however, only use terminology if you know exactly what it means. The glossary section of this book should provide a means of constantly checking your knowledge of specific terms.

Informality of tone or language

The tone of your piece is an important factor in how it is received by your examiner. You will have spent time revising subject matter and considering possible lines of argument appropriate to your essay topic. It would, be a shame, therefore, to spoil all this hard work by framing your ideas within language that undermines them. Try not to offer too many anecdotal references to your own experiences (these are usually found within sentences which begin, 'I think . . . ', 'In my opinion . . . ', 'When I watch/read/listen to . . . ' because your essay will begin to read as unsubstantiated opinion.

Obviously reference to yourself as a particular type of media consumer (with a particular profile) can be relevant, but only if you then move on to discuss the wider issues connected to viewing practices or consumption modes. Nevertheless, you are encouraged to show personal engagement with texts that you have studied and present your views.

Humorous asides!

No matter how tempting it may seem during the exam, a humorous quip or comical aside will never make your answer more palatable or impressive to an examiner!

Direct addresses to the examiner

Again, this is a question of keeping in mind what is appropriate within an exam context. Your essay should be clear, concise and well substantiated. If it is all these things, you will not need to solicit the examiner's agreement or approval by using phrases such as, 'I am sure that we both agree that ... ' or 'You know what I mean when ... '

Over-long or meandering sentences

Syntax (the way sentences are organised) is an important factor in retaining clarity and sense in an essay. It is very important, therefore, that your sentences are not too complex or lengthy. Try to follow the paragraph model described earlier in this chapter and include no more than one relevant point in any one sentence.

Vague or absent substantiation

Appropriate and unambiguous examples will provide clear evidence that you have understood the essay title, constructed an informed debate and identified an accurate frame of reference for your essay. Do not be vague when giving textual or institutional examples. If you are referring to a scene from a film, for example, provide a precise reference for it: 'The final Coliseum confrontation, in which Maximus ... ' is a much more precise introduction to an example from the film *Gladiator* than, 'The last fight scene in the film ... '

Once you have completed the writing for your essay, the final stage during any exam should be close checking for grammar, punctuation, spelling, appropriate reference and relevant argument.

The Media Issues and Debates Exam

Questions, plans and essay examples

The Media Issues and Debates section of this book will give you clear guidance on how to approach each of the set topic areas. For the purposes of this section, we will look at a few examples of essay questions and discuss how they might be approached. The focus will not be on detailed content but on planning, structure and fluency of writing. The examples below are created from one topic from each of the main section headings of Broadcasting, Film and Print. They include sample essay plans, as well as practice questions that you could use as timed essays to revise.

Case Study: Broadcasting

What is the function of music video?

Essay plan example

Your plan for this essay should include notes on the following:

- Your definition of music videos – comment on why they exist and their role for the band, the music industry, for TV and the audience.
- Comment on audience expectations of conventions.
- Two or three examples of music video and examples of conventions used.

Your response to the title could include the following:

Introduction

The introduction should include a statement of the range of interests served by music videos. It could also show your examiner that you understand that music videos have conventions which distinguish them from other types of TV and advertising.

Paragraph 1

In your first paragraph you could discuss their function for the music industry and for the artists.

Paragraph 2

Discussion of the function of music videos for TV.

Paragraph 3

Discussion of the function of music video for the audience.

Paragraphs 4, 5 and 6

The next series of paragraphs should give details concerning your specific music video examples. For example, if you consider boyband videos, you will need to discuss the impact of conventions such as costume changes, direct addresses to camera, location changes and dance routines on the music video audience. Consider examples of videos you think meet audience expectations, those that you think fail to deliver, and those that you might identify as developing or extending conventions.

Conclusion

The conclusion should include a reiteration of your response to the question and a summary of your main arguments.

Questions for your own practice

How do conventions of television news presentation affect the audiences for news programmes?

How has government legislation affected British broadcasting since 1990?

Case Study: Film

'A knowledge of a genre's conventions can enhance an audience's appreciation and understanding.'
Discuss.

Essay plan example

Taking the slasher horror genre as a case study, your plan for this essay should include notes on the
following:

- Your response to the question, that is, whether or not you think it is true.
- Comments on how an understanding of genre conventions can affect/enhance the viewing of a
  film.
- Details of the conventions of the slasher genre.
- Details of how each convention might aid understanding and enhance appreciation.

Your response to the title could follow the structure below.

Introduction

The horror genre has many subdivisions and this essay will concentrate on slasher films to discuss the
importance of a knowledge of generic conventions. Conventions act as basic ingredients within a
particular genre, but how they appear in different films can vary significantly. A writer or director may
decide to subvert a convention or use it ironically to make a particular point. What may enhance an
audience member's appreciation and understanding of a particular film is the recognition of
conventions and the debates which their use may indicate. If we recognise a set of elements within a
film, it can make the film seem less alienating and more accessible. The particular way a convention is
used may help the viewer to understand the messages and values of the film and may even indicate its
ideological context.

Paragraph 1

Convention: The frightening place. Details of how this convention has developed and what
constitutes the frightening place in different films. For example, *Psycho* (1960) (the Bates Motel/Bates
House), *Halloween* (1971) (the suburban domestic space), *Nightmare on Elm Street* (1984) (dreams).

Paragraph 2

Convention: The final girl. Details of the characteristics of the final girl. Links, for example, Laurie in
Halloween and Sidney in *Scream* (1996).

Paragraph 3

Convention: The monster. Differences in representation from 'the internalised monstrous' (Norman
Bates), to 'the masked, unstoppable inhuman' (Michael Myers), to 'the supernatural assailant' (Freddy
Krugger).

Paragraph 4

Convention: Camera work.

1. The floating camera. Details of the disorientating effect, the positioning of the audience, use in film examples (e.g. *Halloween*).

2. Fragmented killer shots. You will need to discuss examples of slasher films in which the killer is only gradually revealed and is shot for the majority of the film in fragments.

However, this is not consistent across all of the films you have studied and Norman Bates is an example of a killer who is 'seen' from the outset. It would be worth discussing the differing ways in which slasher films gradually reveal their monsters.

Paragraph 5

Convention: Iconography. Analysis of the use (actual and symbolic) of masks, knives, and so forth. This paragraph should also discuss iconographic or emblematic images, for example, 'the screaming face' and iconography which sharpens our understanding of character (e.g. the stuffed birds in Norman Bates's parlour).

Paragraph 6

Convention: Obscuring *mise-en-scène*. Discuss the ways in which mists, fogs and shadows are used to create tension and disorientate the viewer.

Paragraph 7

Convention: Narrative movement from disequilibrium to disturbance to a new equilibrium. Why is it that slasher films have a tendency to offer closure and resolution, only to offer a shock finale?

Paragraph 8

Convention: Atmospheric use of **diegetic** and **non-diegetic** sound. You will need to discuss the similarities between various 'monster' character themes, the use of soundtrack to build tension, the use of diegetic sound to signal danger and the use of soundtrack to express the interior workings or motivations of the killer.

Paragraph 9

Convention: Representations. There are certain groups who are often depicted within the slasher genre, for instance, the family, teenagers, the church and the police. Try to examine any differences in the ways that these groups are represented. What does the film intend to indicate by representing these groups in particular ways?

Paragraph 10

Convention: Discussion of certain themes. Slasher films often discuss themes such as death, sex, religion and the effectiveness of institutions of protection. Try to examine what the individual films you have chosen offer in terms of their discussions around these areas. For example, the equation of sex with death is quite common in slasher films. Does this mean that slasher films are intrinsically conservative?

Paragraph 11

You should have been considering the implied ideology and historical context of each of your films as you discussed them in this essay. It may be useful at this point to summarise some of your thoughts on this subject. Do you think viewers of slasher films would interpret the use of conventions as a statement challenging dominant ideas and opinions or do you think they might see a reinforcement of traditional values in these films? Does the time in which the various films were made have any bearing on their treatment of the conventions you have identified?

Conclusion

Having explored your ideas, the conclusion is where you summarise your thoughts about the essay title. Does a knowledge of conventions aid understanding and increase appreciation or does it create a different kind of viewing process, that is, one in which the viewer is self-consciously looking for recognisable conventions rather than suspending their disbelief?

Filmography

Referenced films:
Psycho (1960)
Halloween (1971)
Nightmare on Elm Street (1984)
Friday 13th (1980)
The Texas Chainsaw Massacre (1974)
Scream (1996)

Questions for your own practice

Are the British cinema products since 1990 recognisably different from those produced by Hollywood during the same period?

To what extent do shifts in legislation related to censorship reflect changing social ideologies?

Case Study: Print

How important is it to have a local press?

Essay plan example

Your plan for this essay should include notes on the following:

- Identification of your specific local press examples.
- Comments on how local newspapers reflect the needs of the local community.
- Discussion of how the local community contributes to local newspapers.
- Role of local newspapers for local businesses.
- Relationship between local and national press.

Introduction

Your introduction should begin with a general comment on how important you consider a local press to be – for creating a sense of community, giving a public forum for local views, as an advertising medium for local businesses, and so on. It should also state which local press examples you are going to discuss (two examples would be an appropriate number).

Paragraphs 1 and 2

Discussion of how local newspapers reflect the needs of the local community. You should identify specific examples of content type which fulfils a certain purpose for the local community. For example, you could discuss examples of articles from your chosen papers which foster a sense of local pride in local achievements, or those which inform the local community about important local issues.

Paragraphs 3 and 4

These paragraphs could discuss how the local community contributes to local newspapers and the importance of these contributions within the attitude of the local community to the local press. How important, for example, do you think letters pages are? Does having an arena to voice their opinions within the local paper make readers feel more of a part of their local community? Again, you will need to give specific examples of content for these points.

Paragraph 5

The role of the local newspapers for local businesses is an important area within the consideration of this essay title. You could comment on what percentage of the advertising in your local newspaper examples is for local businesses. Are local businesses involved in any sponsorship of local events within the area? Do you think that the relationship between paper and business is mutually beneficial? Do you think that local press advertising is essential for local businesses?

Paragraph 6

The last point you will need to discuss within an essay such as this is the nature of the relationship between the local and the national press. It would be very useful here to use some statistics from your chosen local press areas which indicate the circulation figures of your local papers and those of national press examples. Do people in your chosen areas seem to read both a national and a local paper? Do they read these for different reasons? Is there any crossover between content (local newspapers also report on national stories, often giving them a local focus)?

Conclusion

Your conclusion should state again your response to the essay title and clearly summarise your main arguments.

Questions for your own practice

How influential are regulatory bodies on the British press?

What strategies does the magazine industry use to target specific groups of consumers?

GLOSSARY

The following glossary offers brief definitions of key words and should be used in conjunction with the index and more detailed definitions of key terms within the book as a whole. Some of the terms have not been used in the book, but you may come across them in your further reading.

ABC – Audit Bureau of Circulation is an independent organisation that provides circulation figures for magazines and newspapers.

Aberrant readings – when a reading of a text is entirely different from the intended meaning. Such a reading may be mistaken or deliberate.

Advertorial – in a magazine or newspaper this is an advertisement that has the appearance of an article.

Aerial shot/bird's-eye view – shots filmed from aircraft or helicopter, from an extremely high angle.

Ambient sound – natural background noise on television, film or radio. In the same manner, ambient light refers to natural, available light that is not enhanced in any way.

Anchorage – Roland Barthes suggested that all images are open to a variety of interpretations or meanings. He referred to this as polysemy. However, if an image is anchored by written text or sound, then this restricts the possible meanings.

Art-house cinema – a cinema that shows films of acknowledged artistic merit, typically low- to medium-budget films that address the aesthetics of film and are produced mainly, although not exclusively, outside the mainstream.

Artificial lighting – any lighting that is used to light a film or television programme that is not available from a natural light source.

Audience – all those who receive or interact with any media product. A target audience is the group of people at whom a product is particularly aimed. It may be identified as either mass (or mainstream) if it is targeted at a very large number of people or niche if it is targeted at a smaller, more specific group of people.

Auteur – a French term meaning 'author'. It is used to refer to a film director who may be said to direct his or her films with distinctive personal style.

Avant-garde – innovative or experimental work made outside the mainstream.

BARB – Broadcasters' Audience Research Board is an independent organisation that is used to measure audiences for television companies. BARB is owned jointly by the BBC and the ITCA (the Independent TV Companies Association).

BBFC – British Board of Film Classification. This organisation, established in 1913, was originally named the British Board of Film Censors. It was founded in response to chaotic and inconsistent practices of censorship in different local authorities. In 1982 the word 'Censors' was replaced by 'Classification' and in 1985 the Video Recording Act brought video into the Board's remit. The BBFC gives a film a specific classification, either U, PG, 12, 15 or 18. The Motion Picture Association of America is the organisation that produces a similar set of classifications for the USA.

British New Wave – the name given to the films

of a small group of British directors (Lindsay Anderson, Karel Reisz and Tony Richardson) produced from the late 1950s to the mid-1960s. Many of the films were also referred to as kitchen-sink dramas or social realist films, offering progressive treatments of the working class and of gender and sexuality.

Broadsheet – the term strictly refers to the size or format of the newspaper, although it is frequently used as a synonym for the 'quality' press.

Camera angle – this refers to the position of the camera in relation to the main subject. It could be a high angle, low angle, worm's-eye view or aerial view.

Chromakey – this technique enables a secondary image or set of images to be superimposed over part of the original camera shots. The original action must be filmed against a background of a single colour. Chromakey is used to superimpose a weather map behind the weather forecaster and was also used to make Superman appear to fly. Although green and yellow are sometimes used, the most commonly used colour is blue (hence blue-screen). It is important that any subject filmed is not wearing the same shade as the background. A substantial amount of action in *The Lord of the Rings* (2001) was filmed using blue-screen.

Cinematographer – the person in film who is responsible for cameras and lighting. Often referred to as the director of photography.

Connotation – Roland Barthes uses this to refer to the meanings that words, images and sounds suggest beyond the literal description or denotation.

Continuity editing – sometimes referred to as invisible or academic editing, this is the unobtrusive style of editing developed by Hollywood and still employed in most commercial productions. The basis of continuity editing is to cut on action so that the whole sequence looks natural.

Convergence – the coming together of different communication devices and processes. With the aid of a modem, the telephone and computer converge to enable us to access the internet, that is the 'new' means of communication.

Crane shot – a shot filmed quite literally from a high angle and from a crane.

Cross-media ownership – when corporations own different businesses in several types of media, for example, News Corporation, which has interests in television film and the press.

Demographics – demographic data refers to the social characteristics of the population studied, according to groupings such as social class, gender and age.

Denotation – the simple description of what can be seen or heard (see **Connotation**).

Depth of field – the distance between the furthest and the nearest points that are in focus. A wide-angle lens will have a much greater depth of field than a telephoto lens.

Diegetic/non-diegetic sound – diegetic sound appears to come from a recognisable source within the narrative of a film, radio or television text. Non-diegetic sound would include a film musical score.

Digital – the conversion of sound and visual to transmit information in a code using the numbers zero and one.

Discourse – a discourse offers a set of statements about a particular area for discussion and organises these statements, giving specific structure to the way the subject is discussed. Discourses, therefore, give expression to the meanings and values of institutions or social groups. This can refer to the way in which a particular social group may construct discussion, for example, 'feminist' discourse.

Disequilibrium – see **Equilibrium**.

Dissolve – a form of transition in editing when one image gradually begins to fade and the second image begins to appear. For a brief time the two images can be seen simultaneously. This is not to be confused with fades or wipes, which are different forms of transition.

Dope sheet – a type of storyboard used for animation, with information about what is in each cel of the animation, layer by layer and with detailed information about camera position, sound and layout. A dope sheet looks like a table, with information for each frame of the animation, unlike a film storyboard which only uses key frames.

Dubbing – a process whereby sound is added to film. This may take the form of adding music or additional sound to dialogue or it may refer to the addition of an entire soundtrack, including dialogue.

Editing – the selection of material to make a coherent whole. It may refer to the editing of copy and still images for a print product or sound for radio, or images and sound for television or film. In film and television an editor will use a variety of methods of moving from one sequence to another, which is referred to as a transition.

Editorial – this may refer to a statement by the editor in any publication or it may refer to any feature material, that is, not advertising.

Enigma – a question or puzzle that may be posed at the beginning of and throughout a text. It refers to one of Roland Barthes' codes of narrative that he called the 'Voice of Truth', also called the hermeneutic code. These puzzles work to maintain the interest of the audience; they are there to be solved or to delay the pleasure of reaching the end of the story.

Equilibrium, disequilibrium, restoration of equilibrium – tensions within a narrative. A secure and balanced state is often used to begin a narrative, but this is soon disrupted by tensions or events that cause disequilibrium. A typical happy ending will result in a restoration of balance or equilibrium. The Bulgarian theorist Tzvetan Todorov is most frequently referred to in relation to this narrative theory.

Establishing shot – a long shot or extreme long shot that establishes the location, general mood and relative placement of main subjects within a scene.

Fade – when the image gradually grows dim or faint and then disappears. This form of editing transition is not to be confused with a dissolve. A fade is usually to a blank black screen, hence 'fade to black'. This is the most common fade, although fades to white or red are used for special effects. If an image gradually appears from a blank screen this is called a 'fade up' or 'fade from'. Fade to and from black is commonly found as a standard feature in camcorders.

Fish-eye lens – an extreme wide-angle lens covering 180°. This gives a high level of distortion (see also **Lenses**).

Form – this term means the structure or skeleton of a text and the narrative framework around it. For example, a feature film commonly has a three-act structure. Some structures are determined by a genre and its corresponding codes and conventions.

Frame – as a noun this refers to the single area on a strip of film that holds a single image (or a single still image on video). As a verb it means to adjust the position of the camera or to adjust the camera lens in order to compose the required image. You would frame your image to construct a close-up, long shot or medium shot. If the framing of a shot is at an angle this is referred to as a canted frame or Dutch angle.

Gatekeeping – the process by which news stories are selected or rejected. A gatekeeper is a journalist, usually the editor, who filters the news stories in order to present them in the most successful way possible to the audience. The term is also applied to other major decision makers in the media industries.

Gaze – at its most basic this refers to the act of looking that takes place as part of the experience of watching films and the process of looking between the actors on the screen and the audience. Since the 1970s the term has been a key term for film theorists. Much feminist film theory takes the starting point that cinema was constructed around male scopophilia and that the camera operated through a male gaze, looking at women as objects.

Genre – this is the classification of any media text into a category or type, such as news, horror, documentary, soap opera, docusoap, science fiction or lifestyle. Genres tend to have identifiable codes and conventions that have developed over time and for which audiences may have developed particular expectations. Media texts that are a mixture of more than one genre are called generic hybrids.

Hegemony – the process by which dominant ideology is maintained. This concept owes much to the work of the Italian political theorist Antonio Gramsci. It is a form of consensus that is initially constructed by institutions that wield social and political power, such as government organisations, the mass media, the family, the education system and religious groups. It is a form of consensus that is frequently renegotiated between the powerful and the dominated.

High-/low-key lighting – high-key lighting is an even lighting scheme that emphasises bright colours, giving a cheerful effect, often used in comedies and musicals. Low-key lighting is where the scene appears under- or dimly lit. The overall appearance is of darkness and shadow. This style of lighting is characteristic of thrillers, horror movies and *film noir*.

Hooks – refers to any device used in the construction of a media product to attract or hold onto the attention of the audience. For instance, these devices are most frequently used at the beginning of a film to make sure the audience is enthralled.

Horizontal integration – when an organisation owns different companies of the same type, for instance, Rupert Murdoch owns several newspapers. This occurs when a company takes over a competitor at the same level of production within the same market sector (see **Vertical integration.**)

Iconography – familiar symbols in works of art have a cultural meaning that has a resonance beyond the individual work. In film, iconography may refer to particular objects, stars, archetypal characters, actors or even specifics of lighting, sets and props.

Ident – in broadcasting this refers to a jingle or logo that identifies the channel, station or programme.

Ideology – often referred to as the system of ideas, values and beliefs which an individual, group or society holds to be true or important. These are shared by a culture or society about how that society should function. Ideas and values that are seen to be shared, or perpetuated, by the most influential social agents (churches, the law, education, government, the media, etc.) may be described as dominant ideologies.

Infotainment – a colloquial term used to identify the trend towards increasing the entertainment value of factual programmes in order to increase their popularity with audiences, despite accusations of trivialisation.

Intertextuality – often related to postmodernism and its culture and criticism, the notion being that we now understand texts by their relationship or reference to another text, or that a text is successful principally because of its intertextual references (e.g. *The Simpsons*, *Scream*). One of the effects on the audience of recognising intertextuality is that it flatters their ability to recognise references and feel superior, or to feel part of a group who share the same joke.

Jumpcut – a break in the continuity of editing. The cut goes from one shot to another in such a way as to disorientate the viewer. This may break the continuity of time by leaping immediately forward from one part of the action to another even though it is clear that they are separated by an interval of time. Jumpcuts can also break the continuity of space in the same way.

Lenses (telephoto, wide-angle) – a telephoto lens enables objects to appear closer to the camera without moving the camera itself. It is the camera's equivalent to a telescope. A short telephoto is flattering for faces in close-up. A long telephoto can also give crowded streets the appearance of being even more congested. A wide-angle lens offers a range of more than 60°. It offers a certain amount of distortion, magnifying the foreground and reducing the size of images in the background. Used for close-ups, this lens will distort the image.

Mainstream – refers to a commercially orientated media product that appeals to a wide audience demographic (or refers to the people who consume them). The term is sometimes used derogatorily to suggest products lacking in flair, imagination or innovation.

Manga – a distinctive genre of Japanese comics that mix reality and fantasy. Anime is the animated version of manga.

Masthead – the title of a magazine or newspaper, usually placed at the top of the front cover.

Mise-en-scène – literally everything that is 'put in the scene', or frame, to be photographed (appropriate to the time or era portrayed). This usually includes production design, set, location, actors, costumes, makeup, gesture, proxemics/blocking, extras, props, use of colour, contrast and filter. Lighting is often included within *mise-en-scène*. Camera shot composition, framing, angle and movement is sometimes referred to as mise-en-shot.

Montage – taken from the French, 'to assemble', it has several meanings in the context of film and is not exclusively used to refer to Soviet montage.

(1) As a synonym for editing. (2) In Hollywood cinema to edit a concentrated sequence by a series of brief cuts that use a series of transitions to create the effect of the passage of time or movement over large distances or for expressionistic moods. (3) Thematic or Soviet montage was developed by Sergei Eisenstein by arranging striking juxtapositions of individual shots to suggest an idea that goes beyond meanings within the individual shots. He called this 'collision' montage. (4) Any sequence that creates a particularly significant effect mainly through its editing. The shower scene in *Psycho* (1960) would be such an example.

Moral panics – individuals, social groups or even patterns of behaviour can be presented by the mass media as a threat to society's status quo. Moral panics reflect the fear of society that the dominant culture might be subverted and are often presented by the mass media in a hysterical or stereotypical manner.

Narrative – the way in which a plot or story is told, by whom and in what order. Flashbacks or flash-forwards and ellipsis may be used as narrative devices. Tsvetan Todorov, Richard Branigan, David Bordwell and Kristin Thompson and Robert McKee all have interesting points about narrative development.

Narrowcasting – contrasted with broadcasting, where product makers aim their programmes and advertisements at a specialist interest audience.

Naturalism – this term is frequently used synonymously with realism. However, realism means something much broader, using more generalised methods of trying to represent the 'real'. Naturalism is a narrower and more focused strategy that involves trying to recreate faithfully the exact conditions of location and exact representations of character through performance. With naturalism the audience is offered the opportunity to observe as if viewing through a one-way mirror. We see a copy of life based on very close observation.

Newsgathering – the process by which news is collected from its source in order to be treated or packaged for presentation.

News values – the process by which news stories or features are selected and their priority and style of presentation, also referred to as gatekeeping. These are sometimes categorised as 'hard' or 'soft'. Galtung and Ruge's definitions (recency, currency, negativity, etc.) are commonly used to categorise news values in greater detail. The news values are usually determined by the producers and editors, to reflect the values of the target audience and what they are interested in reading about or looking at. However, it could be asserted that they also influence and determine the agenda of the readers.

NRS – National Readership Survey is an organisation that sets out to provide information on the number and nature of readership of magazines and newspapers.

Pan and tilt – pan is to turn the camera from a fixed position horizontally on the axis of its mount. Tilt is to move the camera from a fixed position vertically on the axis of the mount. A whip or zip pan is the movement done rapidly rather than the usual slow and smooth movement.

Parody – a media text that ridicules another more serious product by humorous imitation. Mel Brooks' *Blazing Saddles* (1974) is a perfect example of a parody. A parody is frequently referred to colloquially as a spoof. A parody is not the same as a pastiche. A parody deliberately sets out to ridicule the original whereas a pastiche is a text composed in the recognisable style of another maker. If you were to make a film in the style of Alfred Hitchcock then this would be a pastiche.

Plugs – information about the contents of a magazine or newspaper given on the front cover.

Pluralist – a view that modern societies comprise populations that are increasingly different in kind (i.e. heterogeneous), divided by such factors as ethnic, religious, regional and class differences.

Point-of-view shot (POV) – a shot that shows the point of view of a character. This will often be shown as an over-the-shoulder shot. A subjective point of view is when the camera functions as if it were the eyes of the character.

Polysemy – the possibility of a sign to have several meanings (see **Anchorage**).

Postmodernism – a movement or phase in twentieth-century thought. The term is complex and difficult to define in simple terms. It is applied to all the arts and at its most basic refers to the way that new products can be constructed by making reference to already existing ones.

Post-production – the period and the processes that come between the completion of principal photography and the completed film or programme. This involves the editing of a film or programme, including titles, graphics, special effects, and so on.

Preferred reading – this term describes the way in which a media text offers a reading or meaning that follows the intentions, either conscious or unconscious, of the maker or the reading 'preferred' by the dominant forces in society (see **Ideology**).

Pre-production – the entire range of preparations that take place before a film or television programme can begin shooting.

Primary research – research information or data that you collect yourself. Sources for this may include interviews, questionnaires, analysis of original photographs or other media texts that you undertake yourself (see **Secondary research**).

Production – either the product itself or the actual process of filming.

Properties – more commonly referred to by the abbreviation props, the term refers to any object that can be carried and used by the actors, as opposed to the larger items of furniture that are considered to be part of the decor of the set itself. In the singular, property is also used to refer to any copyrighted text – anything from a complete novel to a song title or synopsis of a plot.

Public Service Broadcasting – broadcasting that is intended to 'entertain, educate and inform' but does not have a primary commercial intent.

Puff – words or phrases on the cover of a magazine used to boost its status.

Pyrotechnics – all explosive devices used in films, television or in theatrical stage productions. They are commonly referred to by the abbreviation pyros. In common usage pyrotechnics is a term more narrowly applied to fireworks.

Qualitative research – research undertaken through observation, analysing texts and documents, interviews, open-ended questionnaires and case studies. It is reasoned argument that is not based on simple statistical information. Overall qualitative research enables researchers to study psychological, cultural and social phenomena.

Quantitative research – primarily statistical data most frequently obtained from closed questions in questionnaires or structured interviews. Qualitative research may estimate how many 15–25-year-old males watch *EastEnders*, but quantitative research is necessary to determine why they watch it.

RAJAR – Radio Joint Audience Research is an organisation involving the BBC and commercial radio, similar to BARB, that is responsible for controlling the system of calculating audience figures for radio.

Ratings – the estimated numbers of people who watch or listen to broadcast programmes, seen to be a guide to the relative success of broadcast material (see **BARB** and **RAJAR**).

Readership – this does not simply refer to those

who buy a newspaper or magazine, but to the total number of people who are likely to read the publication: usually considered to be three or four times the number of copies actually sold.

Realism – the dominant mode of representation in television, mainstream films and print. The term usually implies that the media text attempts to represent an external reality: a film or television programme is 'realistic' because it accurately reproduces that part of the real world to which it is referring. The concept is, however, much more complex than this brief definition.

Representation – the process of making meaning in still or moving images and words/sounds. In its simplest form, it means to present or show someone or something. However, as a concept for debate, it is used to describe the process by which an image or similar may be used to represent or stand for someone or something, for example, a place or an idea. Inherent in this second definition is the notion that there may be a responsibility on the part of the producer for any representation, with regard to accuracy, 'truth' and the viewpoints and opinions that such a representation may perpetuate.

Saturated colour – colours that are extremely rich and vivid. Desaturated colours are pale and watery.

Scheduling – the process by which programmes are broadcast at particular times and in particular sequences to maximise their potential audiences.

Scopophilia – literally 'the pleasure of looking', and often discussed in conjunction with the term 'voyeurism', meaning to observe people without their permission or knowledge. Many theorists have considered the whole basis of cinema through scopophilia and voyeurism, with the audience, sitting in the dark, watching the action unfold. Many films have used the act of voyeurism as an integral part of the action, such as Alfred Hitchcock's *Rear Window* (1954) and Michael Powell's *Peeping Tom* (1960).

Secondary research – research into information or opinions already in existence, including material from books, study guides and other resources, such as newspapers, magazines, journals, videos, DVDs and television documentaries, (see **Primary research**).

Semiology/semiotics – the study of sign systems and their function in society.

Shot-reverse shot – a standard technique for filming a conversation in which shots from one character's point of view are intercut with those of the second speaker.

Signifier – the Swiss linguist Ferdinand de Saussure established a division of signs into two constituent parts: the signifier (the physical form that we perceive through our senses) and the signified (the mental concept of what it refers to or means). Barthes gave the example of the rose – we perceive it as a flower (the signifier), but if given to a girlfriend by a young man it becomes a sign (the signified) and signifies his romantic passion.

Social realism – a form of realism that attempts to capture in a 'true to life' manner, the lives of urban working-class communities, (see **British New Wave**).

Stereotype – an oversimplified representation of people, places or issues, giving a narrow set of attributes. Stereotypes are frequently thought to be entirely negative but this is not necessarily the case.

Stop-motion – this technique may be used as a simple special effect, initially used by George Méliès. By stopping the camera during a shot, adding or removing something from view and continuing to shoot, the impression is given of objects appearing or disappearing from the frame. When used with a series of single frames this creates the illusion of animation and is called pixelation.

Storyboard – the planning of a moving-image text by using a series of drawings with written instructions for the methods of filming.

Stripping – (also occasionally referred to as stranding) the form of scheduling on television whereby the same strand or genre of programming (e.g. sport, soap opera, consumer programmes) is offered at the same time every day, every week.

Style – this refers to the 'look' of a media text, its surface appearance. It can be recognised (according to the medium) by the use of colour, typography, graphic design and layout, vocabulary, photography or illustration, *mise-en-scène*, lighting, music, camera angle, movement, framing, dialogue, editing, and so on.

Synchronous/asynchronous sound – synchronous sound is where the sound matches the action or speech in film or television. Asynchronous sound is when there is a mismatch – the most obvious example is when lip-synch is out, in other words, when the words spoken and the lip movements of the actor on screen do not match.

Synergy – the establishment of the relationship between different areas of the media for mutual benefit. This may or not be within the same organisation, although conglomerates such as AOL/Time Warner and News Corporation are in enviable positions to make the most of such opportunities. An example might be when the launching of a new film is accompanied by the promotion of a wide range of merchandise, or just a CD of the music. Synergy between films and music is quite common.

Tabloid – a 'half-sized' newspaper. The term is, strictly speaking, related to the size only but is frequently used critically referring to newspapers such as *The Sun* and *The Mirror* (these are also referred to as red-top tabloids). The *Daily Mail* and the *Daily Express* are referred to as mid-market tabloids. It should be pointed out that several broadsheet newspapers have tabloid supplements.

Take – a take is a single run of film (or video) as

it records a shot. In commercial film-making several takes of the same shot would be filmed until a satisfactory one has been achieved. A long take is a single uninterrupted shot that lasts longer than the usual few seconds to half a minute or so.

Teasers – short phrases on the front cover of a newspaper or magazine to tempt a reader to buy the publication. Teaser trailers are short film or television trailers shown before a full-length trailer is released.

Terrestrial – transmissions of radio and television from land-based transmitters.

Tone – the overall impression that is given by a media text such as serious, comic, romantic, sensationalist, and so on.

Tracking shot – (also referred to as a dolly shot) originally used when a camera was moved along on rails or tracks to follow the action. When the camera was removed from the rails and placed on a platform with wheels or castors, the platform was referred to as a dolly, hence a dolly shot. These shots are also referred to as trucking or travelling shots.

Two-shot – literally a shot with two people in the same frame.

Typography – the typeface or font that is used in print texts.

USP – unique selling point refers to the distinctive feature or features of a media product that helps to make it stand out from the competition.

Vertical integration – a term used to describe how one company owns all stages of production and distribution (and in the world of film, exhibition). The Hollywood Studio System from approximately the late 1920s to the 1950s was organised in this way. In print publication it could refer to a company that owns the paper mills that make the paper through to chains of newsagents who sell the magazines and newspapers.

Vox pop – the opinions on current issues or topics recorded from members of the public. From the Latin *vox populi* meaning 'voice of the people'.

Wide shot/wide-angled shot – a shot that takes in more than 60° of vision rather than the 'normal' range of the camera at 45–50°.

Wipe – a transitional device for editing in which one scene appears to push another off the screen. In early film-making the only possibilities were the vertical or horizontal wipe, but with developing technology a wipe can be done in an almost infinite variety of patterns.

Wrap – (1) The conclusion of a day's filming or the entire production. (2) An item in a news programme that begins with the newsreader, cuts to a location reporter and/or an actuality sequence and then returns to the newsreader.

Zoom lens – a lens of variable length used to give the illusion of moving the camera closer to or further away from a subject without moving the camera itself. A zoom shot should not be confused with a dolly or tracking shot where the camera is physically moved.

Bibliography

Books

Alden C, *The Media Directory 2006*, Guardian Books, 2006.

Altman R, *Genre: The Musical*, Routledge, 1982.

Barker M and Petley J, *Ill Effects: The Media / Violence Debate*, Routledge, 1987.

Bordwell D and Thompson K, *Film Art: An Introduction*, McGraw-Hill Publishing Company, 2000.

Buckingham, D. *After the Death of Childhood: Growing Up in the Age of Electronic Media*. Polity, 2000.

Cook P and Bernink M (eds), *The Cinema Book*, BFI Publishing, 1999.

Corner J (ed.), *Popular Television in Britain: Studies in Cultural History*, BFI Publishing, 2001.

Creeber G (ed.), The *Television Genre Book*, BFI Publishing, 2001.

Curran J, *Media and Power*, Routledge, 2002.

Dyja E (ed.), *BFI Film and Television Handbook*, BFI Publishing, 2005.

Galtung J and Ruge M, 'Structuring and Selecting News' in Cohen and Young (eds), *The Manufacture of News: Deviance, Social Problems and the Mass Media*, Constable, 1973.

Gauntlett D, 'Ten things wrong with the "effects model"' in Dickinson R, Harindrananth R and Linne O (eds), *Approaches to Audiences*, Arnold, 1998.

Gauntlett D, *Media, Gender and Identity – An Introduction*, Routledge, 2002.

Gillmoor D, *We, The Media*, O'Reilly, 2004.

Goodwin A, *Dancing in the Distraction Factory: Music Television and Popular Culture*, University of Minnesota Press, 1992.

Hanley P (ed.), *Striking a balance: the control of children's media consumption*, ITC, 2002.

Hartley J, *Uses of Television*, Routledge, 1999.

Hayward S, *Cinema Studies: The Key Concepts*, Routledge, 2000.

Hodge R and Tripp D, *Children and Television*. Polity, 1996.

Holland P, The *Television Handbook*, Routledge, 2000.

Jencks C, *Culture*, Routledge, 2005.

Johnson S, *Everything Bad is Good for You*, Penguin, 2005.

Keeble R, *The Newspapers Handbook*, Routledge, 2001. (Reprinted several times, this is probably the best book to start with; it is almost a definitive work about newspapers).

Kendall A, *The reading habits of 16–19 year olds – initial findings*, paper presented at the BERA conference, University of Exeter, 2002.

Kress K and Van Leeuwen T, *Reading Images: The Grammar of Visual Design*, Routledge, 1996.

Lacey N, *Narrative and Genre*, MacMillan, 2000.

Lacey N, *Image and Representation*, MacMillan, 2000.

Lacey N, *Media Institutions and Audiences*, MacMillan, 2004.

Livingstone S, *Young People, New Media*, LSE report, 1999.

McKay J, *The Magazines Handbook*, Routledge, 2000.

McNair B, *News and Journalism in the UK*, Routledge, 2003.

Nelmes J (ed.) (1996) *An Introduction to Film Studies*, Routledge, 1996.

Nelmes J (ed.), *An Introduction to Film Studies*, Routledge, 1999.

Newman J, *Videogames*, Routledge, 2004.

Raynor P, Wall P and Kruger S, *Media Studies: The Essential Introduction*, Routledge, 2001.

Reiss S, Feineman N, Stipe M, *Thirty Frames Per Second: The Visionary Art of the Music Video*, Harry N. Abrams, Inc., 2000. Lots of pictures and some good inspiration.

Selby K and Cowdery R, *How to Study Television*, MacMillan, 1995.

Stafford R and Branston G, *The Media Student's Book*, Routledge, 2004.

Stafford R (ed.), *Film Reader 2: British Cinema*. In the Picture Publications, 2000.

Strinati D, *An Introduction to Theories of Popular Culture*, Routledge, 1995.

Tyrell H, 'Bollywood in Britain' in *Sight and Sound* (August 1998), BFI Publishing, 1998.

Watson J and Hill A, *Dictionary of Media and Communication Studies*, Arnold, 2003.

Weaver D and Wilhoit G, *The American Journalist: A Portrait of U.S. News People and Their Work*, Indiana University Press, 1986.

Wilby P and Conroy A, *The Radio Handbook*, Routledge, 1999.

Winship J, *Inside Women's Magazines*, Pandora, 1997.

Websites

Film

http://www.imdb.com

Probably the most useful film archive on the web. Contains information for almost every film produced globally, with a fully searchable archive and links to useful institutional and textual information.

http://www.movies.real.com

Trailers, clips, photos and other useful information about (mostly) big studio releases

http://www.movieflix.com

Source of clips, information and free viewing material for a range of films – useful supporting research, but some obscure films

http://www.darkhorizons.com

Another good site for access to streaming films and downloadable trailers

http://www.apple.com/trailers/

The official Apple site for trailers

http://www.bbfc.org.uk

British Board of Film Classification, with excellent educational resources

http://www.ukfilmcouncil.org.uk

UK Film Council website

TV

http://www.bbc.co.uk/TV

Homepage for all BBC TV channels

http://www.granadamedia.com

Granada television site – access to all Granada channels and television-related pages

http://www.itv.com

ITV portal site

http://www.nbc.com

NBC television (USA)

http://www.sky.com

Sky TV site

http://www.barb.co.uk

TV audience research data

Comics

http://www.dccomics.com

Home site for many comic heroes

http://www.marvel.com

Home site for some of the most well-known comics and comic heroes

Newspapers

http://www.newscorp.com/operations/newspapers.html

Launch site for the corporation's newspapers

http://www.thesun.co.uk/

http://www.express.co.uk

http://www.mirror.co.uk

http://www.people.co.uk

http://www.guardian.co.uk/

Magazines

http://www.emap.com/

Leading magazine publisher

Radio

http://www.bbc.co.uk/radio/

Homepage for all BBC Radio stations

http://www.virginradio.co.uk/

Homepage for a major commercial station

http://www.radio-locator.com/cgi-bin/home

Good programme for finding a wide variety of (primarily) US-based programmes which broadcast live across the internet

http://www.radio-now.co.uk

UK-based programme giving information about streaming programmes in the UK, information about local radio stations, live football commentaries, press releases and much more information relating to UK local radio

http://www.rajar.co.uk

UK radio audience research site

Music Video

http://www.mtv.com/music/video/

> A good range of videos, good for dipping in and researching themes and trends. Reasonably strong on British bands and a fair contemporary coverage

http://www.video-c.co.uk/

> Excellent and informative UK music video site

Animation

http://www.awn.com

> Animation world network

http://www.pixar.com

> Homepage for Pixar

http://www.animationartist.com

> Site with useful links/articles about animation

http://looneytunes.warnerbros.co.uk

> Warner Brothers cartoon homepage

http://www.aardman.com

> Homepage for Aardman

Other useful websites

http://www.aber.ac.uk/media

> Daniel Chandler's Media and Communications site

http://www.blogger.com

> Blogger.com website

http://www.cpbf.org.uk

> Campaign for Press and Broadcasting Freedom website

http://www.ccsonline.org.uk

> Centre for the Study of Children, Youth and Media website

http://www.discover.co.uk/NET/NEWS

> Internet Newspaper Directory

http://www.indymedia.org.uk/

> Indymedia UK website

http://www.longroadmedia.com/

> Long Road College Media site

http://longroadmedia.blogspot.com

> Long Road College Media blog

http://www.mediamagazine.org.uk

> Media Magazine website

http://www.mediauk.com/

> Media UK website

http://www.mediazoo.co.uk

> Media Zoo website

http://www.newmediastudies.com

New Media studies website
http://www.ofcom.org.uk
OFCOM website
http://www.ofcomwatch.co.uk/
OFCOM Watch website
http://www.ourmedia.org
Our media website
http://www.theory.org.uk
Theoryorg website
http://en.wikipedia.org/wiki/Wikimedia
Wikimedia Foundation website

INDEX